# Having Words with God

# Having Words with God

## The Bible as Conversation

**Karl Allen Kuhn**

**Fortress Press**
MINNEAPOLIS

*For my son, Joshua,*
*daily reminder of Yahweh's saving grace*

HAVING WORDS WITH GOD
The Bible as Conversation

Cover design by Diana Running
Cover art: Chagall, Marc (1887-1985). *Moses before the burning bush,* oil on paper. Musée National message biblique Marc Chagall, Nice, France, © 2008 Artists Rights Society (ARS), New York / ADAGP, Paris. Photo © Réunion des Musées Nationaux / Art Resource, NY.
Book design by Michelle L. N. Cook

*Library of Congress Cataloging-in-Publication Data*
Kuhn, Karl Allen, 1967–
  Having words with God: the Bible as conversation / Karl Allen Kuhn.
    p. cm.
  ISBN 978-0-8006-6280-6 (alk. paper)
  1. Bible—Reading. I. Title.
  BS617.K84 2008
  220.6—dc22       2007047078

The paper used in this publication meets the minimum requirements of American National Standard for Information Sciences—Permanence of Paper for Printed Library Materials, ANSI Z329.48-1984.

Manufactured in the U.S.A.

12    11    10    09    08    1    2    3    4    5    6    7    8    9    10

# Contents

# Acknowledgments

**Many people have helped me shape this work** into the form in which it now appears. Lakeland College colleagues Paul White and Suzanne House and clergy colleagues David Moyer and Jeri Behringer read drafts of early chapters, providing encouragement and sage advice. Walter Brueggemann and J. Clinton McCann generously took time out of their schedules to read several chapters and recommended the project to potential publishers. Mark Allan Powell's work on "real reader response criticism" inspired much of chapter 5. He reviewed that chapter and the introduction, and my conversations with him about the chapter and the work as a whole affirmed the direction I was taking. Four individuals served as my primary readers, each of whom carefully read nearly the entire work: my wife, Rev. Kathryn O'Connor Kuhn; and dear friends Rev. Marilyn Stavenger of Eden Seminary; Rev. Larry Balleine, Pastor of Zwingli United Church of Christ in Monticello, Wisconsin; and Will Mathes, member of Bethlehem United Church of Christ in Schlesswig, Wisconsin. To them I owe great thanks for their generous gifts of time, encouragement, and numerous insights that led to many improvements in the work. I am also grateful to Fortress Press for taking a chance on a first-time author, and especially to Neil Elliott and Marissa Bauck for their part in improving the work and shepherding it through the stages of publication. I give thanks for the many blessings I receive in my ministry of teaching and learning at Lakeland College, including a sabbatical leave in the fall of 2007, during which I completed final edits on the book. As a college of the United Church of Christ with an undergraduate program in religion and a graduate program in theology, Lakeland has granted me many opportunities to shape my understanding of Scripture and faith in conversation with students, colleagues, and members of the wider church community. Above all, I give thanks to my wife, Kathryn, and our children, Joshua and Clare, whose support and love in this and many other endeavors are a source of tremendous blessing and joy.

# Scripture: An Invitation to Sacred Dialogue

## introduction

**Contentious conversation has often** accompanied the practice of Christian faith, as those of us who are members of churches must admit. According to the Gospels, even Jesus' own ministry led him into perpetual and eventually deadly conflict with some of the religious authorities of his time over differing understandings of what it meant to follow God's torah (instruction). The disciples argued among themselves, even while Jesus was still with them. Not surprisingly, those who joined the faith after Jesus' death and resurrection also argued. They disagreed over what foods could be eaten, the function and comparative value of spiritual gifts, which Christian teachers were the better ones to follow, how to celebrate the Lord's Supper, whether or not Gentiles (non-Jews) needed to be circumcised, which sexual activities were sinful and which were allowable, whether to marry, what women should wear and how they should behave in worship, and many other things. As any historical account of the church will amply illustrate, such disagreement was not characteristic of Christianity merely in its infancy. It continued in the centuries to follow, leading to divisions both great and small in the body of Christ, even tragically at times to bloody persecution. Despite our differences, the church has often been a steward of God's grace and love. But how we have argued!

This part of our heritage as Jesus' followers is alive and well today. We who are Christians are divided on many issues—war, divorce, abortion, homosexuality, conflict in the Middle East, marriage, and capital punishment, to name a few. Beyond these major issues, many individual congregations often find themselves in disagreement over other matters, of greater or lesser importance, that impact their ministry. Should we have pews or chairs in the sanctuary? Should small children be allowed to receive communion? Should the pastor stay or go? Could the next minister be a woman? Should we use paper or Styrofoam products? Can nonmembers be buried in the church cemetery? May girls play the role of the magi in the Christmas Eve program? Should the children's program even be on Christmas Eve? There are a lot of things, big and small, on which Christians disagree.

To be sure, whenever a group of human beings gather together for any extended period of time there is going to be disagreement. What distinguishes the church from other organizations, however, (at least on its better days) is the reason for our disagreements and how we seek to resolve them. Ideally, when we Christians argue with one another about some feature of their common ministry, we are not simply pushing for our personal preference or "defending our turf." Instead, we are arguing about mission: how this or that issue impacts our corporate witness to God's truth, grace, and love made known in Jesus. We are seeking the course that most closely aligns with God's will for us and the people to whom we minister.

Attempts to resolve issues typically lead Christians to Scripture, prayer, church doctrine, tradition, and reflection on their own experiences as people of faith. Though most of these sources are commonly regarded as important, in many Christian communities Scripture emerges as the highest authority. It is the word of God, the story of our faith, the embodiment of what we profess about God and what it means to be God's people. At its most basic yet ideal level, when Christians argue, it is about how best to serve as God's people and looking to Scripture for direction.

Yet here we come to still another area of disagreement among Christians, one that is the focus of this book: How are Christians to regard and read Scripture? Nearly all Christians agree that Scripture is to play a central role in the life of faith. Nearly all agree that we should thoughtfully attend to its teachings as we seek to discern how to live as God's people. How exactly Scripture is to perform that role, however, is variously understood. I am referring not simply to differences in the interpretation of individual passages but to differences that are more fundamental. What, exactly, is Scripture? What do Christians mean when we refer to it as the "word of God?" And in light of what we think Scripture might be, what are some useful and faithful strategies for reading it?

This book is an attempt to provide a helpful contribution to the ongoing discussion among Christians about the nature of Scripture and how best to engage the sacred traditions we claim as God's word. It presents an approach to the Bible that understands Scripture as embodying and inviting a *sacred dialogue*. Its primary task is to demonstrate the various ways in which Scripture manifests dynamic conversation both between God and humanity and between human beings, and calls for this same faithful conversation among believers today. This introduction sets out the approach to Scripture as sacred dialogue that I will explore in the following chapters. First, it contrasts the "dialogical" or "conversational" approach presented here with what I call a "monological" understanding of Scripture. Then it anticipates the discussion to follow by briefly overviewing the tendencies of Scripture that lead us to regard it as sacred conversation, and the key principles that guide the way of reading the Bible presented in these pages.

## Word of God—A "Monological View" of Scripture

For millennia, Christians of all persuasions have boldly claimed that the body of ancient traditions they regard as sacred Scripture is the "Word of God." Like the eloquent phrase of 2 Tim 3:16, "all Scripture is God-breathed," the expression "word of God" captures well the traditional Christian claim that in some very intimate way God was involved in the writing, gathering together, and reception of these texts and the story they tell. It captures well the sense of many Christians that when they humbly open their hearts to these words, it is God's voice they hear, calling them to a more truthful understanding of reality and to a new way of life that is at times comforting and at other times unsettling.

Yet despite its usefulness and truthfulness, the expression *word of God* can also obscure another very important dimension of the Bible. That expression gives the impression—an impression regarded as a basic tenet of faith for some Christians—that Scripture is only *God's* word. To be sure, all Christians will readily acknowledge that within Scripture there are many voices recorded other than that of God. The words of human characters abound. At times, animals speak. Even Satan gets in a few lines! But my point is that many view Scripture as a "divine monologue," as if it is God alone who has composed the story, word by word, letter by letter. Many view Scripture as if every part of it was directly scripted by God into a flawlessly unified and wholly consistent declaration of who God is and what it means to be God's people. The following is one way of diagramming this "monological" understanding of Scripture.

**God**

> God inspires inerrant/infallible teaching, reporting, and interpretation of events among faithful believers and the biblical authors through the Spirit.

**Biblical Authors**

> God preserves the inerrancy/infallibility and unity of sacred revelation as it is passed on, written down, and gathered into the canon.

**Bible**

> Result: inerrant/infallible word of God preserved in the Bible. Spirit aids interpretation and application.

**Believers**

As the diagram indicates, according to this view there is basically one source expressing the truths Scripture conveys: the voice of God. Human authors play an essential role, of course, in the formation of the biblical traditions. But God directs their contribution to such a degree that the outcome of their service is nothing other than an infallible replica or faithful reproduction of the revelation that God alone intends to speak. The object of interpretation, then, is faithfully to discern the one voice of God that speaks in individual passages and Scripture as a whole.

This view of Scripture is attractive in its straightforward simplicity and clarity. It provides the many Christians who hold it the assurance of knowing that when they read Scripture they are hearing the very words of God. There is much power and security in this assurance. It emboldens proclamation and perseverance. It grants believers the confident sense that answers to many of life's questions (from the profound to most mundane) can be found in this sacred text. Scripture is for them an infallible source of instruction about God and what God desires for God's people.

I deeply respect Christians who hold this view of Scripture. They are among my students, family members, friends, fellow church members, and clergy. They are among the most sincere and committed Christians that I know. I also deeply respect the fact that their understanding of Scripture as God's word nourishes and strengthens their faith in Jesus as Savior and their embrace of God's love, compassion, and truth.

## Word of God—Sacred Speech in Conversation

I also know many other Christians for whom a "monological" view of Scripture does not fit with their view of the Bible and how God interacts with humanity. They are uncomfortable with what they perceive to be the monological view's insistence that we are to "read the Bible literally" and its apparent rejection of the idea that God can teach us new things that may conflict with portions of the biblical witness. These Christians tend to emphasize both the divinely inspired *and* human character of Scripture, and argue that those who view the Bible as a wholly divine work ignore obvious indications to the contrary. Some Christians even go so far as to regard the Bible as not any more "inspired" than many other classical literary or religious works, and consider it as simply one among many possible sources of meaning and truth. They claim that we are free to take from Scripture what we want, and set aside the rest.

I do not share this piecemeal approach to Scripture. Neither would I say that the Bible should be regarded by Christians as simply one source of meaning and truth alongside many others, as though it has no more authority for Christians than do the *Upanishads, The Tibetan Book of the Dead,* or *The Iliad*. At the same time, I do not believe that a "monological view" of Scripture is the most helpful way to understand the nature of Scripture and its essential role in our lives of faith. What I and many other Christians (I think) are after is a view of Scripture somewhere between the extremes represented by a monological approach on the one hand, and one that regards Scripture as simply another human work on the other. I offer this book for those Christians (and perhaps even some non-Christians) who are similarly searching for a view of Scripture that lands somewhere between these ends of the theological spectrum and is also consistent with the Bible's own nature and intent.

Scripture, in my view, is not simply a divine *monologue*. Instead, both the history of its development and its final, canonized form bear witness to its character as a *sacred dialogue*. Yet, to claim this is not to dismiss the confession that God was intimately involved as the guiding force behind the creation of Scripture. I believe God was. It is rather to say that Scripture reflects, with its multitude of voices, a sacred conversation between God and humanity, and a sacred conversation among believers about God, God's will, and what it means to be God's people. This way of viewing Scripture is, I submit, more consistent with the

Bible's own character than either the insistence that Scripture is a divine monologue or the dismissal of God's active involvement in the creation of Scripture and its central role in Christian faith.

### How the Scriptures Came to Be

Several observations commend the view of Scripture as a sacred dialogue. One is our developing understanding of how Scripture came to be. Many, perhaps most, biblical scholars believe that a good number of the biblical texts—and the Scriptures as a whole—underwent rather long, dynamic, and complex processes of development. These include the Pentateuch (the first five books of the Old Testament), some of the prophetic books, the historical books, the Gospels, and a few of the New Testament epistles. During their development, many sacred traditions were told, shaped, reinterpreted, and recast over years as oral tradition before being placed into written form. Then many of those written traditions were reinterpreted and reshaped in varying degrees before finally becoming integrated into the larger work we know as the Bible. One key element often driving the dynamic development of the Old Testament traditions was Israel's desire to understand its identity and calling as God's people in light of new situations it encountered. In the aftermath of an extraordinary or tragic event, the faithful of Israel (often guided by their prophets) turned to their sacred tradition and retold their story as God's people in ways that helped them make sense of their present circumstances and gave them hope for the future. In many such instances, this process of re-engaging and retelling their story not only led them to reshape their story in response to the needs of the day; it also led them to develop new traditions. In turn, some of these new articulations of who God is and what it means to be God's people came to be embraced as part of their repertoire of sacred speech about God. And so, throughout the centuries, Israel's sacred tradition grew and evolved until it reached its final form in the shape of the Jewish Scriptures, what Christians embrace as the Old Testament.[1]

One example of this traditioning process, often cited by scholars, is Israel's shaping, recasting, and composition of its sacred traditions in the aftermath of one of the most destructive tragedies in its history. In the early sixth century B.C.E., Zedekiah, the king of Israel, made the brash move of refusing to pay tribute to the Babylonian Empire, which controlled most of the Mediterranean region, including Asia Minor and Palestine. This was especially bold (and foolish) since the Babylonians had invaded, defiled the temple, and carried off King Jehoiakim and a large segment of the population into exile just ten years before. This time, the Babylonian response to Israel's rebellion was far more brutal. In 587 B.C.E., their armies came marching into Jerusalem, leveled the city, killed many of the inhabitants, razed the temple, and took nearly all the survivors, including the king, with them back to Babylon. Suddenly, nearly everything that defined Israel as a nation and people was gone: land, holy city, temple, monarchy. Not destroyed, however, were their sacred stories and traditions preserving their history and heritage as God's people. Many scholars believe that during their time in exile and in the years following, Jews gathered and reworked these traditions into a written collection (the Pentateuch) and codified other traditions as well (such as the prophetic and historical books), forming the core of what would later become the Jewish Scriptures. This reshaping and production of sacred tradition did not take place in a vacuum, removed from the painful experience of destruction and exile. Rather, in very tangible ways the shaping of these traditions was influenced by an emerging understanding of the crisis. Two elements of this understanding loomed large: Guided by the prophets, the Jewish community reflected on its sacred traditions and came to realize first of all that the tragedy of destruction and exile was a result of the people's unrelenting sin against God and one another. They also came to believe that, despite all appearances, God still cared deeply for the people and would one day restore them. This twofold understanding of their failure as God's people and of God's redeeming love served as a "template" of sorts for retelling their entire history. (For clear examples of this perspective at work, see Nehemiah 9; Deut 30:1-5; Leviticus 26; 1 Kgs 8:46-53). To be sure, these two elements were already an important part of Israel's sacred traditions—they were, after all, what led them to view the exile in this manner. But now, with a greater degree of emphasis and clarity than likely existed before, many of their sacred traditions were reshaped in order to tell the story of a people who struggle to live rightly with God and one another, and of a God of steadfast love, mercy, and grace who does not abandon them to the destruction wrought by their deeds, but time after time forgives and reclaims them.

A similar process of rereading and recasting sacred tradition took place among the earliest believers in Jesus as the Christ, and played a significant role in shaping the New Testament writings. Confronted with the in-breaking of God's reign among them in the life, death, and resurrection of Jesus and guided by Jesus' own teaching, these Jewish believers sought to make sense of these extraordinary events in light of their sacred traditions. For this reason, nearly every page of the New Testament is filled with either direct references or allusions back to the Jewish Scriptures. That the New Testament authors' use of the Jewish Scriptures often involved the dynamic reshaping of these traditions is quite apparent. In numerous instances, it is clear that the Old Testament tradition in view has been reinterpreted or even modified in order that it might more clearly illuminate the fulfillment of God's promises in Jesus (see the text box). But the Jewish Scriptures were not the only sacred traditions the New Testament writers both embraced and adapted. Many of the traditions recounting Jesus' ministry, death, and resurrection were also reshaped by the Evangelists as they were gathered into the Gospel texts, as a comparison of the Gospel accounts easily shows. The reason the Gospel writers molded these traditions somewhat differently is so that each of their portrayals of the gospel story would effectively address the concerns facing the particular communities to whom they were writing. The Gospels, in other words, were shaped in order to contribute to an ongoing conversation among Christians about what it means to proclaim Jesus as Savior and to follow him as Lord in their present time and place. The same could be said for the New Testament epistles, as Paul and the other letter writers boldly and creatively proclaim the good news in ways that respond to the crises and issues facing particular churches or larger segments of the early Christian community.

---

### Modifications of Old Testament Traditions by New Testament Writers

The intuitive sense of many Christian readers when they come across an Old Testament passaged cited by the New Testament authors is that the Old Testament passage must have been originally and directly about Jesus. Along with many biblical scholars, I consider it unlikely that any Old Testament tradition was first uttered with the specific person of Jesus or the particular circumstances of his ministry, death, or resurrection in view. Rather, in most cases it is quite clear that any Old Testament tradition, when read in its original context, is very much focused on realities the Israelites faced hundreds of years prior to the time of Jesus (see examples below). Thus, in nearly every case in which a direct quotation of or allusion to an Old Testament tradition appears in the New Testament, it has been at least conceptually, if not literally, modified by the New Testament writers (or other early Christians from whom they received the tradition).

This is not to say that there is little correspondence between the hopes and expectations of the Old Testament traditions and Jesus. Quite the contrary is true. But in most cases, this correspondence is on a more general level. In constantly citing and alluding to various Old Testament traditions, the New Testament writers both present the story of Jesus as the continuation of the story of Israel and also proclaim that Israel's hopes and expectations for God's deliverance are now fulfilled in Jesus. At times, as illustrated below, the precise nature of the hope found in those older traditions (especially those which spoke of the defeat of

Israel's enemies and the restoration of Israel as a nation) underwent considerable transformation as they came to be applied to the ministry, death, and resurrection of Jesus. The following examples are just a few of a multitude.

## Mark 1:2-3 (compare with Isaiah 40:3 and Malachi 3:1)

Scholars have long perceived that Mark 1:2-3 is a composite quotation from two sources, despite the fact that Mark identifies it as coming from Isaiah. Of special note is how Mark (or someone before him) slightly altered the Isaian text in v. 3 so that "make *his* paths straight" replaces "make straight in the desert a highway for our *God*" (Isa 40:3). The use of the personal pronoun "his" rather than "God" allows Mark to apply the Isaian text to Jesus' advent. Similarly, "*your* way" in v. 2 replaces "*my* way" in Mal 3:1.

## Matthew 2:16-18 (compare with Jeremiah 31:15)

Within the context of Jeremiah, the verses quoted by Matthew clearly apply to the devastation Israel suffered at the hands of the Babylonians and are followed by the prophetic promise that God will restore Israel and bring the Israelites out of exile to their own land. By applying the passage from Jeremiah to Herod's brutal massacre of Jewish infants, Matthew weaves together these two eras of Israel's history and further strengthens the connection between God's long-standing promise to redeem Israel and the arrival of Jesus.

## Luke 1:68-79

In this beautiful hymn, Zechariah celebrates God's salvation of Israel in response to the birth of John and the awaited birth of the Messiah, composing a pastiche of numerous Old Testament themes and images. Note, however, the transformation of Israel's ancient hopes that is already taking place here in the hymn. Zechariah rejoices that God "has raised up a mighty savior in the house of his servant David" (v. 69) through whom they will be "redeemed" (v. 68) and "rescued from the hands of our enemies" (vv. 74, 71). This, of course, corresponds well to the Jewish hope often expressed in the Old Testament and in the years leading up to Jesus that God would reestablish the Davidic monarchy, deliver Israel from its earthly enemies, release them from their bondage to foreign rule, and reestablish them as an independent nation (see, for example, Mic 5:1-6; Isa 9:1-7; 11:1-9; Jer 33:10-36; Ezek 36:16-37). But, as we know, Luke and the rest of early Christianity do not maintain that Jesus delivered Israel in quite this way. Appropriately, Zechariah's hymn gathers other elements of ancient Jewish hopes that more closely correspond to the salvation Luke proclaims: hopes for serving God in holiness and righteousness (v. 75); for the coming day of the Lord (v. 76); for forgiveness of sins (v. 77); for the merciful gift of God's favor (v. 78); for light in the midst of darkness, for guidance in the way of peace (v. 79). In doing so, the traditional Jewish hopes for deliverance are recast by the hymn in ways that will more closely correspond to the salvation the New Testament writers claim Jesus accomplished.

### Romans 8:36 (compare with Psalm 44:11, 22)

Paul can be quite creative in his use of Old Testament traditions (see also Gal 3:15-18; 4:21-31), employing interpretive techniques that bear some resemblance to Jewish exegetical procedures of his day but at the same time also represent a distinct understanding of the Old Testament's witness to Jesus Christ (more on this in chapter 4). Here in Romans 8, Paul draws from a lament psalm reflecting Israel's horrible experience of defeat and exile (see Ps 44:9-22) in which the psalmist offers a desperate plea for God to hear and act on behalf of God's people (vv. 23-26). Paul's use of the psalm draws a comparison between the trials and tribulations of that tragic time and the persecution and trials believers face as Christians. Yet instead of desperate lament, Paul erupts in jubilant celebration: these trials will be more than overcome through the love of God in Christ Jesus our Lord (Rom 8:37-39).

The dynamic development of sacred tradition we see reflected in both Old and New Testament traditions is summed up well by Paul Achetemeier:

> All of our biblical texts are therefore the products of interpretation of the will of God as that is illuminated in a new time by earlier traditions. Struggling to understand new revelations of God's purpose for them, Israel and the church turn to older traditions to find some clue to how they may cope with such a dynamic God. Our Scriptures reflect that process and enshrine that quest. The real threat to a proper understanding of the Bible is therefore to fail to see it in the light of its own origins in this process of interpretation and reinterpretation.[2]

The significance of this for our present discussion is to recognize that Scripture itself is the result of a dynamic refinement of sacred tradition as believers struggled to discern God's character and will in new times and places. In other words, much of Scripture was composed through a "dialogical" process of reflection and re-engagement among God's people over the course of their history. This does not mean, however (as some scholars presume), that such was a purely human endeavor. Rather, many who hold this view of how Scripture came to be also profess that God was actively involved in this process of dialogue and discernment; that God, in fact, was one of the dialogue partners in the many "conversations" that led to the formation of sacred traditions and eventually to the creation of Scripture.[3] To pull all these observations together, I propose that the creation of the biblical books is best viewed not as the result of God simply providing human authors the exact words to write down but as *a culmination of a dynamic process.* That process consisted of *many people over centuries inspired by God to form, rework, and recast their sacred traditions in ways that provided them with hope, guidance, and understanding of God and God's will.* In short, the very creation of Scripture stemmed from an ongoing dialogue between God and God's people, and of God's people with one another, as they sought to know God and God's workings in the world and faithfully to respond to God's call.

## The Conversational Character of Scripture

Also commending a view of Scripture as sacred dialogue is the recognition that *Scripture itself embodies and invites dynamic conversation between God and humanity and conversation among believers about God.* Three observations concerning Scripture's conversational character are the focus of this book. I will treat these three observations in a preliminary way here in the introduction, providing enough details to indicate what will be discussed in the pages to follow.

### 1. Conversations of Biblical Proportions

The first of these three observations is that Scripture itself contains or reflects conversations between God and humanity and among the biblical authors. As will be discussed in chapter 1, many biblical stories not only present God's character being disclosed through pronouncement and God's will being taught through commandment but also present God engaged in intimate dialogue with humanity and even moved to action by conversation with human creatures. To put it simply, the stories of Scripture do not present a God who does all the talking, but a God who does a lot of listening. In the book of Psalms, we encounter God's people in intimate engagement with God, expressing the whole range of human experience and emotion, from jubilant praise and heartfelt devotion to gut-wrenching disappointment, pain, and calls for vengeance. In the case of the Psalms, the fact that these raw human words to God have, in becoming Scripture, become God's words to us stands as an unequivocal invitation for us to enter into honest, intimate—perhaps even "irreverent"—conversation with God. Chapter 1 lays the groundwork for the chapters to follow by inviting us to consider that the nature of Scripture as sacred dialogue would be fittingly consistent with God's own "conversational" character.

There are also conversations in Scripture that convey different and, at times, conflicting understandings of who God is and what it means to be God's people. Frequently, scriptural texts record specific discussions and debates within Israel and the early Christian communities and clearly endorse one side. Such is the case with the people murmuring in the wilderness against God and Moses, with Jeremiah battling the "false prophets," or with Paul confronting the "circumcision crowd" in Acts and Galatians. Less frequently recognized, however, are places where Scripture reflects a debate taking place among the biblical authors (see chapter 2). Examples of such debates include contrasting perspectives on who may be counted among God's people in the Old Testament, disagreements over dietary restrictions for non-Jews in the New Testament, or different understandings of the role of women in the Christian community. Remarkably, these varying perspectives have not been edited out of the biblical witness (as they easily could have been) but have been allowed to remain side by side. The fact that these and other contrasting views have been preserved as a dimension of God's word testifies to the importance granted within the scriptural canon to recognizing diversity and disagreement within the community of believers. In other words, the dialogical character of the canon is not simply accidental—it results from the dialogical character of God and the Judeo-Christian tradition, and the compilers of the canon recognized this as an integral element of their faith. In bringing these discordant voices together in dialogue, the biblical texts affirm both the reality and the normality of God's people being in sometimes-disputatious conversation about who God is and what it means to be God's faithful people.

## 2. God's Dynamic and Reforming Instruction

A second observation, which builds on the first and also supports an understanding of Scripture as an invitation to dialogue, is that the biblical story reveals God's instruction as dynamic and reforming (see chapters 3 and 4). As we move along the Old Testament story, we find new laws being added and old laws recast or set aside. Terence Fretheim regards these changes to Old Testament law as "a canonical witness to the process of unfolding law," leading to the insightful—yet bold—claim that the "development of the law is just as canonical as individual laws or the body of law as a whole."[4] Jesus' and Paul's recastings of God's law throughout the New Testament mark dramatic examples of what Fretheim calls "a canonical witness to the process of unfolding law." While Scripture narrates the history of the relationship between God and

God's people, climaxing in the life, death, and resurrection of Jesus, how humanity is to live out its calling as God's people evolves throughout. This ongoing development of God's torah (instruction) is thus presented as part of God's unfolding plan to bring humanity back into right relationship with God, one another, and creation. Accordingly, Jesus tells his disciples that the dynamic character of God's instruction will continue. God's Spirit will come and teach them all the things he did not have a chance to say and they were not ready to hear (John 16:12-14). Thus, followers of Jesus are called to converse with the Living Word and together to discern what it means to be Christ's disciples in our own time and place.

## 3. From Form to Function

Third, the very form of biblical revelation invites readers into wonderment, ongoing reflection, prayer, and conversation. So much of Scripture is written in forms that do not lend themselves well to simple, precise, and fixed interpretations of "what a text means for us": for example, parables, explosive apocalyptic imagery, or Paul's ruminations on the gospel imaginatively conceived to meet the needs of his churches (see chapter 4). Of course, chief among the forms of biblical revelation is narrative. Storytelling dominates Scripture, and, perhaps more than any other revelatory form, narrative resists once-and-for-all determinations of meaning (see chapter 5). Richard Bauckham puts it well:

> [T]he diversity [of the Bible] is such that readers of Scripture have their own work to do in discerning the unity of the story. Moreover, the diversity of different versions of the story is not the only feature of Scripture that requires such work. There is the sheer profusion of narrative material in Scripture, the narrative directions left unfinished, the narrative hints that enlist reader's imagination, the ambiguity of stories that leave their meaning open, the narrative fragments of the stories of prophets in their books of or writers and churches in the apostolic letters, the very different kinds of narrative that resist division into simply alternatives such as "history" and "myth," or "fiction," the references to stories external to Scripture. Such features, even apart from the bearing of the nonnarrative literature on the narrative, make any sort of finality in summarizing the biblical story inconceivable. . . . The church must be constantly retelling the story, never losing sight of the landmark events, never losing touch with the main lines of theological meaning in Scripture's own tellings and commentaries, always remaining open to the never exhausted potential of the texts in their resonances with contemporary life.[5]

Bauckham's comments on Scripture's narrative form help us to see that the goal of Scripture is not simply to provide us with a set of propositional truth claims or a detailed, one-size-fits-all-for-all-time list of the dos and don'ts of faithful life. Rather, the narrative form of Scripture leads us to lively, imaginative, and humble reflection with God and one another on what it means for us to live into God's will in our time and place. This is its function in our lives of faith. "The church must be constantly telling the story," Bauckham says, "always remaining open to the never exhausted potential of the texts in their resonances with contemporary life." Scripture's narrative form, along with the numerous other ways in which Scripture invites us to invest ourselves and our experiences in our reading of Scripture, serves as another testimony to God's desire to engage us and converse with us about how our lives might more fully reflect the story God has inspired Scripture to proclaim.

The following diagram attempts to portray the understanding of Scripture as sacred dialogue presented in the preceding discussion:

*How the Scriptures came to be—a dynamic, dialogical process . . .*

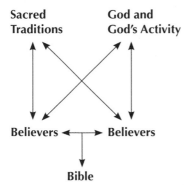

The Bible is the culmination of an ongoing dialogue in which believers, inspired by God and God's activity in their lives and in conversation with God and one another, develop their sacred traditions, evolve new traditions, and reshape them over time. These gathered traditions are eventually embraced by the Christian community as Scripture. God's Spirit is at work throughout this process to help believers shape their sacred traditions in ways that bear witness to God's character and will.

*. . . that is reflected in how we read Scripture today.*

The truth of God and God's ways is discerned as dynamic dialogue continues between believers and Scripture, believers and one another, and believers and Jesus as they pray and reflect on Scripture and God's activity in their lives past and present.

The diagram expresses, in contrast to the preceding diagram of a monological view of Scripture, the dynamic and conversational character of both the development of Scripture and its ongoing role in communities of faith. Just as Scripture came about through many years of reflection and discernment born out of believers' dialogue with God and one another in response to God's activity in their lives, so too are believers to continue this practice of engaging and telling the story of their faith in dynamic dialogue with God and one another. Like our ancestors before us, we who are believers are called to recite the story to one another with ears and hearts open to the Spirit's leading, so that we too may live out this story faithfully in our time and place.

## Three Key Principles

Thus far I have sought to explain why I think Scripture commends the approach introduced here by briefly highlighting several ways in which Scripture itself reflects and invites a sacred conversation between believers and God, and between believers and one another. There are also three fundamental interpretive principles that guide my description and practice of this approach: it is an approach that is, above all, canon-centered, story-centered, and Christ-centered. In the chapters that follow, readers will have numerous opportunities to see these interpretive principles in action. Here I will provide an introduction to each, followed by a brief illustration of how these approaches might guide our engagement with Scripture.

### The Canon-centered Approach

The word *canon* as used here may not be familiar to some readers. It has to do with "canon" in the sense of "rule" or "norm," as in "canon law," not with *cannon*, the large, cylindrical object that hurls round projectiles. When applied to Scripture, *canon* refers to the body of sacred writings that most Christians throughout history have regarded as "normative" or "faithful." These writings, in disclosing to us the character and will of God, provide the "rule" or "norm" for our faith as Christians. The word *canon*, then, is a noun used in a way similar to *Bible* or *Scripture*, and the adjective *canonical* is similar to "biblical" or "scriptural." When *canon* is used of Scripture, however, it often carries and emphasizes the connotation of "rule of faith" or "norm of faith," that which defines what Christians are to believe and how they are to live.

In a similar vein, the approach introduced here regards Scripture as canon in the traditional sense that it provides a rule or norm of faith. I argue also, however, that the canon should not be regarded as normative only in terms of its content, that is, in terms of what it has to say about

God and God's will for creation. It should be regarded as normative also in terms of what it has to teach us, through its own example, about how to embrace the sacred tradition it embodies. This expansion of the meaning of *canon* and focused attention on how Scripture directs us to engage its sacred tradition further separate the approach presented here from the monological perspective. One of the key distinguishing features of the approach to Scripture as sacred dialogue is that it *upholds the dynamic heritage of sacred conversation that led to and is reflected in Scripture as just as "canonical" for Christian faith as the content of Scripture itself.* To put it more simply, it is not only the words of Scripture that matter (and they matter very much!). The dynamic, ongoing, *sacred dialogue* that Scripture reflects and calls believers to take part in is equally canonical, equally essential to biblical faith. Not only does Scripture preserve and proclaim the story of our faith; it also provides for us an implicit "instruction manual" of sorts for how to read and reflect upon it.

This way of reading Scripture is not an attempt to marginalize the Bible's importance or authority in our lives of faith. On the contrary, it is a way of regarding our sacred tradition that takes Scripture so seriously that it seeks to embrace fully what Scripture might teach us about itself and about how we are to live into its story as God's people. Taking our cue from Scripture, we are called to be those who embrace the story of God's saving will and ways, culminating in Jesus, and those who converse humbly, prayerfully, and boldly with God, Scripture, and one another on what it means to live our part of that story. Biblical faith is not about turning the recorded conversations of our spiritual ancestors into a static transcript, as if the word of God were confined only to pages from the past. Biblical faith is about joining our forebears in the sacred conversation they themselves model. It is about listening very carefully to what they have said, cherishing their witness, attending prayerfully to the guidance of the Spirit, and hashing out and living out the story in a way that reflects our own faithfulness to God and devotion to Jesus.

### The Story-centered Approach

Another important principle of the dialogical approach presented here is that as a canon-centered approach, it also takes seriously the story that the canon, as a whole, proclaims about God, God's relationship with humanity, and the culmination of that story in the life, death, resurrection, and continuing ministry of Jesus. Thus, it is also a story-centered approach. Aided by Bauckham, we have already considered the notion that the narrative, or story, form of Scripture is itself an invitation for us to be in continuing dialogue with Scripture, God, and one another about what it means for us to live as those who are part of this story. *At the same time*, Bauckham also emphasizes the importance—the crucial matter, really—of continually rehearsing "the landmark events" and the "main lines of theological meaning" in our rereadings and retellings of this story. This is an essential point. Appreciating the narrative, and dialogical, character of Scripture does not lead to an anything-goes mode of reading, as if the biblical story itself has no core or recurring story lines. It is a mode of reading and reflecting that takes its cues from the dominant themes and the plot of our story (see chapters 6 and 7). It seeks to grasp the import of particular passages in relation to the broad portrait of God's character and will as painted by the story as a whole. It invites readers to consider how their lives and life experiences fit into the contours of the biblical story, and how they may more deeply inscribe themselves into this story (see the conclusion).

## The Christ-centered Approach

Because the story of our faith as set out in the Christian Bible has as its climax the life, death, resurrection, and ongoing ministry of Jesus, the approach presented here is also fundamentally christocentric in character. From the church's earliest moments, Christian believers read the Jewish Scriptures with the goal of understanding their significance in light of God's revelation made known in Jesus. The New Testament texts reflect this process of discernment on nearly every page. Moreover, they celebrate Jesus as the fullest embodiment of God's will, presenting his instruction as that which transcends the teaching of his contemporaries and even the commandments of old. The New Testament authors also confess their faith in the resurrected Jesus as one who continues to abide with and instruct believers.

The Christ-centered character of the biblical story presents two patterns of reading and reflecting on sacred tradition that are especially important for the engagement of Scripture as sacred conversation. First, guided by the witness of the New Testament authors, readers are called to assess every element of tradition through the lens of Jesus' instruction and life example. To read the Bible christocentrically does not mean that one finds in nearly every Old Testament tradition a veiled reference to Jesus. Nor does it mean that one mutes the distinctive witness of Old Testament traditions to the will and character of God. But it does mean that we hold these and all biblical traditions in conversation with the disclosure of God's character and will as most fully made known in the cross of Christ and his teachings. Very often this conversation is wondrously cohesive. At other times, such reflection may lead us to explore more thoroughly dimensions of God's character that we have neglected. At still other moments, we may find that certain elements of our biblical tradition are in sharp tension with features of God's grace, mercy, and character as revealed in Jesus. Then, in conversation with God and one another, we, like our ancestors in the faith, may be led to recast those elements as we subordinate them to the fuller disclosure of God's character and will made known in Jesus and in the biblical story as a whole. (See the discussions of Jesus' and Paul's radical recasting of God's torah in chapter 3, Paul's creative recasting of Jewish tradition in chapter 4, the discussion of God's judgment in chapter 6, and the interpretation of the Jephthah story in the conclusion.)

Second, as those who share with the New Testament authors the confession that the risen Jesus abides with us still, to read christocentrically also means that we remain open to the instruction Jesus, the Living Word, continues to offer on how to live as his disciples in our time and place. Granting Jesus the sovereignty that is due to him as Lord, we are mindful of his freedom to lead us in ways that transcend the teachings of old, perhaps even some of those found in the New Testament (see chapter 2).

## Dialogical and Monological Perspectives: An Important Difference

As the discussion up to this point, and especially the immediately preceding comments, has suggested, one of the implications of engaging Scripture as sacred dialogue that further separates it from a monological approach is that not every single element of Scripture is necessarily regarded as faithfully disclosing the character of God and God's ways. With the approach presented here, there is a greater degree of openness to regarding some elements of Scripture as reflecting a view of God's character and will that sharply contrasts with the portrayal of God provided by Scripture as a whole and revealed in Jesus. This will be amply illustrated in following chapters. For now, by way of example, consider the following passage from Josh 11:16-20, which is part of a larger narrative describing Israel's conquest of Canaan, the promised land, under the leadership of Joshua.

> So Joshua took all that land: the hill country and all the Negeb and all the land of Goshen and the lowland and the Arabah and the hill country of Israel and its lowland from Mount Halak, which rises toward Seir, as far as Baal-gad in the valley of Lebanon below Mount Hermon. He took all their kings, struck them down, and put them to death. Joshua made war a long time with all those kings. There was not a town that made peace with the Israelites, except the Hivites, the inhabitants of Gibeon; all were taken in battle. For it was the LORD's doing to harden their hearts so that they would come against Israel in battle, in order that they might be utterly destroyed, and might receive no mercy, but be exterminated, just as the LORD had commanded Moses.

In the narrative that immediately precedes these verses we hear in unceasing refrain that the extermination willed by God was not restricted to able-bodied Canaanite males who posed a threat to the fulfillment of God's promise to Israel, but included "utterly every person" and "all that breathed" (see Josh 10:28-40 and 11:12-14). All were to be put to the sword, from frail widow to infant child (see also 1 Sam 15:1-33).

One holding a monological view of Scripture is required to embrace this portrayal of God's character and will as though it were God's own self-disclosure: that is, as what God wants us to believe about the divine will and character. In contrast, those holding a canon-centered, story-centered, and Christ-centered view of Scripture (as described above) may be led to view this passage as not fully or even faithfully capturing God's will and character. To them, this story may conflict with the overarching themes and movements of the biblical story as a whole, which present God as equally concerned for all of humanity, not just ancient Israel. They may be hard-pressed to reconcile this story with Jesus' instruction, especially his teaching on enemies, his earnest desire for all of humanity to be reconciled to God, and his example of self-sacrifice that others may be saved. Because a canon-centered approach recognizes that even the biblical authors at times held contrasting views of God's will, and that such diversity bears witness to Scripture as a sacred dialogue rather than a divine monologue, they feel called to adjudicate between these disparate voices and to add their own story- and Christ-formed testimony in support the view of God's character and will that they find more faithful. For them, to discern that this is one instance in which our ancestors in the faith failed to reflect God's character and will is not a statement in opposition to Scripture but one consistent with the way of engaging sacred tradition that Scripture itself embodies and invites us to undertake.

Many, of course, will not be comfortable with this view of Scripture. It invites a level of ambiguity and uncertainty that many may find difficult to accept. After all, someone might object, if not all parts of Scripture truly reflect God's character and will, how do we know which ones to trust? The standards for faithful discernment and boundaries of what constitutes biblical faith presented here (canon-centered, story-centered, and Christ-centered), while having a familiar ring, leave room for readings of Scripture that challenge common monological interpretations. The monological view escapes this disconcerting ambiguity and these troubling readings. In their place it offers the security of knowing that all of Scripture is breathed from the very mouth of God. To the question, What parts are to be trusted? it answers, All of them. What about the teaching of the Holy Spirit? It will never conflict with the written word. What about those believers who are feeling led to different understandings of God's will? They are mistaken.

I like simplicity. Much to my wife's chagrin, I am happiest in a house with white walls and very few adornments. I find beauty in practicality, efficiency, and simplicity of design, and I strive for it in my hobbies of carpentry and woodworking. If I had my preference, the monological view would be the one for me. As I study Scripture, however, and (on my better days) seek to live out my faith in community with other believers, I find that the monological view of Scripture doesn't always square with my encounter of God's word. Very often it does. When reading Scripture, I often hear God's word clear and pure, a double-edged sword that divides with surgeonlike precision the ways of God from the ways of the world, a bright light that unmasks the thoughts and intentions of my heart. At those moments I hear Scripture as an a cappella choir flawlessly singing the melody, clarion, and true. It is beautiful, and sometimes painful. (Double-edged swords have a tendency to cut both ways.)

But at other times, I encounter Scripture and it is more like a symphony orchestra, with all sorts of harmonization, melodies, and countermelodies. It requires much more effort to take it all in. There are also those moments when parts of this orchestra seem off-beat or out of key; when (so to speak) the violins send out a string of sour tones, the woodwinds screech, the trumpets are on the sharp edge of their notes, or the percussionists lose count. Sometimes it can all be quite cacophonous. But even when it is at its most noisesome, there is still beauty and grace to behold, and this is why I and others can't help but still listen. For all instruments of the orchestra offer their music as a witness to God and God's ways. The conductor graciously beckons all of them to play, even those whom we might think the symphony would be better without. The conductor calls all of us to imagine the vision of God and God's kingdom that the various voices of the orchestra offer in song. More often than not, our imaginations and hearts are able to capture the harmony of their witness rising above the discordance. And oh, how wondrous that harmony and vision are!

This book is written as an invitation for readers to explore Scripture as sacred conversation. I present it as a contribution to the ongoing Christian discussion of the nature and authority of Scripture. If, however, you are not a Christian, or if you are being forced to read this text against your will by an ogre posing as a college or seminary professor, I also hope that you will find something of value in these pages and perhaps even become interested in the discussion. At the very least, I trust the book will serve as a witness to the fact that not all Christians regard and read Scripture in the same way.

The chapters to follow will further elaborate on the various ways sacred dialogue is inscribed in Scripture, and the joys and challenges facing those who accept the invitation to join the conversation. As a means of illustrating the dynamic, conversational, and often disputatious character of Christian sacred tradition, I begin each of the chapters (except chapter 7, which continues the argument of chapter 6, and the conclusion) with a brief, imaginative vignette, based on a particular biblical passage, inviting the reader to "hear" part of the conversation that I suggest lies behind or beneath the biblical text.

# Having Words
# with God

_____

## chapter one

*"O Lord, why does your wrath burn hot . . . ?"*
*(Exod 32:11)*

**Following the golden calf affair and Moses'**
own drastic response to the Israelite's egregious betrayal of Yawheh
(see Exodus 32), I imagine Moses having ruminations similar to what
follows.

*Why did Yahweh listen to me? When I saw with my own eyes that
hideous form Aaron had sculpted and the people dancing before
it, when I heard with my own ears their cries of adulterous adora-
tion, "These are your gods, O Israel, who led you out of Egypt!"
suddenly the bold words of petition I had spoken to Yahweh rang
hollow in my heart. The emptiness was filled with a seething rage.
The betrayal! The utter lunacy! The abject, mindless depravity!
Then I knew how Yahweh had felt. Then I knew righteous rage
bent on destroying those who so quickly had turned to utter evil.
But unlike Yahweh, I did not relent. I did not put aside my thirst to
see evil consumed before me, not until a multitude had fallen by
the sword. Yahweh listened to my words, but I forgot them. Yahweh sent me to the people with his commands in my hands, and
I smashed them. I smashed the tablets, for these stiff-necked fools
did not deserve God's torah. Then I smashed the people, for they
did not deserve life. How could Yahweh not have done the same?
Why did Yahweh listen to me when I said, "Turn from your fierce
wrath and change your mind"?*

## A Divine Change of Mind

Among the many biblical accounts that portray the descendants of Abraham turning away from God and God's ways, the story of the golden calf affair (Exodus 32–34) stands out as one of the most thick-headed and egregious.[1] The artistry of the narrator in leading us to appreciate the utter depravity of the people's actions in Exod 32:1-6 is apparent at a number of points. The opening chapters of Exodus tell the story of Yahweh hearing the cries of his oppressed people, Israel, and with a mighty hand delivering them from their slavery to Pharaoh. God leads them out of Egypt by cloud and fire, through water and desert to Mount Sinai. In God's own words, "I bore you on eagles' wings and brought you to myself" (Exod 19:4). There God announces God's intentions to renew the covenantal relationship with them (19:1-6). Of all the peoples of the earth, they are to be God's "treasured possession." They are to be for God a "priestly kingdom" and a "holy nation," a nation set apart (holy) for a particular purpose: to serve as priests for the rest of the world, bearing witness to God and God's ways. What a calling for an oppressed people—from a ragtag group of slaves to those who will mediate the will and ways of God to humanity! They need only to trust God's voice and keep God's statutes. The Decalogue (Ten Commandments) comes next, spoken by God directly to the people. The commands begin with what is most central: "I am Yahweh your God who brought you out of the land of Egypt, out of the house of slavery; you shall have no other gods before me" (Exod 20:2). This is followed by the command to "not make for yourselves an idol . . . you shall not bow down to them or worship them" (20:4-5). After God gives Israel the Ten Commandments, Moses goes back up the mountain to receive other instructions from God, statutes that are to guide the people into living rightly with God, one another, and also creation (Exodus 20–23).

In Exodus 24, the time for ratifying the covenant is at hand. Moses comes down from the mountain to give the instructions to the people. The narrator is careful to note the unanimity of the people's devotion: "and all the people answered with one voice, and said, 'All the words that Yahweh has spoken, we will do!'" (24:3). After final preparations are made for ratifying the covenant, Moses once again reads the book of the covenant to the people, and once again the people affirm, "All that the LORD has spoken we will do, and we will be obedient!" (24:7). Moses then departs from the people and ascends Mount Sinai to receive detailed instructions from God on the construction and maintenance of the tabernacle, the portable sanctuary that Israel will take with them through the wilderness embodying God's presence with the people (Exodus 25–31). God's instruction is painstakingly precise, emphasizing the sacredness of the tabernacle and the importance attached to its purpose: Yahweh dwelling among them. Moses is with God on the mountain for forty days and nights (24:18).

Thus, the background is set for the golden calf affair. This people, the descendants of Abraham, have just been delivered by God from Egypt. Yahweh, the Lord of the universe, the God who covenanted with their ancestors, has heard their cries and led them out into the wilderness to be God's treasured possession. God has instructed them on how to walk rightly in relationship with God and one another. The people pledge their devotion to God. The marriage is enjoined, and now God is helping them to prepare a place where God's very presence will dwell among them. All seems to be going so well. If at this point in the story you were to ask, What would be the most outrageous thing the people could do to threaten their renewed relationship with God? It would be difficult, I think, to come up with something more destructive than what happens next. The people tire of waiting for Moses to return from the mountain. They now command Aaron, "Come, make gods for us, who shall go before us; as for this Moses, the man who brought us up out of the land of Egypt, we do not know what has become of him" (Exod 32:1). Aaron, without a hint of resistance to the people's demand, collects gold from them (part of their plunder from Egypt) and forms it into an image of a calf. Then comes the line that really stings. With the golden calf before them, the people bow down before it proclaiming, "These are your gods, O Israel, who brought you up out of the land of Egypt!" (Exod 32:4).

Perhaps Aaron tries to salvage some semblance of devotion to God when he announces, "Tomorrow shall be a festival to Yahweh" (Exod 32:5). But the "reveling" that characterizes the people's "worship" (Exod 32:6; see also vv. 18-19) clearly indicates that the Yahweh they had come to know as Savior has—*in essence if not in name*—been co-opted by a new god, and one designed according to the worst angels of their nature.[2] Remember the people's words the very last time they spoke in the narrative. They devoted themselves to the covenant, saying "All that Yahweh has spoken we will do, and we will be obedient!" They couldn't even get past the first two commandments! Note how the people's words and actions together form a direct repudiation of those two commands.

> I am Yahweh, your God, who brought you out of the land of Egypt, out of the house of slavery; you shall have no other gods before me. You shall not make for yourselves an idol, whether in the form of anything that is in heaven above, or that is on the earth beneath, or that is in the water under the earth. You shall not bow down to them or worship them. (Exod 20:2-5)

> When the people saw that Moses delayed to come down from the mountain, the people gathered around Aaron, and said to him, "Come, make gods for us, who shall go before us; as for this Moses, the man who brought us up out of the land of Egypt, we do not know what has become of him." Aaron said to them, "Take off the gold rings that are on the ears of your wives, your sons, and your daughters, and bring them to me." So all the people took off the gold rings from their ears, and brought them to Aaron. He took the gold from them, formed it in a mold, and cast an image of a calf; and they said, "These are your gods, O Israel, who brought you up out of the land of Egypt!" (Exod 32:1-4)

Not only are the people transgressing the first commands given to them; in doing so they are also rejecting and betraying everything that God has revealed God's self to be. It is Yahweh as has been revealed to them through plague, flame, and water, not Pharoah or golden figurine, who is Lord of the universe. Yahweh has delivered them from Egypt and hence from this time onward is to be known to them as Savior. Yahweh has "brought them to myself" and renewed the covenantal relationship with them. But in an act of folly that defies comprehension (well, at least until we take a good, critical look at ourselves) the people throw all of that aside. They get tired of waiting for Moses, cast away their special relationship with Yahweh, Lord of all, and bow down before a lump of gold. In one of the worst ways imaginable, they betray Yahweh, their Creator, Savior, and Lord, who desires to dwell with them.

Students in my courses are often taken aback by the harshness of Yahweh's response to the people's betrayal. God immediately distances God's self from the people, in effect, disowning them. Yahweh commands Moses, "Go down at once! *"Your* people, whom *you* brought up out of the land of Egypt have acted perversely" (Exod 32:7). After relaying a full account of the people's actions to Moses, culminating in their cry "These are your gods, O Israel, who have brought you up out of the land of Egypt!" Yahweh pronounces their doom: "I have seen this people, how stiff-necked they are. Now let me alone, so that my wrath may burn hot against them and I may consume them; and of you I will make a great nation."

Yahweh's response of judgment is indeed harsh. Yet from the perspective of the biblical writer, I think we are to see it as justly commensurate with the people's crime. The people, after having just pledged their full devotion to God, now betray God in one of the worst ways imaginable. In a dramatic replay of humanity's distrust of God in the garden of Eden (see Genesis 3), the people once again fail to trust in God, even though they have been given every reason to do so. Instead, they follow their insecurities and misplaced passions and cast aside the very source of blessing: a trusting relationship with their Creator. So egregious is their betrayal, so warped have they revealed themselves to be, that their destruction, and God's attempt to begin again with a new people, seems the only fitting option. The people, from the perspective of the biblical author, deserve no more. They have completely forfeited any covenantal claim that could be made on their behalf.

Noting this, I think, not only helps us to understand the harshness of Yahweh's response to the people's betrayal (Exod 32:7-10), but also helps us rightly hear Moses' words to God (Exod 32:11-13) as both bold and outlandish. Moses, in effect, calls Yahweh to abide by the covenant promises even when the people—in a most incredible manner—have failed to do so.

> But Moses implored the LORD his God, and said, "O LORD, why does your wrath burn hot against your people, whom you brought out of the land of Egypt with great power and with a mighty hand? Why should the Egyptians say, 'It was with evil intent that he brought them out to kill them in the mountains, and to consume them from the face of the earth'? Turn from your fierce wrath; change your mind and do not bring disaster on your people. Remember Abraham, Isaac, and Israel, your servants, how you swore to them by your own self, saying to them, 'I will multiply your descendants like the stars of heaven, and all this land that I have promised I will give to your descendants, and they shall inherit it forever.'"

Moses reminds Yahweh of Yahweh's own intentions in delivering Israel from Egypt. One intention was to reveal to Egypt and the rest of the world that Yahweh, not Pharaoh, is Lord of creation (see Exod 5:1-2; 9:14, 15:11, 18:10-12). Moses now says to God, in effect, "What will the Egyptians and the rest of the world think of you if you destroy this people? Will anyone want to follow you?" But God's primary intention was to act on the promises God had made to Abraham and his descendants, to call out this people as God's own, to grant them provision, security and land, so that they may multiply and eventually be a source of blessing for all the peoples of the earth (see Gen 12:1-3; Exod 3:1-17). Knowing this, Moses calls Yahweh to take back the people and to claim them once more as God's own: "O LORD, why does your wrath burn hot against *your* people, whom *you* brought out of the land of Egypt with great power and with a mighty hand? . . . Turn from your fierce wrath; change your mind and do not bring disaster on *your* people." In light of how the narrator has carefully crafted the narrative to highlight the depravity of the people's betrayal, it seems to me that the response the narrator is expecting from the reader at this point is along the lines of: "Forgive them? How could God do so? There's just no way!" But

Moses knows the deep desires of God's heart for Abraham's descendants and the rest of humanity. His plea manages to undo Yahweh's adamant resolve to destroy this stiff-necked rabble. He tells God to embrace them once more, despite their utter rejection of God. He tells God, in effect, to remember the relationship. Then come those startling words: "And the Lord changed his mind about the disaster he planned to bring on his people" (v. 14).

This is remarkable. Divine intention is reversed by human intercession. And yet in the very next chapter we see God change God's mind once again. God commands Moses and the people to leave Mount Sinai and to resume their journey to the promised land (Exod 33:1). He tells Moses, "Go, leave this place, you and the people whom *you* have brought out of the land of Egypt," using the second person singular pronoun again to signal that Yahweh still refuses to reclaim the people. Although an angel will be sent before them to drive out the inhabitants of the land, Yahweh will not go with them, "or I would consume you on the way, for you are a stiff-necked people!" (33:3). Once again, Moses intercedes, this time appealing to the intimate relationship that he and Yahweh share, and again urging Yahweh, "Consider too, that this nation is *your* people" (33:12-13). Yahweh relents once more and assures Moses, "My presence will go with you, and I will give you rest" (33:14).

Judgment is also a part of this story. In Exod 32:35 we learn that "the Lord sent a plague on the people, because of the calf—the one that Aaron made." But this reference to the judgment God imposes is mild in comparison with what God had initially threatened and also pales in comparison with Moses' actions preceding the plague. Upon coming down from the mountain after interceding on behalf of the people, Moses sees with his own eyes the Israelites reveling before the calf. He smashes the tablets written by God's hand, grinds the idol into powder, spreads the dust into the water, and makes the Israelites drink it (32:19-20). When the people still run wild with idolatrous frenzy, Moses gathers the sons of Levi around them, and tells them to take up their swords: "Go back and forth from gate to gate throughout the camp and each of you kill your brother, your friend, and your neighbor . . . and about three thousand of the people fell that day" (32:27-28). Readers disagree on whether Moses' drastic actions were commanded by God. That Moses claims to act on God's behalf is clear: "Thus says the Lord, the God of Israel, put you sword on your side . . ." (32:27). But in nearly every other case in which Moses speaks with divine authority, the narrator tells us that Yahweh has directed Moses to do so. Here, we are never told that God has issued such a command. Instead, we go from Yahweh relenting from anger and the threat of destruction to Moses, once he sees for himself how bad things have become, responding with bloody vengeance. The point of the contrast (as illustrated in the imaginative vignette at the beginning of the chapter) seems to be that Moses, despite his great love for and loyalty to the people, was incapable of the mercy that Yahweh displays. Such forgiveness and forbearance are possible only for God.

This section of Exodus, extending through chapter 34, is about as theologically dense as they come, and we will have the opportunity to reflect further on it in chapters 6 and 7. This story poignantly speaks to the character of God as "merciful and gracious, slow to anger and abounding in steadfast love and faithfulness" (34:6-7), a profession that from this point on becomes basic to the Old Testament's portrait of God. It also highlights the fickleness and "stiff-neckedness" of God's people, who time and time again are quick to turn away from Yahweh. However, the reason I want to begin this chapter with the story of the golden calf affair is because it also bears striking witness to the nature of God as one who seeks out an interactive and dynamic relationship with human creatures. That relationship is one in which humanity is called to trust and obey God in order that they might enjoy the blessings God intends to bestow upon them. It is one in which humanity is to attend carefully to the revelation God provides about the divine character and instruction on what it means to be God's people. But it is not a relationship characterized by one-way conversation. God also invites humanity into unabashed dialogue. God listens to human creatures and is willing to be moved by them, even in situations in which human sinfulness threatens God's relationship with and loving intentions for humanity. It is no coincidence that in this story, and just before God's second change of mind, the narrator pauses to describe for us Yahweh's practice of conversing with the people, and the intimate dialogue shared between Moses and God (Exod 33:7-11a):

> Now Moses used to take the tent and pitch it outside the camp, far off from the camp; he called it the tent of meeting. And everyone who sought the Lord would go out to the tent of meeting, which was outside the camp. Whenever Moses went out to the tent, all the people would rise and stand, each of them, at the entrance of their tents and watch Moses until he had gone into the tent. When Moses entered the tent, the pillar of cloud would descend and stand at the entrance of the tent, and the Lord would speak with Moses. When all the people saw the pillar of cloud standing at the entrance of the tent, all the people would rise and bow down, all of them, at the entrance of their tent. Thus the Lord used to speak to Moses face to face, as one speaks to a friend.

The interaction described here between Moses and God is but one of countless depictions of God engaged in dialogue with humankind. What we find throughout the biblical story, in fact, is God frequently in conversation with individuals and the people as a whole, either directly or through mediums such as visions or prophecies. God is not silent and removed, but obtrusively interactive in the lives of human creatures, from Adam and Eve, to Cain, Noah, Abraham, Hagar, Jacob, Joseph, Moses, Joshua, Deborah, Hannah, Samuel, Elijah, Elisha, David, and the prophets— the list goes on, leading to, as the New Testament authors would claim, the ultimate manifestation of God's interaction with humankind in Jesus. And, as we find in Exodus 32–34, God is willing to change God's course of action in response to human petition. In Numbers 14, a passage that in many ways mirrors Exodus 32–34, Moses once again intercedes on behalf of God's people and once again God relents from threatened destruction. Sometimes even the repentance and prayers of the wicked lead God to relent, as in the case of the reprobate King Ahab (1 Kgs 21:27-29) or the inhabitants of Ninevah (Jonah 3:10). The story of Abraham interceding on behalf of Sodom and Gomorrah is still another wonderfully dramatic account that reveals God's desire to engage human creatures. It begins with God involving Abraham in discerning the fate of those wicked cities (Gen 18:17-19).

> The LORD said, "Shall I hide from Abraham what I am about to do, seeing that Abraham shall become a great and mighty nation, and all the nations of the earth shall be blessed in him? No, for I have chosen him that he may charge his children and his household after him to keep the way of the LORD by doing righteousness and justice; so that the LORD may bring about for Abraham what he has promised him."

But Abraham is far from compliant. He boldly challenges God's plan (Gen 18:24-25):

> "Will you indeed sweep away the righteous with the wicked? Suppose there are fifty righteous within the city; will you then sweep away the place and not forgive it for the fifty righteous that are within it? Far be it from you! Shall not the Judge of all the earth do what is just?

God responds to Abraham's petition with a generous offer: "if there are fifty righteous in the city, I will forgive the whole place for their sake." But Abraham is not satisfied. He bargains and cajoles until Yahweh finally accepts the number that Abraham considers more in keeping with what is just: "For the sake of ten I will not destroy" (Gen 18:32).

Unfortunately for the evil cities, not even ten righteous could be found, and only a portion of Lot's family is spared. But here again we find God in dialogue with humanity and open to changing God's course of action in response to human petition. Once more, it is a conversation that God initiates. Here too, the human character responds with boldness, challenging God's actions based on what he knows about God's character and intentions for humanity. Once more, God changes God's mind.

## God—the Unmoved, or *Most* Moved Mover?[3]

While engaging, these dramatic tales of human characters leading God to change God's mind have been a source of discomfort for many readers. It is easy to understand why. How is it that an all-knowing, perfect, and unchanging God could actually change his/her mind? Would not this imply that God, in essence, made a mistake, or at least had initially chosen a course of action that was not the best option? If God is all knowing, should not God have known the course of action that God would eventually take, making the initial choice pointless and illogical?

The problems some readers have with the notion that God could change God's mind stem from traditional ways of understanding God's character that are more closely aligned with Greek philosophy than with biblical revelation. Over the course of Christian history, major thinkers making formative contributions to Christian theology often drew from Platonic and Aristotelian thought when constructing their paradigms for God. Theological giants such as Augustine, Thomas Aquinas, Anselm, and Calvin (and countless others drawing from their works) found the philosophical constructs of omniscience (all knowingness), omnipotence (all powerfulness, all controllingness), and immutability (unchangingness) useful for conceiving of the basic dimensions of God's nature. Still today, these concepts remain so integral to our understandings of God that for many they go unquestioned as essential to any proper definition of God. These concepts, however, are in tension with the *biblical* construal of God's character and actions. As well summarized by Clark Pinnock,

> What took place was that the attributes of God contained in Scripture were shaped and amplified under the influence of Greek thought. On the one hand, there was a Hellenic [Greek] ideal of God as absolute, timeless and unchangeable being, a view which assumes God to be unconditioned, unchanging, impassible and totally in control; a Being that cannot be affected by anything outside of itself. On the other hand, there was the biblical ideal of God as a dynamic, relational person; vulnerable, sympathetic, accessible and committed to relationships. This is a picture of a God who loves covenant and chooses dialogue over monologue.[4]

The struggle between these two paradigms for God—the immutable, monological God of Greek thought versus the relational, conversational God of Scripture—is quite apparent in my discussions of Exod 32:1-14 with layfolk and students. Invariably, many feel the need to rescue God from the biblical notion that God would—or could—actually change God's mind. Creative solutions are frequently offered. Most common among them is the explanation that God already knows that God will not end up destroying the people, but is testing Moses here to see if he will stick up for the people and thus faithfully embrace his role as a mediator between God and Israel (similar explanations are given for the negotiation between God and Abraham in Genesis 18). Another common resolution is that God is simply posturing to let Moses and the people know the seriousness of their betrayal—a divine "bluff," if you will. Still others have concluded that God is "just blowing off steam," indicating what God would like to do—but does not really intend to do—to God's stiff-necked people.

While imaginative, these attempts to preserve God's immutability and omniscience are fraught with problems. If God always knew what God was going to do, and is unchangeable, what would be the point of a mediator who sticks up for the people? What type of real mediation could ever take place? A divine "bluff" amounts to a falsehood, and a God who needs to "blow off steam" by making hollow threats hardly coheres with any notion of a perfectly composed, immovable, deity. More importantly, these explanations and the conception of God that motivates them fail to take seriously the portrait of God presented in Scripture. The text of Exod 32:14 is clear: "And the Lord changed his mind about the disaster that he planned to bring on his people." Moreover, as framed well—and passionately—by Pinnock:

> The god of the gospel is not the god of philosophy, at least not of Hellenic philosophy. The God and Father of Jesus Christ is compassionate, suffering, victorious love. The god of philosophy is immutable, timeless and apathetic. We must speak boldly for the sake of the gospel: Augustine was wrong to have said that God does not grieve over the suffering of the world; Anselm was wrong to have said that God does not experience compassion; Calvin was wrong to have said that biblical figures that convey such things are mere accommodations to finite understanding. For too long pagan assumptions about God's nature have influenced theological reflection. Our thinking needs to be reformed in light of the self-revelation of God in the gospels and we must stop attributing to God qualities that undermine God's own self-disclosure. Let us not treat the attributes of God independently of the Bible but view the biblical metaphors as reality-depicting descriptions of the living God, whose

very being is self-giving love. When we do so, God's unity will not be viewed as a mathematical oneness but as a unity that includes diversity; God's steadfastness will not be seen as a deadening immutability but constancy of character that includes change; God's power will not be seen as raw omnipotence but as the sovereignty of love whose strength is revealed in weakness; and God's omniscience will not be seen as know-it-all but as a wisdom which shapes the future in dialogue with creatures.[5]

While an honest appraisal of the biblical portrait of God may lead us to think about God in ways that are unusual or uncomfortable for some of us, it is important to note that the approachable, conversational, and even vulnerable nature of God's character is what enables God and humanity to be in genuine relationship with one another. In order for humanity to respond to God with genuine devotion and love, humanity must have the freedom to either trust and embrace God, or distrust and reject God. Otherwise, we are simply automatons, capable of neither genuine devotion nor betrayal. And in order for God to respond to humanity in ways that foster the survival and strengthening of God's relationship with God's human creatures—especially in response to human betrayal—God must also have the freedom to act dynamically, contingent not only upon the abiding features of God's character but also upon the actions of God's covenant partner. Accordingly, the future for humanity and God must have at least some degree of openness to it, and the biblical story as a whole revolves around this view of reality. What is the biblical story about if not the failures and triumphs in humanity's calling to live rightly with God and one another, and the myriad of ways in which God responds to human betrayal and faithfulness in order lead humanity more deeply into God's blessing? As a whole, the biblical story presumes free will on the part of both humanity and God, and thus by necessity presumes that the future of the relationship between God and humanity has not yet been fully scripted. The part of the script that is not in doubt is the future for those who devote themselves to God and seek God's mercy. They shall find themselves delivered into God's loving care. But the ways in which God's desires for humanity will be realized in the present, and the specific contours of God's work among humanity in the future, are in large measure shaped by the extent to which humanity embraces God's guidance and provision.

In sum, what we find in the Old Testament passages we have briefly considered thus far, and the biblical story as a whole is a God in conversation with God's human creatures. It is a dialogue that God initiates, but not for the sake of controlling human response to God's preordained plan. Instead, *it is a dialogue God invites and takes so seriously that God is open to courses of action made possible through that conversation, even courses that at times cause God to repent, change God's mind, and move in a new direction.* It is an invitation to dialogue which reveals that our interactions with God and our own participation in God's intentions for humanity shape in large measure how our future with God will unfold. It is a conversation through which humanity discovers more deeply, and God claims more steadfastly, what is most essential and unchanging about God's character: God's mercy and love for creation.

## The Psalms of Lament: Instruction for Faithful Dialogue

Stories such as the ones we have considered provide concrete examples of the words we find in Jas 5:16: "the prayer of the righteous is powerful and effective." They illustrate Jesus' words to his disciples: "Ask and it will be given you; search, and you will find; knock, and the door will be opened for you" (Matt 7:7). Throughout the biblical story we also encounter God hearing the call of the oppressed or afflicted and responding to their cry for help with decisive, life-changing action on their behalf as well as with judgment for their oppressors. So consistent is this pattern that whenever we come across a cry to God in the biblical story, we can be sure that God's saving actions will follow. This is good news and a source of hope for those who seek God's aid. For those causing the oppression, the message is not so positive.

The Old Testament Psalter is filled with the cries of the oppressed faithful. The psalms of lament are a type of psalm in which the psalmist offers a lament, or complaint to God. There is something terribly wrong in the psalmist's life, some affliction or persecution, and the psalmist calls upon God for deliverance. Now, as just mentioned, there are numerous stories in Scripture of the oppressed crying out to God, and we could profitably turn to these to learn more about what it means to be in dialogue with God in times of distress (for example, Israelites in Egypt [Exodus 3], widows and orphans [Exodus 22], oppressed laborers [Deuteronomy 24], Hannah [1 Samuel 1], David [2 Samuel 22], Jehoshaphat [2 Chronicles 20], Job, Jeremiah). But the psalms of lament are especially well suited for this purpose for two reasons. First, the psalms in general began as human words to God that, in becoming Scripture, were embraced by the community of faith as God's words to us. In other words, generations of believers have found in these ancient prayers and hymns faithful instruction on what it means to be in conversation with God—this is central to their purpose.[6] They serve as prayers to recite *and* paradigms to follow when in our lives of faith we are led to erupt in praise, rejoice in thanksgiving, sue for pardon, or cry out in distress.[7] Thus, we do well to consider them at this point in our discussion. Second, the psalms of lament provide us with some of the most astonishing examples of impassioned speech with God. In doing so, they help us to realize that the boundaries of what constitutes sincere, faithful words with God are drawn very wide indeed, wider than we might have imagined.

Despite their tremendous usefulness and the fact that they are the most common type of psalm in the Psalter, the psalms of lament are frequently underutilized and even neglected by Christian communities. Christian liturgy instead gravitates toward the psalms of thanksgiving and praise, and verses from these psalms fill Christian hymnals. The Revised Common Lectionary also heavily favors the psalms of praise and thanksgiving, and thus these are the psalms most frequently read and recited in worship. There are probably a number of reasons why the psalms of lament are not all that popular among us. One reason might be that these psalms speak to situations of pain and distress, and we would rather focus on what we consider positive and uplifting in worship. Another likely reason behind their unpopularity is that in these psalms the psalmists sometimes speak to God in a manner that we might find "irreverent," perhaps even offensive.

The language employed by the laments matches the dire situations and feelings of distress experienced by the psalmists. What we typically find in them are not polite, meek, deferential pleas for God's assistance, as if the psalmist is saying: "Ahem, excuse me, God. If it pleases you, Sir, would you mind, when you have chance, giving me a little assistance down here. You see, I've got this problem and just thought that you might, if it's not too much to ask. . . ." Rather, these are characteristically desperate, even outraged, door-battering complaints in which the psalmist cries: "Hey God, WAKE UP!! These guys are after my neck! What are you waiting for?! If you don't do something soon, I'm DEAD!"

Consider the plea of Ps 13:1-4, one of the more well known psalms of lament, which demands that God "pay attention" to the psalmist's distress:

> *How long, O L*ORD*, Will you forget me forever?*
> > *How long will you hide your face from me?*
> *How long must I bear pain in my soul,*
> > *and have sorrow in my heart all day long?*
> *How long shall my enemy be exalted over me?*
>
> *Consider and answer me, O L*ORD *my God!*
> > *Give light to my eyes, or I will sleep the sleep of death,*
> *and my enemy will say, "I have prevailed";*
> > *my foes will rejoice because I am shaken.*

The passionate complaints of Ps 10:1-4, 12-13 call upon God to take note of the dark deeds of the wicked and to deliver the faithful.

*Why, O Lord, do you stand far off?*
    *Why do you hide yourself in times of trouble?*
*In arrogance the wicked persecute the poor—*
    *let them be caught in the schemes they have devised.*

*For the wicked boast of the desires of their heart,*
    *those greedy for gain curse and renounce the Lord.*
*In the pride of their countenance the wicked say,*
        *"God will not seek it out";*
    *all their thoughts are, "There is no God."*

*. . . Rise up, O Lord; O God lift up your hand;*
    *Do not forget the oppressed.*
*Why do the wicked renounce God,*
    *and say in their hearts, "You will not call us to account"?*

As reflected in these and other psalms, common to the laments are complaints that God is nowhere to be found. In essence, the lament psalms frequently identify God as part of the problem that needs to be fixed. God is not attentive. God needs to be spurred to action. We encounter this poignant petition in Ps 42:1-3, 9-10:

*As a deer longs for flowing streams,*
    *so my soul longs for you, O God.*
*My soul thirsts for God,*
    *for the living God.*
*When shall I come and behold*
    *the face of God?*
*My tears have been my food,*
    *day and night,*
*while people say to me continually,*
    *"Where is your God?"*

*. . . I say to God, my rock,*
    *"Why have you forgotten me?"*
*Why must I walk about mournfully*
    *because the enemy oppresses me?"*
*As with a deadly wound in my body,*
    *my adversaries taunt me,*
*while they say to me continually,*
    *"Where is your God?"*

In Psalm 77, the psalmist's disgust with God's absence and inaction reaches such depths that the very thought of God leads him to moan with despair. The psalmist's anguished complaint moves to the chilling conclusion that the very nature of God has changed.

> I cry aloud to God,
>> aloud to God, that he may hear me.
> In the day of my trouble I seek the Lord;
>> in the night my hand is stretched out without wearying;
>> my soul refuses to be comforted.
> I think of God, and I moan;
>> I meditate, and my spirit faints. Selah
>
> You keep my eyelids from closing;
>> I am so troubled that I cannot speak.
> I consider the days of old,
>> and remember the years of long ago.
> I commune with my heart in the night;
>> I meditate and search my spirit:
> "Will the Lord spurn forever,
>> and never again be favorable?
> Has his steadfast love ceased forever?
>> Are his promises at an end for all time?
> Has God forgotten to be gracious?
>> Has he in anger shut up his compassion?" Selah
> And I say, "It is my grief
>> that the right hand of the Most High has changed!"
> (Ps 77:1-10)

In some laments, the psalmist is so distressed the he accuses God of being the enemy from whom he needs rescue. Psalm 88 is one of the very few laments that is so relentless in its complaint against God (see also Psalm 89) that it does not close with an expression of confidence in God's eventual deliverance. The following excerpt picks up the psalm in v. 6 and continues to its conclusion in v. 18.

> You have put me in the depths of the Pit,
>> in the regions dark and deep.
> Your wrath lies heavy upon me,
>> and you overwhelm me with all your waves. Selah
>
> You have caused my companions to shun me;
>> you have made me a thing of horror to them.

*I am shut in so that I cannot escape;*
    *my eye grows dim through sorrow.*
*Every day I call on you, O LORD;*
    *I spread out my hands to you.*
*Do you work wonders for the dead?*
    *Do the shades rise up to praise you? Selah*
*Is your steadfast love declared in the grave,*
    *or your faithfulness in Abaddon?*
*Are your wonders known in the darkness,*
    *or your saving help in the land of forgetfulness?*

*But I, O LORD, cry out to you;*
    *in the morning my prayer comes before you.*
*O LORD, why do you cast me off?*
    *Why do you hide your face from me?*
*Wretched and close to death from my youth up,*
    *I suffer your terrors; I am desperate.*
*Your wrath has swept over me;*
    *your dread assaults destroy me.*
*They surround me like a flood all day long;*
    *from all sides they close in on me.*
*You have caused friend and neighbor to shun me;*
    *my companions are in darkness.*

While many laments speak to the unmet needs and suffering of individuals, laments were also offered on behalf of Israel as a whole. As
is typical with all the psalms, it is difficult to locate most communal
laments in a specific historical context. However, many of the communal laments preserved in the Psalter were likely written or utilized in
response to the tragic defeat and exile of God's people at the hands of the
Babylonians in 587 B.C.E. In them we find some of the boldest expressions
of complaint to God and outrage against Israel's enemies. For example,
in Psalm 44:9-13 the psalmist blames the defeat of Israel by its enemies
on God's willful neglect.

*You have rejected us and abased us,*
    *and have not gone out with our armies.*
*You made us turn back from the foe,*
    *and our enemies have gotten spoil.*
*You have made us like sheep for slaughter,*
    *and have scattered us among the nations.*
*You have sold your people for a trifle,*
    *demanding no high price for them.*

*You have made us the taunt of our neighbors,*
  *the derision and scorn of those around us.*
*You have made us a byword among the nations,*
  *a laughingstock among the peoples.*
*All day long my disgrace is before me,*
  *and shame has covered my face*
*at the words of the taunters and revilers,*
  *at the sight of the enemy and avenger.*

The psalmist responds to God's inaction with an urgent call for God to act on behalf of God's people (vv. 23-26):

*Rouse yourself! Why do you sleep, O LORD?*
  *Awake, do not cast us off forever!*
*Why do you hide your face?*
  *Why do you forget our affliction and oppression?*
*For we sink down to the dust.*
  *our bodies cling to the ground.*
*Rise up, come to our help.*
  *Redeem us for the sake of your steadfast love.*

In addition to brash demands for God to change God's course of action and respond to the people's needs, some of the communal psalms of lament also contain startling, vengeance-seeking calls for God to destroy the enemies of God's people. Psalm 58 is an example of what are often called "imprecatory psalms," psalms in which the psalmist imprecates, or curses, his enemies.

*Do you indeed decree what is right, you gods?*
  *Do you judge people fairly?*
*No, in your hearts you devise wrongs;*
  *your hands deal out violence on earth.*

*The wicked go astray from the womb;*
  *they err from their birth, speaking lies.*
*They have venom like the venom of a serpent,*
  *like the deaf adder that stops its ear,*
*so that it does not hear the voice of charmers*
  *or of the cunning enchanter.*

*O God, break the teeth in their mouths;*
  *tear out the fangs of the young lions, O LORD!*
*Let them vanish like water that runs away;*
  *like grass let them be trodden down and wither.*

*Let them be like the snail that dissolves into slime;*
*    like the untimely birth that never sees the sun.*
*Sooner than your pots can feel the heat of thorns,*
*    whether green or ablaze, may he sweep them away!*

*The righteous will rejoice when they see vengeance done;*
*    they will bathe their feet in the blood of the wicked.*
*People will say, "Surely there is a reward for the righteous;*
*    surely there is a God who judges on earth."*

One of the more commonly known of the imprecatory psalms, and one no less ruthless in its call for retribution, is Psalm 137. This psalm clearly identifies exile in Babylon as its specific historical setting. The psalmist mourns the loss of the temple and Jerusalem (Zion), and calls for God to execute bloody vengeance upon those who rejoiced in Jerusalem's ruin.

*By the rivers of Babylon—*
*    there we sat down and there we wept*
*    when we remembered Zion.*
*On the willows there*
*    we hung up our harps.*
*For there our captors*
*    asked us for songs,*
*and our tormentors asked for mirth, saying,*
*    "Sing us one of the songs of Zion!"*

*How could we sing the LORD's song*
*    in a foreign land?*
*If I forget you, O Jerusalem*
*    let my right hand wither!*
*Let my tongue cling to the roof of my mouth,*
*    if I do not remember you,*
*if I do not set Jerusalem*
*    above my highest joy.*

*Remember, O LORD, against the Edomites*
*    the day of Jerusalem's fall,*
*how they said, "Tear it down! Tear it down!*
*    Down to its foundations!"*
*O daughter Babylon, you devastator!*
*    Happy shall they be who pay you back*
*    what you have done to us!*
*Happy shall they be who take your little ones*
*    and dash them against the rock!*

Given their passionate expression of complaint and wrath, it is probably not too surprising that the psalms of lament are not popular ones among most Christians. In some, the psalmist is angry at God, accusing God of being absent, uncaring, or even the cause of the psalmist's suffering. In a few others, such as here in Psalms 58 and 137 (see also Psalm 109) the psalmist calls upon God to act with violence against the psalmist's enemies. Contemporary readers might respond, "This is no way to talk to God!" And, to be sure, this is nothing like the polite, measured, meek style of prayer that many of us have been taught. We suffer great loss, however, if we push these psalms aside and do not tend to what they might teach us about sincere and faithful words with God.

First of all, these psalms teach us that it is important for us to name those things in our lives and our society that are not right. In an article aptly titled, "The Costly Loss of Lament," Walter Brueggemann argues that when we neglect the psalms of lament we risk neglecting the permission and even the calling to cry out against injustice and evil in our world, and to do so with the expectation that God will hear us and act. As Brueggemann helpfully puts it:

> The lament Psalms, then, are a complaint which makes shrill the insistence:
> 1. Things are not right in the present arrangement.
> 2. They need not stay this way but can be changed.
> 3. The speaker will not accept them this way, for it is intolerable.
> 4. It is God's obligation to change things.[8]

God desires abundant life for all creatures, and yet there are many forces in this world that work against God's will for creation. The psalms of lament join with other scriptural texts teaching believers to get upset and cry out when God's will for them, for their community, and for their world is not being realized. For this reason, the lament psalms have served for generations as a faith-filled resource for those facing all sorts of trials and sufferings. Many have found that in reciting and praying the psalms, they are able to give voice to their deepest hurts and struggles and move God to action.

Just as important, these psalms teach that Yahweh values honesty over misplaced piety. When coming before God in prayer, it is not the right words that matter. Neither is God eager to hear only from those who come with a gentle disposition and meekness. Rather, these troubling psalms announce that God wants to engage believers—and wants believers to engage God—no matter how they feel, no matter what their complaint. In short, God wants human creatures to be real with God. They are called to bring it all before God, the good and the bad, the beautiful and the ugly. The Psalter as a whole teaches us that thanksgiving and praise are essential to the discourse of genuine faith, but also appropriate are disappointment, anger, and even blood-thirsty rage.

There is another imprecatory lament, Psalm 139, that helps us to appreciate still another important function of lament in our lives of faith. Now many of us have likely never heard Psalm 139 read in its entirety or even thought of it as a lament. When the psalm is featured in the Revised Common Lectionary, a portion of it is missing. Not included are the rather disturbing words of vv. 19-22, an exclusion that actually (and unfortunately, in my view) changes the psalm from a lament into a psalm of confidence or trust. In the psalm's complete form, the psalmist's celebration of God's all-encompassing presence and care (vv. 1-18) suddenly gives way to an outburst of bitter invective against his enemies, beginning with a call for God's vengeance (vv. 19-22).

> *O that you would kill the wicked, O God*
> *And that the bloodthirsty would depart from me –*
> *those who speak of you maliciously*
> *and lift themselves up against you for evil.*
> *Do I not hate those who hate you, O Lord?*
> *And do I not loathe those who rise up against you?*
> *I hate them with a perfect hatred;*
> *I count them my enemies.*

With these verses *included*, Psalm 139 is rightly regarded as a psalm of lament (or at least a psalm of mixed form that contains lament). Unlike in some laments, here in Psalm 139 the psalmist does not question God's faithfulness. In fact, most of the psalm (vv. 1-18) is a jubilant, and most eloquent, celebration of God's ever-present care and concern (if you do not remember the psalm, stop here and read it!). But then without warning the psalmist issues a bold demand for God's action that seems to fly in the face of conventional piety and who we are called to be as God's people. The psalmist calls upon God to respond to the suffering caused by the "wicked" and "bloodthirsty," by annihilating them: "O, that you would kill the wicked, O God!" (v. 19).

Now, I just said above that the purpose of the lament psalms is to teach believers that even their deepest and darkest emotions and thoughts are to be brought before God. To that we should add that such thoughts are to be *turned over to God*. Notice how Psalm 139 reveals this as the psalmist's motivation. The psalmist opens with the proclamation that he or she is intimately known by God (vv. 1-6). This is followed by the psalmist's celebration of God's unyielding presence and another section that traces God's knowledge of the psalmist to the psalmist's very creation in the womb (vv. 7-18). All of this, all this rejoicing in God's knowledge of and presence with the psalmist, then suddenly leads to the disturbing plea to wipe out the wicked and bloodthirsty. To many, these harsh verses just don't seem to fit. Their sudden appearance is jarring; their focus on vengeance seems completely unrelated to what has just preceded. Many have even speculated that these verses were added to the psalm at a later time, and thus not original to what was initially simply a psalm of trust. But it seems to me that they do fit, and fit very well. Note what the psalmist says next after his call for God's vengeance to conclude the Psalm (vv. 23-24):

> Search me, O God, and know my heart
> test me and know my thoughts,
> See if there is any wicked way within me,
> and lead me in the way everlasting.

What the psalmist does in Psalm 139 is just what the psalms of lament teach all believers to do: to dare to bring before God their deepest struggles, fears, and even feelings of hatred—to lay them there before God, and then to say, "OK, God, here it is. I've laid it all before you. Now, search me and know my heart, test me and know my thoughts, see if there is any wickedness in me, and if so, lead me in *your* ways." The Psalmist knows that he is known by God. The Psalmist knows that God is with him and desires abundant life for him. And because of this trust that God is truly by his side in good times and in bad, the psalmist dares to speak even these unsettling words to God. He offers God his darkest thoughts. He gives these thoughts over to God, he *relinquishes* them to God and asks God to guide him in the ways of justice and mercy. In his reflection on Psalm 109, another imprecatory psalm, Brueggemann offers these words about the practice of submitting one's vengeance to God.

> Now in submitting one's rage as this speaker does, two things become clear. The submission to Yahweh is real and irreversible. It cannot be tentatively offered to Yahweh and then withdrawn if Yahweh does not deal as we had hoped. Such a submission carries with it a relinquishment, a genuine turning loose of the issue. When God is able to say, "Vengeance is mine" (Deut 32:35; Rom 12:19), it implies, "not yours." The submitting partner is no longer free to take vengeance—may not and need not. So the submission is an unburdening and freeing from pettiness and paralysis for praise and thanksgiving. The second fact is that submitting to Yahweh is submitting to Yahweh's free action. Yahweh will avenge, but in God's own way and in God's own time— and perhaps not as we would wish and hope. Yahweh is not a robot.

Yahweh does not implement our violent yearning, but passes it through his sovereign freedom, marked by majesty, faithfulness and compassion. Thus what could have been a barbarian lashing out against a neighbor becomes a faithful activity in which the venomous realities are placed squarely in God's hands. God is permitted to govern as he will. And the speaker is again free to start living unencumbered.[9]

That the psalms of lament are about a transformation of the heart is indicated also by a common characteristic of their form. With few exceptions, the psalms of lament contain an abrupt, even jarring, transition from lament to a concluding section of praise or a vow to offer thanksgiving for God's eventual salvation. In one second the psalmist is calling for God's attention and deliverance; in the next the psalmist is praising God and thanking God for the deliverance God will accomplish or has accomplished. Below is Psalm 13 in its entirety, offering a typical example of this abrupt shift from lament to praise.

> *How long, O Lord, Will you forget me forever?*
> *How long will you hide your face from me?*
> *How long must I bear pain in my soul,*
> *and have sorrow in my heart all day long?*
> *How long shall my enemy be exalted over me?*
>
> *Consider and answer me, O Lord my God!*
> *Give light to my eyes, or I will sleep the sleep of death,*
> *and my enemy will say, "I have prevailed";*
> *my foes will rejoice because I am shaken.*
>
> *But I trusted in your steadfast love;*
> *my heart shall rejoice in your salvation.*
> *I will sing to the Lord,*
> *because he has dealt bountifully with me.*

Many a scholar has wondered what has happened in the life or consciousness of the psalmists to lead to such a startling transformation in their manner of address to God. Has there been an interlude during which God's deliverance has been experienced, and so now thanksgiving is appended to the lament? Was this a common liturgical practice, to conclude lament with thanksgiving as a sign of trust in God's deliverance? We may never be able to discover—from a historical perspective—the reasons why the lament psalms contain this sudden transition from lament to praise. However, in their final form—the form known to generations of Jews and Christians—the psalms of lament embody the profession that in the midst of trial and tragedy, God's people are called to bring it all before God. They are to bring it all to God, and then listen for God's voice and wait on God's action, knowing that salvation is found in nothing else. In short, trust, thanksgiving, and praise are somehow renewed in the midst of this sometimes brash and painful dialogue with God.

Anna Carter Florence helps us to summarize the kind of conversation God and our ancestors in the faith continue to invite from God's people:

> The biblical family story includes creations and floods, covenants and betrayals, enslavements and liberations, wanderings and homecomings. The people of God have seen it all. Moreover, they have refused to keep quiet about any of it, understanding that families need to talk to one another and to God, most of all. Not all of the talk is pretty, but then neither is life. Some days the only thing you can do is praise God on your knees; other days you just bow your head and cry. The only rule in God's family is that the talk has to be really and truly *yours*, which means that it's no good if you pretend to say *Thank you!* when the honest-to-God truth is that you are so fed up that you could spit. God's people do not hold back *anything*—not ferocious love or ferocious grief. "Restraint" is therefore not a word they use with much success. On the other hand, "intimacy" and "honesty" they do very well.[10]

## Jesus' Teaching: Instruction through Dialogue

Still another clear biblical witness to the conversational nature of God, and to our call to be in conversation with God and one another, is Jesus' method of teaching. From the perspective of the New Testament writers, Jesus' instruction represents the fullest manifestation of what God desires for humanity. Jesus is the "fulfillment of the law," Paul says (Rom 10:4). Jesus' authority as the teacher of God's torah even outstrips that of Moses, as Jesus radically recasts or even *sets aside* some commandments of old (as we shall explore further in chapter 3). It is by following Jesus' commands that true righteousness is found, a righteousness that exceeds that of the Scribes and Pharisees (Matt 5:19-20) and that which provides a foundation for life and living that will not fail (Matt 7:24-29). John presents Jesus as the fullest disclosure of the will and ways of the Father, in both his actions and words (see, for example, John 8:21-30; 17:14).

Given the importance of Jesus' instruction, it might surprise readers of Scripture to find that much of Jesus' teaching takes place in rather pedestrian and sequestered settings. To be sure, Jesus is presented by the Gospel writers as doing a lot of "preaching" in front of large crowds or in the temple precincts. However, most of his instruction takes place in private conversation with his disciples and even his adversaries. The ways of the kingdom are shared with those who walk with Jesus on the dusty back roads of Palestine, or dine with Jesus in the homes of folk as diverse as Pharisees, tax collectors, common laborers, and widows. In fact, more than one scholar has suggested that, given Jesus' fondness for "dinner parties," he might have been a rather large fellow. I would imagine that Jesus liked food as much as the rest of us. But in the ancient Mediterranean world, such meal times were about much more than just food and drink. They were social affairs that revolved around debate and discussion. It is in these intimate settings that Jesus did much of his teaching about the kingdom of God. Moreover, Jesus' words are often initiated in response the questioning, searching, even accusation of Jesus' conversation partners, such as we find in many of the "controversy dialogues" involving Jesus and the religious elite. In short, Jesus valued interaction and conversation.

Not only does much of Jesus' teaching take place in the context of conversation, but the form of Jesus' teaching as presented by the Gospel writers calls his hearers to further discernment. The monological view of Scripture summarized in the introduction implies that God's instruction consists primarily of straightforward propositional truth claims that are readily integrated into a cohesive vision of God and faith. But Jesus teaches mostly in parables! Jesus is not a systematic theologian but more of a storyteller, offering little parabolic vignettes that call his listeners to see the truths of the kingdom in and through their experience of life; stories that might mean different things to different people in different times and places (see chapter 5).[11] The point of all this indirection in his instruction, it seems to me, is to get his followers to start thinking—to start thinking in ways that invite the reality of God's reign into their lives. He wanted to begin cultivating in them *the disposition of discernment in dialogue.* That was, after all, the work he said his Spirit would continue to inspire in them (John 14:26; 16:12-15). Jesus did not want his followers simply to parrot theological maxims back and forth, but to reflect creatively with one another, as he did with them, what it means to welcome the saving rule of God in their lives.

## Implications: Called into Conversation

The essential point this chapter has sought to emphasize is that God invites God's people into sincere dialogue. It is a dialogue that matters very much to God. It is a dialogue that shapes God's response to human sin and to human suffering. It is a dialogue in which humanity is to be real with God, and through which humanity is able to remember and understand God's saving care more fully.

That such conversation should be so central to humanity's relationship with God might be inferred from the creation stories (Genesis 1–2). It was by God's word that creation itself came into being (Genesis 1). In the second creation story (Genesis 2), we find Adam given the charge of naming the animals. God brings the creatures to Adam "to see what he would call them; and whatever the man called every living being, that was its name" (Gen 2:19). The spoken word, that of God *and* of humanity, was to play a role in ordering creation. From the very beginning God and humanity were to be partners in shaping the world in accord with the life-giving designs for which Yahweh called it into being.

Scripture then reveals to us a God who continually and in manifold ways invites us into dialogue, values our conversations, and is moved by our words so that we and others might receive God's blessing more fully, even words of complaint, doubt, anger, and accusation. To draw again from Clark Pinnock, Scripture paints us a "picture of a God who loves covenant and chooses dialogue over monologue."[12] The God of Scripture is not so much a God of immutable poise and pronouncement as a God of dynamic engagement and unyielding care. Yahweh is not a God unmoved by the desperate and triumphant vagaries of our lives that pulse us toward joy or despair, rejoicing or rage. Emmanuel, God with us, is one who becomes so completely enmeshed in our human affairs that God becomes one of us, lives with us, teaches us, shares table with us, walks with us, suffers with and for us.

Scripture's portrayal of God's character not only invites believers into conversation with God; it also invites us to consider the kind of Scripture that this same God would inspire among God's people. I have no doubt that those holding to a monological view of Scripture also recognize and value the way in which Scripture calls us into conversation with God. But the character of God as one who pursues interaction with God's human creatures seems to me more fully and consistently represented in the approach to Scripture as sacred dialogue presented here than in an approach to Scripture as a divine monologue. In the pages to follow, Scripture is viewed as a paradigmatic manifestation of the intimate exchange that is to characterize our relationships with God and one another, rather than as a divine monologue that God bestows upon humanity. Therefore, and in contrast to a monological perspective, *the form of Scripture is not seen as an exception to the conversation God pursues with and calls for among humanity but as revelation that bears witness to, participates in, and invites dialogue.*

The chapters to follow will demonstrate several ways in which Scripture presents its sacred tradition in a dynamic, conversational context. Chapter 2 will show that contentious dialogue about what it means to be God's people—so often found among the characters of Scripture—is also found among the biblical writers themselves. Chapter 3 points out that Scripture portrays God's instruction to God's people as dynamic and ongoing. Although human testimony to God's will, in response to God's revelation, is essential to our heritage as God's people, this testimony is open to reformation as believers receive God's revelation and together discern the witness of the risen Christ in their midst. Chapter 4 follows this up with Paul's own example of Spirit-led and context-driven conversation about the gospel in response to the needs of his communities. Chapter 5 explores the numerous ways in which Scripture invites us to invest ourselves and our experiences into our reading of Scripture, serving as still another testimony to God's continuing engagement with believers in their own times and places. The present chapter lays the groundwork for these and later chapters by emphasizing the conversational nature of God's very own character. For it stands to reason that the Scriptures inspired by a God such as ours would similarly participate in and invite sacred conversation.

# Sacred Traditions
# in Tension

_____

## chapter two

*"Do not let the foreigner joined to the LORD say . . . "*
*(Isa 56:3)*

**Ezra 9-10 recounts the story of the Israelites**
sending away their non-Jewish wives and their children, as commanded
by the officials of the recently restored Jerusalem. Below is a small slice
of that story the book of Ezra does not tell.

*Two days have passed since that horrible morning. Wives torn from
husbands. Children torn from fathers. Wailing. Sobbing. Screams
of disbelief and dismay. They were actually going to go through
with it. "Yahweh demands it!" they said. "We are to be a holy
people. 'Do not mix with the peoples of the lands,' the commandments say! Do you want God to bring destruction upon us once
again?" Like unclean refuse we were swept away. Many husbands
also wept. Their final, feeble glances betrayed their doubt. Others
simply turned and walked proudly back into town, back to their
empty homes.*

*So here I am, and here are my children. A family with no name
and no future. Where did they think we would all go, roaming
bands of women and children in the wilderness with provisions
that could hardly last a week? Did they think that the Lord would
provide, as though we were all Hagars and Ishmaels? Well, perhaps God has provided. Several of the outlying villages have welcomed us into their homes. They, too, believe in Yahweh. Some of
our officials had looked down on these villages, saying they were
lax in their devotion to God's torah. But they have saved us. I'm not
sure how they could meet the needs of such a multitude. But they
have fed and sheltered us and do not speak of sending us away.*

*They too believe in Yahweh. They are part of God's holy people. I
see that now. And so, I see, are we. They are not going to send us
away.*

No one knows what really happened to the refugees of Jerusalem and
surrounding towns, the non-Israelite wives and their ethnically mixed
children separated from their Israelite husbands and fathers as recorded
in Ezra 9–10. Were some wives able to return to their families of origin?
Did others find shelter in nearby towns or villages? If so, did they acquire
it through the generosity of others or by others' exploitation of them? Or
worse, were they simply turned away by village after village and left to
a desperate existence in the wilderness? An element of the biblical witness that gives us some hope of their survival is that Jewish folk in Ezra's
day were not of one mind on the issue of mixed marriages. Perhaps a
sympathetic Jewish village (or group of villages) did take them in. Perhaps a non-Jewish village. Perhaps some of those who sent their wives
and children away, overcome with guilt and guided by other sources of
instruction, changed their minds and reclaimed their families before it
was too late. We will never know.

What we do know is that Scripture preserves for us two very different perspectives on the matter of whether those of non-Israelite descent
can be part of the community of God's people. Now, it is not uncommon
for us to find differences of opinion recorded in Scripture. Disagreements abound. But in the vast majority of cases, these disagreements
take place between characters in the narrative, and it is clear which side
of the argument Scripture is endorsing. When the Israelites murmur in
the wilderness against God and Moses, we might feel some sympathy
for them, but it is obvious with whom the biblical author sides (Exodus
16; Numbers 11). The same is true with the debate between Jeremiah
and the false prophets (Jeremiah 26–28) or Paul and the Christians who
insisted that Gentile converts be circumcised (Galatians; Acts 15). Less
common are those instances in which the biblical authors hold contrasting opinions on the very same matter. In this chapter, we will focus on
two such instances: the post-exilic (fifth–sixth century B.C.E.) debate
over mixed marriages as it surfaces in Ezra, Nehemiah, Ruth, Isaiah,
Malachi, and Jonah; and different perspectives on whether non-Jews
needed to adhere to certain dietary restrictions reflected in the New
Testament.

## Who Belongs in the New Jerusalem?

### Ezra and Nehemiah

As mentioned in the introduction, in 587 B.C.E. the Babylonian armies invaded and leveled the city of Jerusalem, killing many of the inhabitants, razing the temple, and taking most of the survivors, including the king, with them back to Babylon while others fled to Egypt. Suddenly, nearly everything that defined Israel as a nation and a people was gone: land, holy city, temple, king. During their time in exile, the Jewish people reflected on their experience guided by their sacred traditions and several of the prophets. They came to discern first of all that the tragedy of destruction and exile was a result of their unrelenting sin against God and one another. They also came to believe that, despite all appearances, God still cared deeply for them and would one day restore them. The book of Ezra tells about the Jewish people in Jerusalem after they were allowed by King Cyrus of Persia to return to their homeland (539 B.C.E.), about the rebuilding of the temple, and about the people's recommitment to following God's torah. Despite a delay in the reconstruction of the temple—a seventeen-year hiatus due to problems caused by their enemies in the north—and the numerous hardships the people faced, it must have been for many an exciting time. Many likely saw in these events the hand of God at work, moving the people closer to that glorious restoration of Jerusalem promised by the prophets.

Some years after the temple was completed and rededicated, still other Jews, including the scribe Ezra and the heads of many leading families, returned to Jerusalem with the blessing of the Persian king, Artaxerxes. Ezra is celebrated by the biblical writer as a "scribe skilled in the law of Moses that the Lord the God of Israel had given; and the king granted him all that he asked, for the hand of the Lord his God was upon him" (Ezra 7:6). Soon after he arrives, however, Ezra is confronted with unwelcome news. Many Israelites, including priests, Levites and officials, have taken non-Israelite wives. In the words of the officials, "the holy seed has mixed itself with the peoples of the lands" (9:1-2). Ezra rends his garments, pulls hair from his head and beard, and leads the people in an impassioned prayer of confession (Ezra 9:6-15). Ezra praises God for allowing them to return to the devastated city. He recognizes that it was more than they deserved, for "from the days of our ancestors to this day, we have been deep in guilt, and for our iniquities we, our kings, and our priests have been handed over to the kings of the lands, to the sword, to captivity, to plundering, and to utter shame, as is now the case" (v. 8). With great anguish Ezra acknowledges that they have once again broken God's law, for God has commanded them concerning the peoples of the land "not to give daughters to their sons, neither take daughters for your sons, and never seek their peace and prosperity" (v. 12). He begs for God's forgiveness, lest God bring destruction upon them once again. The people add their own voices to Ezra's earnest confession: "While Ezra prayed and made confession, weeping and throwing himself down before the house of God, a very great assembly of men, women and children gathered to him out of Israel; the people also wept bitterly" (10:1). Then, Shecaniah son of Jehiel steps forward to address Ezra and proposes a remedy: "let us make a covenant with our God to send away all these wives and their children, according to the counsel of my lord and of those who tremble at the commandment of our God. Take action, for it is your duty, and we are with you. Be strong, and do it!" (10:3-4). Ezra stands and makes all of Israel swear that they will do as had been said (v. 5).

The reader can certainly appreciate Ezra's and the people's earnest desire to abide by the will of God in all things. After all, they are just beginning to put their lives as a people back together again and piece together their holy city, which was destroyed, they understand, because of their unfaithfulness. Now, having just taken a major step forward in reclaiming their identity as a people and rededicating themselves to God with the completion of the temple, they once again find themselves living in sin. Perhaps it was an oversight. Perhaps some thought that this particular law prohibiting marriage to foreigners was relevant only for an age now passed. But now, thanks to Ezra, they know God's will, and they steel themselves for the grim task of ripping families apart in the name of the LORD. A census is taken. Then the non-Jewish women and their children are sent away (10:44).

The book of Nehemiah is believed by most scholars to have been written by the same author who produced Ezra, and the two books were likely created as a single volume. Nehemiah, who became governor of the Jews in Judea, may have been a contemporary of Ezra (as the narrative implies) or may have arrived at a time shortly after Ezra. One of the main features of the author's portrayal of these two leaders is the complementary character of their respective tenures. Accordingly, Nehemiah's policy on relations with non-Israelites parallels that of Ezra:

On that day they read from the book of Moses in the hearing of the people; and in it was found written that no Ammonite or Moabite should ever enter the assembly of God, because they did not meet the Israelites with bread and water, but hired Balaam against them to curse them—yet our God turned the curse into a blessing. When the people heard the law, they separated from Israel all those of foreign descent. (Neh 13:1-3)

Later on in the same chapter (vv. 23-27), Nehemiah also condemns mixed marriages between Israelites and non-Israelites with words as uncompromising as those of Ezra:

In those days also I saw Jews who had married women of Ashdod, Ammon, and Moab; and half of their children spoke the language of Ashdod, and they could not speak the language of Judah, but spoke the language of various peoples. And I contended with them and cursed them and beat some of them and pulled out their hair; and I made them take an oath in the name of God, saying, "You shall not give your daughters to their sons, or take their daughters for your sons or for yourselves. Did not King Solomon of Israel sin on account of such women? Among the many nations there was no king like him, and he was beloved by his God, and God made him king over all Israel; nevertheless, foreign women made even him to sin. Shall we then listen to you and do all this great evil and act treacherously against our God by marrying foreign women?"

The closing of the book follows, with Nehemiah offering a summary of the work that he has accomplished, beginning with, "Thus I cleansed them from everything foreign" (v. 30), and concluding with the petition, "Remember me, O my God, for good" (v. 31).

The "good" that the biblical author believed Nehemiah and Ezra were accomplishing in cleansing Israel from all that was foreign is based on torah traditions found in the Pentateuch. When renewing the covenant with Israel following the golden calf affair (Exod 34:11-35), God instructs the people to avoid the inhabitants of the land that God is going give to them. They are not to make a covenant with them, lest they be led astray to worship their gods and take wives from among them (vv. 11-16). In Deut 7:1-6, with Israel on the verge of entering the promised land, Moses gives these commands concerning non-Israelites they will encounter:

[W]hen the LORD your God gives them over to you and you defeat them, then you must utterly destroy them. Make no covenant with them and show them no mercy. Do not intermarry with them, giving your daughters to their sons or taking their daughters for your sons, for that would turn away your children from following me, to serve other gods. Then the anger of the LORD would be kindled against you, and he would destroy you quickly. But this is how you must deal with them: break down their altars, smash their pillars, hew down their sacred poles, and burn their idols with fire. For you are a people holy to the LORD your God; the LORD your God has chosen you out of all the peoples on earth to be his people, his treasured possession. It was not because you were more numerous than any other people that the LORD set his heart on you and chose you—for you were the fewest of all peoples.

Later, in Deut 20:16-18, Moses orders Israel,

But as for the towns of these peoples that the LORD your God is giving you as an inheritance, you must not let anything that breathes remain alive. You shall annihilate them—the Hittites and the Amorites, the Canaanites and the Perizzites, the Hivites and the Jebusites—just as the LORD your God has commanded, so that they may not teach you to do all the abhorrent things that they do for their gods, and you thus sin against the LORD your God.

The motivation consistently given for Israel's need to avoid non-Israelites in these and similar passages is the fear that they will lead Israel astray to worship other gods. Thus, the peoples of the land are to be avoided at all costs, even at the cost of their very existence. We find this exterminatory policy put into practice during Israel's conquest of the promised land, as reflected in several passages from Joshua. Here, again, is that difficult text from Josh 11:16-20 that we considered briefly in the introduction:

So Joshua took all that land: the hill country and all the Negeb and all the land of Goshen and the lowland and the Arabah and the hill country of Israel and its lowland, from Mount Halak, which rises toward Seir, as far as Baal-gad in the valley of Lebanon below Mount Hermon. He took all their kings, struck them down, and put them to death. Joshua made war a long time with all those kings. There was not a town that made peace with the Israelites, except the Hivites, the inhabitants of Gibeon; all were taken in battle. For it was the LORD's doing to harden their hearts so that they would come against Israel in battle, in order that they might be utterly destroyed, and might receive no mercy, but be exterminated, just as the LORD had commanded Moses.

The "cleansing" that Ezra and Nehemiah pursued, while different in its method (divorce and deportation, or segregation), is rooted in the very same policy of cleansing commanded in Deuteronomy and enacted in the conquest traditions, a cleansing that was ethnic in character, exhaustive in scope, and brutal in its implementation. Scholars question to what extent these genocidal practices were actually employed by Israel during the conquest. But for our purposes—examining the shaping of the canon in its final form—it is sufficient to establish that the author of Ezra-Nehemiah, *who cites the very same torah commands as the motivation for Ezra and Nehemiah's actions*, understands these exclusionary and exterminatory policies as consistent with the will of God.

## Other Voices

These policies, however, do not exhaust the perspectives provided by the writers and compilers of the Old Testament on the matter of non-Israelites. We also find in the Old Testament writings a much more inclusive, even welcoming, stream of tradition. Non-Israelites have been included among God's people since the time of the exodus ("a mixed crowd also went up with them" [Exod 12:38]). Commonly referred to as "aliens," they are also called to abide by many of the commandments of the law (Lev 17:12; 18:26; 24:22; Num 9:14; 15:11-16; Deut 5:14; cf. 1 Kgs 8:41-43). This may seem to us a burden, but the law was given to Israel as a means of setting them apart from the nations and molding them into God's special possession (Exod 19:1-6). By following the law, aliens are called to participate in that identity. In addition, and in sharp contrast to the exterminatory policies enacted later, Israel is repeatedly called upon to provide sustenance for the aliens living among them (for example, Lev 19:10; 33-34; 23:22; Deut 24:17-21; Jer 22:3; Ezek 22:29). Moreover, Moses himself takes a Midianite wife, and his father-in-law, Jethro, provides his inexperienced son-in-law with sage advice (Exod 3:1; 18:1-27).

One could argue that such positive regard for non-Israelites was to be granted to only those aliens who joined God's people prior to their entrance into the land. Because they did not pose a threat to Israel's religious fidelity, they were not singled out for exclusion as were the "peoples of the land." However, non-Israelites from among the "peoples of the land" play key roles in the history of God's people after the conquest begins. In Joshua 2, Rahab the prostitute shelters and saves the lives of those sent to spy out the land. She professes faith in Yahweh: "The LORD your God is indeed God in the heaven above and on earth below" (Josh 2:11). In return for her kindness and faith, she and her family are spared. Thus, enmeshed in the very account of Israel's conquest of Canaan and the slaughter of its inhabitants lest they lead God's people into sin, stands the story of a God-fearing Canaanite woman (a prostitute no less!) who plays an important role in Israel's entrance into the promised land.

## Ruth

The story of Rahab is thick with irony, but the irony gets thicker with the story of Ruth. Ruth is a Moabite woman and thus non-Israelite.

She marries into an Israelite family from Bethlehem that settled in Moab, consisting of two sons and their widowed mother, Naomi. After both of Naomi's sons die (including Ruth's husband), Naomi prepares to leave Moab and her widowed daughters-in-law, Orpah and Ruth, and return to Judah. She instructs Orpah and Ruth to remain in the land and return to their own relatives. Orpah heeds Naomi's words and bids farewell. But Ruth clings to Naomi. Once again Naomi urges her to depart: "See, your sister-in-law has gone back to her people and to her gods; return after your sister-in-law." But Ruth will not be dissuaded. In response, she proclaims these now famous words:

> "Do not press me to leave you or to turn back from following you! Where you go, I will go; where you lodge, I will lodge; your people shall be my people, and your God my God. Where you die, I will die— there will I be buried. May the LORD do thus and so to me, and more as well, if even death parts me from you!" (Ruth 1:16-17)

What makes these words especially poignant is not simply the fact that this happens to be a moving scene, filled with pathos. Read over these words again, or better yet get out your Bibles and read the whole of the book of Ruth. Now imagine that you are reading this story in the house of the Judean governor, in the mid-fifth century B.C.E., to a group that includes Ezra, Nehemiah, and the leading officials of the restored Jerusalem. Imagine their reaction to the story as it unfolds, their discomfort with the statement that Naomi's Israelite sons "took Moabite wives." Imagine their approval when Naomi commands Ruth, the Moabite, to turn away from her and instead follow her sister-in-law "who has gone back to her people and to her gods." Imagine their surprise and dismay when Ruth again refuses to leave, and instead announces, "your people shall be my people, and your God my God." And then, imagine their consternation as the obstinate, non-Israelite, Moabite Ruth once again marries a Jewish man, and an upstanding one at that, named Boaz. Now, if you have an active imagination, you may also be feeling a little uncomfortable at this point, since you are finding yourself in front of all these important, imposing folk reading a story that they very likely do not care to hear. But they are likely more uncomfortable than you. For they are likely by now beginning to remember how the story of Ruth is part of the larger story of Israel. They remember that this mixed couple, Ruth and Boaz, bears a son. His name is Obed. They remember that he becomes the father of Jesse, who becomes the father of a ruddy-looking youth, highly gifted with a slingshot. They remember that the Moabite Ruth is the great-grandmother of the great King David, whose "holy seed" Ezra, Nehemiah and the leading officials are hoping will one day return to the throne of Israel! (Ruth 4:18-22).

Many scholars conclude, based on its genre and style of writing, that the story of Ruth was written down sometime after the exile (or, if written earlier, that it was likely being recirculated as an important and sacred tradition during the post-exilic era). Consider what this potentially means. Around the same time many were following Ezra and Nehemiah's exclusionary policies, including the biblical author as he was approvingly penning his account, some other Jewish writer was recording the story of Ruth, shaping it and using language that was sure to catch the ear of his fellow Jews. Remember Ruth, he tells them. Remember how she left her gods, pledged her devotion to Yahweh, and became joined with an upstanding, God-fearing, Jewish man. Remember the Moabite great-grandmother of King David.

## Isaiah

The writer of Ruth was not alone in his welcoming attitude toward Gentiles. The oracles found in the later chapters of Isaiah are dated by most scholars to the same period as Ezra and Nehemiah.[1] With expression both eloquent and moving, Isa 56:1-8 proclaims that all those who devote themselves to Yahweh, even those who were formerly not included among the people of Israel—foreigners and the genitally deformed (in this case, eunuchs; see Deut 23:1)—are now to be welcomed and included among God's people.

> *Thus says the LORD:*
>> *Maintain justice, and do what is right,*
> *for soon my salvation will come,*
>> *and my deliverance be revealed.*
> *Happy is the mortal who does this,*
>> *the one who holds it fast,*
> *who keeps the sabbath, not profaning it,*
>> *and refrains from doing any evil.*
>
> *Do not let the foreigner joined to the LORD say,*
>> *"The LORD will surely separate me from his people";*
> *and do not let the eunuch say,*
>> *"I am just a dry tree."*
> *For thus says the LORD:*
> *To the eunuchs who keep my sabbaths,*
>> *who choose the things that please me*
>> *and hold fast my covenant,*
> *I will give, in my house and within my walls,*
>> *a monument and a name*
>> *better than sons and daughters;*

*I will give them an everlasting name*
*    that shall not be cut off.*
*And the foreigners who join themselves to the LORD,*
*    to minister to him, to love the name of the LORD,*
*    and to be his servants,*
*all who keep the sabbath, and do not profane it,*
*    and hold fast my covenant—*
*these I will bring to my holy mountain,*
*    and make them joyful in my house of prayer;*
*their burnt offerings and their sacrifices*
*    will be accepted on my altar;*
*for my house shall be called a house of prayer*
*    for all peoples.*
*Thus says the Lord GOD,*
*    who gathers the outcasts of Israel,*
*I will gather others to them*
*    besides those already gathered.*

Note how the language employed by the prophet or group producing these oracles invites us to hear its instruction with Ezra and Nehemiah's exclusionary practices in mind: "Do not let the foreigner joined to the Lord say, 'The Lord will surely separate me from his people.'" Here the Hebrew verb for "separate" (badal) is the same as that used in Ezra 10:11 in reference to the Israelites separating themselves from foreign wives and their children and in Neh 13:3 in reference to their separation from all those of foreign descent. Verse 8 strengthens the likelihood of an intended connection as it specifically holds in view the congregation of returned exiles and those "others"—namely, the foreigners and eunuchs—whom God will gather to join them: "Thus says the Lord GOD, who gathers the outcasts of Israel, I will gather others to them besides those already gathered." Note too the all-encompassing embrace God offers to faithful foreigners: "these I will bring to my holy mountain and make them joyful in my house of prayer; their burnt offerings and their sacrifices will be accepted on my altar" (v. 7). They are to partake fully in the life of God's people. Placed in the framework of a book attributed to the eighth-century prophet Isaiah, this oracle announces that God's plan for restored Israel did not fit the exclusion of an earlier age, nor does it fit the exclusion some are advocating in the present age. Yahweh announces, "my house shall be a house of prayer for all peoples." According to the framers of these oracles, that time has now come: "Thus says the LORD: Maintain justice and do what is right. . . ."

## Malachi

The book of Malachi is another post-exilic, prophetic text offering instruction that is often viewed by scholars in connection with the exclusionary policies of Ezra and Nehemiah. Most scholars, however, argue that, like Ezra and Nehemiah, Malachi condemns mixed marriages when he chastises Judah for profaning the sanctuary and "marrying the daughter of a foreign god" (2:10-12). Yet the phrase "marrying the daughter of a foreign god" need not refer to the practice of Israelites marrying foreign women. Instead, it may refer simply to idolatrous activity in general, similar to the common prophetic use of sexual impropriety as a metaphor for religious infidelity (for example, Ezekiel 16; Hosea 2). I believe that if we suspend the assumption that Mal 2:10-12 condemns mixed marriages between Jews and non-Jews, we find that numerous features of the text instead suggest that Malachi is actually defending these mixed marriages and condemning the marital policies of Ezra and Nehemiah.

Let's begin with what comes immediately following this phrase in Mal 2:10-12. In 2:13-16, the prophet rails against divorce. Malachi is the only prophet to address the issue, and what seems apparent from the prophet's rebuke is that the practice had become rather widespread during this time.

> And this you do as well: You cover the Lord's altar with tears, with weeping and groaning because he no longer regards the offering or accepts it with favor at your hand. You ask, "Why does he not?" Because the Lord was a witness between you and the wife of your youth, to whom you have been faithless, though she is your companion and your wife by covenant. Did not one God make her? Both flesh and spirit are his. And what does the one God desire? Godly offspring. So look to yourselves, and do not let anyone be faithless to the wife of his youth. For I hate divorce, says the Lord, the God of Israel, and covering one's garment with violence, says the Lord of hosts. So take heed to yourselves and do not be faithless.

If we read these verses with the policies of Ezra and Nehemiah in mind, without assuming that the phrase "marrying the daughter of a foreign god" in v. 11 refers to Jews marrying non-Jews, the possibility that Malachi is instead supporting those mixed marriages and condemning the marital policies of Ezra and Nehemiah presents itself. Twice the prophet rebukes those who have been unfaithful to "the wife of your youth," as if to say, "You know, that wife to whom you were first married and with whom you had children." The concern for "godly offspring" underscores the destructive and tragic consequences of divorce. The children who have been sent away are not only dishonored, they have been sent away from the people who are charged with the task of guiding them in the ways of God. The phrase "covering one's garment with violence" may refer to the rather heartless manner in which the wives and children were cast out.

Moreover, if Malachi were condemning mixed marriages in vv. 10-12, then it would seem counterproductive for him immediately to condemn divorce in the strongest possible terms ("For I hate divorce, says the Lord, the God of Israel"), when divorce was the very means being used by the returned exiles to rectify that "sin." Some scholars attempt to resolve this problem by arguing that the returned exiles must have been divorcing their Jewish wives in order to marry foreign women, and that is why Malachi condemns both mixed marriage and divorce. However, there is nothing in Jewish writings of this era to confirm this theory. In fact, if this were a common occurrence among post-exilic Jews, then it surely would have been raised by Ezra and Nehemiah as yet another reason for condemning mixed marriages. But they never hint that Jews were divorcing their Jewish wives in order to marry foreign women. The problem as the author of Ezra-Nehemiah describes it is that many Jews were simply marrying foreign women *instead of* Jewish women. Accordingly, Ezra and Nehemiah do not condemn divorce; they advocate it in this instance as a means of disposing the mixed marriages.

Equally revealing is the focus and development of the text leading up to 2:10-12. At first glance these verses may seem simply to address the problem of priests bringing blemished or less than desirable offerings to God. But there is more going on here. Let's zero in on Mal 1:8-12:

> When you offer blind animals in sacrifice, is that not wrong? And when you offer those that are lame or sick, is that not wrong? Try presenting that to your governor; will he be pleased with you or show you favor? says the Lord of hosts. And now implore the favor of God, that he may be gracious to us. The fault is yours. Will he show favor to any of you? says the Lord of hosts. Oh, that someone among you would shut the temple doors, so that you would not kindle fire on my altar in vain! I have no pleasure in you, says the Lord of hosts, and I will not accept an offering from your hands. For from the rising of the sun to its setting my name is great among the nations, and in every place incense is offered to my name, and a pure offering; for my name is great among the nations, says the Lord of hosts. But you profane it when you say that the Lord's table is polluted, and the food for it may be despised.

Notice the reference to seeking the governor's (Nehemiah's?) favor in v. 8, and how that is contrasted with the more important task of imploring the favor of *God* (v. 9), inviting us to see in Malachi's words a critique of cultic practices endorsed by the present leadership. But the LORD takes no pleasure in their vain sacrifices and wishes that the doors of the temple were closed (v. 10). Why? In giving his explanation, the prophet not only cites unworthy offerings (vv. 7-8, 13-14) but also sets up a contrast between two different groups of worshippers. This is an important development, and it helps us to see an additional dimension of the prophet's rebuke. The prophet explains that in contrast to the worship of the returned exiles, God's name is held in great honor by many from among the nations, and God is praised with pure offerings in every place (v. 11). In other words, there are many—including *Gentiles* presumably—besides the returned exiles calling upon and praising the name of the Lord and, in fact, *they* are doing a much better job of it (see also v. 14).

Thus, what the prophet rails against in chapter 1 is the infidelity of Israel's worship marked by (1) the offering of polluted foods (those from animals that are lame, sick, or "taken by violence") *in contrast to* the faithful in other nations who rightly praise and worship God, and (2) an attitude that seems more concerned with the favor of the governor than the favor of Yahweh. The prophet is clearly not, in these verses, endorsing the status quo guarded by the Jewish leadership. This becomes even clearer in 2:1-3, as the prophet rebukes the priesthood in a most degrading fashion: if they persist in their unfaithfulness, the dung of their offerings will be spread upon their faces (v. 3). Two additional features of Malachi's rebuke are important for us to note. In 2:4-9, the prophet goes on compare the current priesthood with Levi, the ancestor of all priests (2:4-9). They are so unlike him. They have turned aside from his pure and upright ways and from the ways of God. How? *"They have shown partiality"* in their instruction and administration of the temple (v. 9). Still later, Malachi includes "those who thrust aside the alien" as among those who will be subject to God's judgment (3:5).

In sum, Malachi's rebuke of the returned exiles displays a positive orientation toward the worship of Yahweh by non-Jews, a rejection of the partiality displayed by the temple leadership, and an urgent reminder to care for the alien among them. These features of the text, coupled with the prophet's scathing rebuke of divorce, hardly cohere with the ethnic exclusivity and attending marital policies endorsed by Ezra and Nehemiah. Furthermore, turn again to 2:10 and note how the words "Have we not all one father. Has not one God created us?" now ring clear. Many scholars suggest that the pronouns "we" and "us" in these phrases refer only to the people of Israel. But given the favorable regard for non-Jews evident in the immediate context and the rebuke against the priest's partiality that comes immediately before the statement, a far more inclusive reading is warranted. In asking, "Have we not all one father. Has not one God created us?" Malachi, like the writers of Ruth and Isaiah 56, exhorts his Jewish contemporaries to broaden their own conceptions of who is to be included among God's people: "are we not all—including Gentiles—children of God?" he asks. Similarly, in his castigation of divorce that follows, the prophet says concerning the wives being sent away, "Did not one God make her? Both flesh and Spirit are his" (2:15).

Therefore, when the prophet refers to the profaning of the covenant and sanctuary again in 2:10-12, he likely has in view the current policy of exclusion and divorce perpetuated by the returned exiles against non-Jews who, in the prophet's mind, have proven faithful in their worship of Yahweh. Then, with a sarcastic and penetrating twist of irony, the prophet boldly claims that it is the exclusionary attitudes and the substandard worship practices of the returned exiles that are, in fact, the stuff of idolatry. In effect, he says, "You are worried about Israel being led astray to worship idols because some are taking non-Jewish wives? When you—*Judah*—reject those who, in contrast to yourselves, rightly worship God, then *you* are the ones acting as those married to a daughter of a foreign god! This must stop. For you are the ones who will be cut off if you persist in this most unfaithful treatment of God's beloved and God's sanctuary" (v. 12). Then, fittingly, follows the prophet's condemnation of divorce: "And you do this as well . . ." (v. 13).

## Jonah

There is still another canonical witness left to consider: the book of Jonah. Although scholars have struggled to date the work, and thus we cannot with confidence assign it to the post-exilic period, it still provides yet another example of an Old Testament perspective toward non-Jews that is in sharp contrast to that of the author of Ezra-Nehemiah and other Old Testament traditions. You know the story. The prophet Jonah is told by God to go at once to Nineveh: to "cry out against it; for their wickedness has come up before me." Jonah's reluctance to go is certainly understandable. The story is set in the eighth century B.C.E., when Nineveh was the great city of the Assyrian empire, the despised and feared enemy of Israel. Who would want to go there to tell them to stop being so mean? So Jonah takes his chances, and runs from God. After a nasty storm at sea, an equally nasty ride in the belly of a fish, and a violent regurgitation, Jonah finds himself on dry land with a renewed—though still reluctant—willingness to listen to God. He travels to dreaded Ninevah and announces God's imminent judgment.

Incredibly, the Ninevites repent. What is perhaps less understandable is Jonah's reaction to his miraculous success in Nineveh. Who had ever before accomplished such an evangelistic coup? But Jonah is not pleased, and here we learn the true reason why Jonah had initially refused to go. It was not because he was afraid that the Ninevites would reject his message and kill him. He was afraid that they might actually listen, repent, and be forgiven by God. He feared that God's forbearance and mercy might also extend to Israel's enemies.

> But this was very displeasing to Jonah, and he became angry. He prayed to the LORD and said, "O LORD! Is not this what I said while I was still in my own country? That is why I fled to Tarshish at the beginning; for I knew that you are a gracious God and merciful, slow to anger, and abounding in steadfast love, and ready to relent from punishing. And now, O LORD, please take my life from me, for it is better for me to die than to live." (Jonah 4:1-3)

Hear God's response in v. 11:

> And should I not be concerned about Nineveh, that great city, in which there are more than a hundred and twenty thousand persons who do not know their right hand from their left, and also many animals?"

## Different Ways of Remembering

What Jonah and the traditions of Ruth, the later chapters of Isaiah, and (likely) Malachi have in common is that they are urging their fellow Israelites to reclaim an element of their calling and heritage that is as ancient as their ancestor Abraham. When God calls Abram in Gen 12:1-3 (his name is changed to "Abraham" in Genesis 17), it is for the purpose of creating a people that will be God's own, a "treasured possession out of all the peoples," as God puts it in Exod 19:5. Yet God's creation of this people from Abram was not simply for their own sake. Along with the gift of blessing, God also gives Abram and his descendants a calling: "and through you all the nations of the earth shall be blessed" (Gen 12:3). Thus, the "treasured possession," by its trust in God and obedience to God's ways, was also to be a "priestly kingdom" and a "holy nation" (Exod 19:6). They were to be a people set apart as priests, those who call the nations to repentance, who instruct the nations in the ways of God, who celebrate the faithful role Gentiles have played in their history, and who rejoice when foreigners and eunuchs are gathered with them into God's household. Israel was to be a dispenser of blessing, that wondrous gift of right-relatedness and abundance that God called into being as the fruit of creation (Genesis 1). We will talk more about this central thread of the biblical story in chapters 6 and 7. Suffice it to say that throughout the biblical narrative, this story line of Israel's calling to be a source of blessing for all nations waxes and wanes and is especially faint during the conquest narratives and in Ezra and Nehemiah when a strong exclusionary focus dominates the story.

Therefore, *what we see reflected in Ezra and Nehemiah on the one hand and Ruth, Jonah, the later chapters of Isaiah, and Malachi on the other is two groups of God's people and two groups of biblical traditions, remembering and living into their sacred story very differently at virtually the same point in time.* The one looks back and believes that for their time and place they are called to focus on those traditions which command Israel to remain separate from the peoples of the land. The other looks back and instead believes that the time was right to embrace those traditions which call Israel to welcome and minister to the people of the land.

As Christians, we are naturally led to consider which way of remembering is endorsed in Jesus's ministry and teaching, as well as in the writings of the New Testament authors. And many will readily conclude that the instruction of Jesus and the New Testament authors on the relationship between Jews and non-Jews is decidedly along the same lines as that offered by the authors of Isaiah, Malachi, Ruth, and Jonah. This is an important point to appreciate, but not the point I wish to emphasize in this chapter. What is most striking to me as I reflect on these very different ways of remembering is that both of them were preserved in the canon. Despite their markedly contrasting understandings of what it meant to live as God's people in the post-exilic world, both perspectives came to be embraced by Jews and Christians as the word of God.

## Who and What Belong at the Table?

Disagreement among the biblical writers is not confined to the Old Testament. In the New Testament as well, we find biblical authors on different sides of an issue—one that once again has to do with non-Jews (those troublesome Gentiles!). It concerns the issue of whether Gentile converts to Christianity need to adhere to some of the dietary restrictions commanded in the law of Moses. This instance of disagreement is more subtly reflected in the biblical text, but instructive nonetheless.

### The Jerusalem Conference (Acts 15)

The issue of whether Gentiles needed to follow some of the dietary restrictions prescribed by the law is part of a larger controversy in early Christianity. From both Galatians and Acts (and other Pauline letters, such as Philippians and Colossians), we learn that a sizable group of

Jewish Christians believed that Gentile converts to Christianity needed to abide by at least parts of the Jewish law, including circumcision and the dietary codes. Paul repeatedly enters into debate with these folk, and when the issue comes to a head in Antioch, Paul and Barnabas are sent to Jerusalem to seek the advice of the apostles and elders (Acts 15:1-3). After arriving in Jerusalem Paul and Barnabas begin to tell the believers there what God is accomplishing among the Gentiles through their ministry (v. 4). Not all are enthused by the report. Some "who belonged to the sect of the Pharisees stood up and said, 'It is necessary for them [the Gentile converts] to be circumcised and ordered to keep the law of Moses'" (v. 5).

A lengthy debate ensues among the elders and apostles. After much discussion, Peter and once again Paul and Barnabas address the crowd, describing how God has blessed the Gentiles though their respective ministries (vv. 6-12). Then James stands and proclaims that what God is now doing among the Gentiles fulfills the prophecies of old, citing from the prophet Amos. Finally, James issues the verdict:

> Therefore I have reached the decision that we should not trouble those Gentiles who are turning to God, but we should write to them to abstain only from things polluted by idols and from fornication and from whatever has been strangled and from blood. For in every city, for generations past, Moses has had those who proclaim him, for he has been read aloud every sabbath in the synagogues. (Acts 15:20; see also v. 29)

The judgment is, in effect, a compromise. Neither circumcision nor following the entire law of Moses is required for Gentile converts. They are, however, required to follow certain parts of that law, including some dietary restrictions and the prohibition against fornication. Concerning food, the Gentile Christians are specifically to avoid:

1. "pollutions of idols" (v. 20), clarified in v. 29 to mean food that has been sacrificed to idols;

2. "what is strangled": that is, meat from animals that have been slaughtered not according to Jewish law (which stipulated the draining of blood); and

3. foods made from blood.

The prohibition to refrain from meat offered to idols, and possibly the prohibition to avoid fornication (if it refers to ritualized intercourse), relates to practices common in the worship of pagan deities. Because of this, some scholars view all of the listed prohibitions together as signifying pagan worship, and thus regard James's instructions as referring only to the practice of idolatry in general and not also to dietary restrictions stemming from Leviticus 17–18. However, James's instructions to avoid meat from strangled animals (see Lev 17:15) and the consumption of blood (see Lev 17:10-11) were standard Jewish dietary practices rooted in torah regulations. It seems to me highly unlikely that James intended his fellow Jews to regard these instructions as simply a collective reference to idolatry. If idolatrous feasts were his only concern, the extended listing of food-related prohibitions is oddly redundant. James could have said simply, "avoid meat offered to idols." Moreover, even if idolatrous feasts were his primary concern (and this is doubtful), we must note that James specifically identifies as part of their problematic character their method of slaughtering and the consumption of blood. Either way, the dietary codes related to consumption of meat are clearly in view, and their observance is upheld as relevant for Gentile converts.

### Paul's Letters

The compromise likely strikes contemporary Christian readers as both fair and wise, and I have no doubt that this is how Luke, the writer of Acts, wished his readers to regard it. His portrayal of James in this scene is wholly in line with his portrayal of faithful characters throughout his Gospel and Acts, who, guided by the Spirit or in response to the Spirit's work, profess the fulfillment of God's will proclaimed by the Scriptures. Paul, however, apparently did not accept James's judgment as intractably binding. For in two letters written after this event he sets these dietary restrictions aside. In 1 Cor 8:1-13, Paul specifically addresses the eating of meat offered to idols, which, presumably, had created some controversy in the Corinthian church. It is likely that a fair number of Corinthian Christians had continued to take part in civic celebrations that typically involved the serving of sacrificial meat as part of the feast. Paul discourages the practice, lest it create division and lead those who are "weak" in their faith to participate in the pagan feasts as though they were eating in honor of a god (vv. 10-13). However, apart from this concern, Paul does not find the practice of eating meat offered to an idol a violation of God's will: "Food will not commend us to God. We are no worse off if we do not eat, and no better off if we do" (v. 8). Later, in 1 Cor 10:14-22, Paul will again exhort the Corinthians not to be enthusiastic participants in sacrificial feasts. But as to the eating of meat, Paul goes on to offer instruction that pays no heed to the dietary codes stipulated by James in Acts 15.

Eat whatever is sold in the meat market without raising any question on the ground of conscience. For "the earth is the Lord's and everything in it." If one of the unbelievers invites you to dinner and you are disposed to go, eat whatever is set before you without raising any question on the ground of conscience. (1 Cor 10:25-27)

In Romans 14, Paul's concern for those who are "weak" in their faith leads him to offer similar instructions to the Roman church. If by what they are eating some believers are causing division in the church and leading others to be scandalized or led astray, then it is better not to partake of the offending foods (vv. 15-23). Yet Paul also tells the church at Rome "I know and am persuaded in the Lord that nothing is unclean in itself" (14:14), and "everything is indeed clean" (14:20). By way of summary, Ben Witherington's comments concerning 1 Corinthians 8–10 are equally applicable to Paul's thought on food presented here in Romans:

Paul does not dispute that the Corinthians have a right to eat such food, so far as the food is concerned. Chs. 8–10 make it clear how far from Judaism Paul had moved on the matter of food. He no longer believed that food commended one to God or offended God. He had come to the view that food was morally and religiously neutral.[2]

Paul has moved far not only from his Jewish upbringing in the matter of food but from other Jewish Christians, including James and Peter. In Paul's account of his argument with Peter at Antioch (Gal 2:11-14) over the issue of table fellowship with Gentiles (eating with Gentiles was another violation of Jewish food laws), he tells us that "certain men from James" led Peter to withdraw from sharing table with Gentile believers. This event likely takes place *after* the Jerusalem conference reported in Acts 15, which Paul appears to describe in Gal 2:1-10. Thus, this passage joins with those in Romans and 1 Corinthians affirming that even after the compromise of the Jerusalem conference, Paul continued to push the envelope when it came to relaxing the stipulations of the law regarding dietary issues, and he pushed harder and faster than James and Peter were willing. Also telling is the fact that in his summary of the conference and its decision, Paul says nothing about James's instructions to avoid meat offered to idols or not properly slaughtered: "They asked only one thing, that we remember the poor, which was what I was actually eager to do" (v. 10).

### The Gospels

Differences of opinion on this matter may be found among the Gospel writers as well. In the next chapter, we will take a look at Mark

7:1-23, a controversy dialogue in which Jesus and the Pharisees butt heads over the issue of what makes one unclean. Jesus declares that it is not what goes into a person that makes one unclean, but what comes out of a person (7:17-23). Yet in the midst of this instruction, the Gospel writer inserts a parenthetical remark lest we miss the full significance of what Jesus is saying: "(thus, he declared all foods clean)" (v. 19). Mark wants to be sure his readers/listeners are rightly following along and catching what he thinks is the logical corollary of Jesus' teaching. Nothing, no substance in and of itself, no food, is unclean. Along with Paul, Mark believes that one's righteousness is not impacted by what one eats, but only by what is in one's heart. However, when we turn to this same story in the Gospel of Matthew, we find that it is, in nearly every detail, exactly the same as that in Mark, with one notable exception—the parenthetical comment Mark supplies is missing. When we turn to Luke, the entire story is missing.

The force of this observation is strengthened when we learn that most scholars believe that Mark was the first Gospel to be written, and that Matthew and Luke used Mark as a source.[3] If the majority of scholars are correct about this, then we have Matthew following Mark's account in nearly every detail but omitting Mark's parenthetical remark pointing out that Jesus just declared all food clean. Why would he do this? Why leave it out? Why would Luke not even include the story? Perhaps they, unlike Mark, were not quite ready to go this far on the matter of dietary restrictions. To be sure, as we will see in the next chapter, both Matthew and Luke, along with Mark, present Jesus radically redefining Jewish understandings of righteousness, even to the point of transcending some of Moses' laws. But with James and Peter, and in contrast to Paul, it appears that these two Evangelists believed that at least some of the laws pertaining to dietary restrictions were to be followed by believers, including Gentiles.

## Implications: Inspired Diversity and Dialogue

A passage that is frequently cited in discussions about the nature and authority of Scripture is 2 Tim 3:14-17:

> But as for you, continue in what you have learned and firmly believed, knowing from whom you learned it, and how from childhood you have known the sacred writings that are able to instruct you for salvation through faith in Christ Jesus. All scripture is inspired by God and is useful for teaching, for reproof, for correction, and for training in righteousness, so that everyone who belongs to God may be proficient, equipped for every good work.

Those holding a monological approach to Scripture often appeal to this passage in order to support their understanding of the Bible as the inerrant, or infallible, word of God. They find in the expression "all Scripture is God-breathed" (or "inspired") justification for their belief that God carefully scripted the written word into a flawless, homogeneous unity. After all, if Scripture came from the very mouth of God, shouldn't we be confident in its complete truthfulness and the unity of its witness?

I share with the monological position the belief that God was actively involved in the formation of our sacred traditions. Guided by the writer of 2 Timothy and my experience of Scripture, I wholeheartedly embrace the claim that these sacred writings are able to instruct us for salvation and that they are useful for teaching, for reproof, for correction, and for training in righteousness. But it seems to me that the expressions "God-breathed" or "inspired" and "useful" are far from clear-cut statements about the nature and authority of Scripture. They may mean something other than what those holding a monological view of Scripture take them to mean. Inspired? Yes, but how, and with what result? Useful? Of course, but in what sense: as inerrant statements or as the story of our faith and our struggle as God's people to walk in the will and ways of God? I believe that we need to look carefully at Scripture itself and the kinds of writings we find in it in order to understand how it is inspired by God, useful, and able to instruct us for salvation.

What we have found in this chapter is that Scripture is far more complex than the statement "Well, the Bible says it, and so it must be true" appreciates. We see that in some telling instances Scripture itself contributes to the diversity and disagreement that often characterize God's people by endorsing opposing perspectives. What are we to make of this? If we understand that God was somehow involved in the process by which Jewish and Christian folk included these conflicting traditions in their canon, how should we account for that fact? How might we find them useful, and what might they teach us about salvation?

Among the various things we might learn from this, three seem to me most important. First, the diversity reflected among the biblical authors underscores an important part of our Judeo-Christian heritage that is already apparent from the stories they record: we are a people who often have conflicting understandings of what it means to live as God's people in our time and place. The right answers will not always—or often—be easy for us. Remember, God's ways are not our ways. In our conversation with God and one another, we will struggle to discern what is faithful and true, and we will disagree. While unsettling and unpleasant at times, this is the path that is ours to walk as God's people in whom the effects of the Fall have not yet been wholly washed away.

Second, the fact that God guided the compilers of the canon to include these divergent traditions is a signal to us that not only will we disagree, but we are also called to keep talking with one another. *These conflicting views among the biblical writers, and the way they play off one another and show themselves to be remembering and recasting the story differently, present a conversation taking place in the very pages of Scripture.* To embrace Scripture as inspired by a God who chooses dialogue over monologue and as formative for our lives of faith is to embrace the example of conversation it embodies. It is to be a dialogue of sharing with one another our attempts to live into the sacred story of our faith in a way that is faithful for our present. It is to be a dialogue mindful of the biblical view that our conversations with one another—however disputatious they might become—are to be regarded and respected as part of our vocation as God's people. They are sacred. As stated well by Allen Verhey,

> There is a diversity of gifts within the interpretive community. And there is also a diversity of interpretations, diverse ways of using Scripture as morally instructive. Reading Scripture in Christian community does not mean that we will always agree. There have been diverse ways of using Scripture in moral discourse for as long as there have been Christian communities. Jewish Christians did not all read Scripture one way, but they read it differently than Gentile Christians did. Within the New Testament canon there are diverse ways of interpreting Hebrew Scripture, of using it for moral instruction. . . . To read Scripture in Christian community, to read Scripture as canon, is not to insist upon unanimity in reading it.[4]

Third, we must note that the biblical writers whose words we have explored in this chapter are, despite their differences, all celebrated as our ancestors in the faith. This, I think, can make us a little wiser about God's gift of salvation. Our inclusion and the inclusion of others into the family of God's people is not dependent on us or them getting all of it right. To be sure, "getting it right" is important. The energy invested in this very pursuit throughout the pages of Scripture makes it clear that we are a people called to discern the ways and will of God for our lives. As far as I can tell, Ezra and Nehemiah, despite their worthy motivations, had it quite wrong, and Isaiah, Malachi, and the writers of Ruth and Jonah had it quite right when it came to the matter of Gentiles (of course, as a Gentile, I am biased!). But there is something more fundamental to our inclusion among God's people than consistently hitting the mark. In the end, we are included not because of how right we are but because God graciously and mercifully accepts us, sometimes despite "the good" we try to do (Neh 13:31).

In our age of division, the polemical rhetoric we often use to strike at one another fails to appreciate these important biblical truths about God's salvation and our vocation as God's people. At times, those of us within the church are on the verge of "writing one another off" as we contend over what is right. Are any of those fellow believers with whom we disagree more "in the wrong" than Ezra and Nehemiah? The compilers of the canon did not write Ezra and Nehemiah out of the story. Such is the wideness of God's mercy. We are called to extend the same grace to one another.

# The Dynamic Character of God's Instruction

## chapter three

*"You have heard that it was said. . . but I say to you . . ." (Matt 5:21-22)*

**The Gospel according to Matthew presents** Jesus' teaching regarding the torah in dramatic contrast to that of the Pharisees. Matthew's portrayal of the Pharisees is distinctive in its sharpness; Luke, in contrast, presents more amicable relations between Jesus and various Pharisees. My interest here is not with a "quest for the historical Pharisees," however, but with the way Matthew presents Jesus in dialogue with another contemporary Jewish interpretation of the law. Let us imagine how some of the Pharisees, as Matthew portrays them, might have responded to the beginning of Jesus' Sermon on the Mount (Matt 5:1-48).

A whole host of folk has gathered to hear Jesus preach, including many teachers of the law. Many among the Pharisees are concerned, and with good reason. They have heard reports about this carpenter turned wandering healer. Charismatics always posed the risk that many could be led astray. And how would Pilate respond if things got out of hand? How many Jews would lose their lives this time?

A group of nervous Pharisees huddles together as they await Jesus' words. "They say he can cure all manner of demon possession and disease. Even paralytics. Imagine that! Limbs now useful that haven't stirred for years." It seemed too incredible to be true. And who could blame them for not believing—they'd seen it before. Someone claiming to be a healer gets lucky once, or fakes it, and soon tongues start wagging and hordes of people start following.

"Before you know it, they'll be hailing him as another Messiah. He probably wouldn't mind, from what the people say. He's
gathered disciples around himself as if he's some prophet. He is
telling them to repent, 'for the kingdom is at hand!' This one could
be dangerous."

Now Jesus stands before the host of folk who have gathered to
hear what he has to say. Not much is yet know about his teaching.
"Rumor has it that he's going to lay it all out here on the mount.
The mountain. A bit presumptuous, don't you think?" The cluster
of Pharisees solemnly nods in agreement. One of them snorts, "But
perhaps he doesn't intend any connection to Moses, or even realize it. How much of the torah could a carpenter from Nazareth
actually know?"

Jesus begins to speak, and the nervous Pharisees whisper their
commentary to one another.

"So he begins with blessings. All right, very good. Well in line
with our teaching. God will favor the lowly and the oppressed. The
righteous among us will receive great reward. Yes, the persecuted.
. . . What did he just say? Did he say those persecuted 'on my
account' will be blessed? What is that supposed to mean?! Now,
a few parables. Salt, light, 'give glory to God.' All right, not bad.
'Not going to abolish the Law and the Prophets.' Well, of course
not, what fool would! Wait a minute: He is going to fulfill the Law
and the Prophets? We do have another messianic nightmare on
our hands! Wait until Herod and Pilate hear of it. There will be a
price to pay!

"'Not one letter, not one stroke of the letter will pass from the
law until all is accomplished.' Good. 'Therefore, whoever breaks
one of the least of these commandments . . .' Well, at least he
respects the law. But what's this? '. . . Unless your righteousness
exceeds that of the scribes and Pharisees, you will never enter the
kingdom of heaven' — what insane words are these?!"

The clutch of Pharisees clench their fists and exchange broiling
glances. But the worst is yet to come:

"You have heard that it was said to those of ancient times, you
shall not murder. . . . But I say to you . . ."

"May the heavens fall upon us! But he says! He says! Who is
he to say? Who is he to add to God's torah? These are the words
of Moses, the words of Adonai. He is supposed to interpret them,
not supersede them!

"That's what he seems to be doing anyway. He's presenting a
common form of interpretation, getting to the underlying intent of

the laws on murder and adultery. Why then does he insist on saying 'But I say to you . . .'? The fool. Thinks he's quite original, better than Moses, does he? What's this? He's tossing aside Moses' teachings on divorce! Also on oaths! Our laws on retaliation? Someone stop him! He's Satan in disguise! What happened to 'not one letter, not one stroke of a letter will pass from the law'? He's shredding the torah to pieces. 'Love our enemies?' Does he mean love the Romans? 'You've heard it was said . . . but I say to you . . .' He must be stopped!"

## The Dynamic Character of God's Instruction

Jesus' Sermon on the Mount (Matthew 5–7) serves as a striking example of the dynamic nature of God's instruction to God's people. Yet the dynamic character of the torah is not seen first here, but is already apparent in the opening books of the Old Testament. As recorded in Exodus, Moses first gives the law—God's torah—to the Israelites shortly after they are delivered from Egypt at the start of their time in the wilderness. God speaks the Ten Commandments directly to the people, and when Moses returns from meeting with God atop Mount Sinai, he teaches the Israelites the remaining commands of God (Exodus 20–23). At a later time, as recorded in Deuteronomy, Moses again lays before the people the entire law. The setting has changed. Israel's wanderings in the wilderness are at their end, and the people are now preparing to enter the promised land. Moses says to them, in effect, "My time with you is up. But before you go into the land God promised to your ancestors, the land flowing with milk and honey, I am going to teach you once again all of God's commands and statutes. Remember them! Follow them! Your very life depends on them!" (See Deut 4:1-40, 30:1-20.) As we compare these two great bodies of instruction from Exodus and Deuteronomy, we notice that certain laws have changed.

**Exod 22:21-24**
Commands not to oppress the resident alien, widow, or orphan.

**Deut 24:17-22**
Also includes instruction about not taking a widow's garment as a pledge and leaving remnants in the field for the alien, widow, and the orphan

**Exod 23:1**
Commands not to spread a false report or not to join hands with the wicked to act as a malicious witness.

**Deut 19:16-21**
Offers instruction on what to do with one who gives a false witness.

| Exod 21:2-7 | | Deut 15:12-18 |
| --- | --- | --- |
| Seventh-year release applies only to male slaves, and specifically not to female slaves. | | Seventh year release applies also to female slaves. |

| Exod 21:2-6; 23:10-11 | Deut 15:1-18 | Leviticus 25 |
| --- | --- | --- |
| Commands that in the seventh year, slaves shall be set free and the land shall lie fallow. | Commands that in the seventh year, remission of debts shall be granted and slaves set free. | Commands that in the seventh year, the land shall lie fallow; very detailed discussion on the redemption of ancestral lands in the fiftieth year (jubilee). |

The changes noted here are not staggering, but they are enough for us to see that as the biblical author portrays God's people entering a new stage of their lives on the eve of their entrance into the promised land, he also portrays God's instruction for them developing as well.[1] Concerning these developments in the law, Old Testament scholar Terence Fretheim states,

> The integration of law and narrative throughout the Pentateuch (see chapter 5 on Leviticus) is a key consideration. God's gift of the law is not drawn into a code, but remains integrated with the story of God's gracious activity in the ever-changing history of God's people. Law is always intersecting with life as it is, filled with contingency and change, with complexity and ambiguity. . . This means that new laws will be needed and older laws will need to be recast or set aside. . . . Internal tensions and inconsistencies between these laws, however, are not ironed out or considered a threat to the law's integrity. Rather, old and new remain side by side as a canonical witness to the process of unfolding law. Hence, *development of the law* is just as canonical as individual laws or the body of law as a whole.[2]

For Christians, perhaps the most revealing examples of the law's development are found in New Testament traditions such as the Sermon on the Mount (Matt 5:1–7:28)—a portion of which was illustrated above—Mark 7, Acts 15, and sections of Paul's letters. In the Sermon on the Mount, for instance, Jesus announces that he has not come to abolish "the law and the prophets" (referring to the Jewish Scriptures as a whole), but to fulfill them (v. 17). He adds that "not one letter, not one stroke of a letter will pass from the law until all is accomplished" (v. 18). But then Jesus goes on to offer his own recasting of several torah commands marked by the refrain: "You have heard it was said . . . but I tell you . . ." (5:21-48). Some of Jesus' reinterpretations simply focus on the underlying spirit of the particular law in view by expanding the application of that law (for example, the laws on murder, and adultery [vv. 21-30]).

"You have heard that it was said to those of ancient times, 'You shall not murder'; and 'whoever murders shall be liable to judgment.' But I say to you that if you are angry with a brother or sister, you will be liable to judgment; and if you insult a brother or sister, you will be liable to the council; and if you say, 'You fool,' you will be liable to the hell of fire.

"You have heard that it was said, 'You shall not commit adultery.' But I say to you that everyone who looks at a woman with lust has already committed adultery with her in his heart. If your right eye causes you to sin, tear it out and throw it away; it is better for you to lose one of your members than for your whole body to be thrown into hell. And if your right hand causes you to sin, cut it off and throw it away; it is better for you to lose one of your members than for your whole body to go into hell."

In broadening the purview of these laws to include behaviors and dispositions that might lead up to the physical acts of murder and adultery, Jesus is engaging in a manner of interpreting torah that would likely not be unique among Jewish teachers of his time. The Pharisees are often caricatured by Christians as strict legalists who woodenly clung to every command of torah. However, rabbinic traditions from as early as the second century c.e. suggest that Jewish interpretation of torah in Jesus' day was quite dynamic and creative in its engagement with Mosaic tradition. The difference, it seems, between Jesus and his fellow Jewish interpreters of torah was not a matter of method. Both likely agreed on a fundamental principle of Jewish interpretation that one is allowed to recast the laws in ways that help to apply it in new times and places. From the perspective of the Gospel writers, what they didn't agree on was Jesus' authority to provide such a radical retelling of God's instruction and *the extent to which* Jesus prioritized the center of the law at the expense (in the Pharisee's view) of the letter of the law.

When Jesus takes up the torah commands on divorce (Matt 5:31-32; see Deut 24:1-4), oaths (Matt 5:33-37; see Lev 19:12; Num 30:2; Deut 23:21), compensation/retaliation (Matt 5:38-42; see Exod 21:24; Lev 24:20), and loving one's neighbor (Matt 5:43-48; see Lev 19:18; esp. Deut 23:6), he departs from the original meaning and intent of the laws so much so that these laws previously given by God are radically recast:

"It was also said, 'Whoever divorces his wife, let him give her a certificate of divorce.' But I say to you that anyone who divorces his wife, except on the ground of unchastity, causes her to commit adultery; and whoever marries a divorced woman commits adultery.

"Again, you have heard that it was said to those of ancient times, 'You shall not swear falsely, but carry out the vows you have made to the Lord.' But I say to you, Do not swear at all, either by heaven, for it is the throne of God, or by the earth, for it is his footstool, or by Jerusalem, for it is the city of the great King. And do not swear by your head, for you cannot make one hair white or black. Let your word be 'Yes, Yes' or 'No, No'; anything more than this comes from the evil one.

"You have heard that it was said, 'An eye for an eye and a tooth for a tooth.' But I say to you, Do not resist an evildoer. But if anyone strikes you on the right cheek, turn the other also; and if anyone wants to sue you and take your coat, give your cloak as well; and if anyone forces you to go one mile, go also the second mile. Give to everyone who begs from you, and do not refuse anyone who wants to borrow from you.

"You have heard that it was said, 'You shall love your neighbor and hate your enemy.' But I say to you, Love your enemies and pray for those who persecute you, so that you may be children of your Father in heaven; for he makes his sun rise on the evil and on the good, and sends rain on the righteous and on the unrighteous. For if you love those who love you, what reward do you have? Do not even the tax collectors do the same? And if you greet only your brothers and sisters, what more are you doing than others? Do not even the Gentiles do the same? Be perfect, therefore, as your heavenly Father is perfect." (Matt 5:31-48)

Another example is also instructive. The controversy dialogue of Mark 7:1-23 begins with the Pharisees criticizing Jesus because his disciples were eating with defiled (unwashed) hands (vv. 1-5). Jesus responds by noting the Pharisee's own inconsistency in following torah (vv. 6-13). Then, in his instruction to the crowd, Jesus teaches that "there is nothing outside a person that by going in can defile, but the things that come out are what defile" (vv. 14-15). When elaborating on this extraordinary teaching with his disciples, Jesus repeats this statement (using gastrointestinal illustrations to drive home the point! [vv. 17-19]). And it is here that the Gospel writer drops a parenthetical bombshell: "(Thus he declared all foods clean)" (v. 19). What served for Jesus and many of his fellow Jews as an important, daily reminder of their distinct identity as Yahweh's own and their sense of duty to God's torah is now set aside. Scores of dietary restrictions rooted in torah provisions are no longer viewed as relevant to the vocation of God's people (see Leviticus 11, 17; Deuteronomy 14). All foods, in Mark's words, are now clean.

Throughout the Gospels, Jesus is repeatedly portrayed as redefining prevailing understandings of what it means to be righteous. Thus, for Jesus, righteousness is marked not by legal rectitude as much as by a repentant spirit (for example, Jesus and the sinful woman in Simon the Pharisee's home [Luke 7:36-50]; the parable of the Pharisee and the tax collector [Luke 18:9-14]). Compassion and attention to human need outrank purity and piety (Jesus healing the man with the withered hand on the Sabbath [Mark 3:1-6]; the parable of the Good Samaritan [Luke 10:29-37]; the healing of the woman suffering from hemorrhaging [Mark 5:24-24]). Many of Jesus' teachings direct his followers to have compassion for and identify with the poor, problematizing wealth in a society where great need exists (the parable of the rich man and Lazarus [Luke 16:19-31]; the repentance of Zacchaeus [Luke 19:1-10]; the beatitudes in Luke 6). Greed is a reflection of one's trust in wealth, not God, as the source of blessing, and is thus another form of idolatry (Jesus' teachings on wealth in the Sermon on the Mount [Matt 6:19-34]). Righteousness is also defined by the Gospel writers as recognizing the presence of God's reign in Jesus and devoting oneself to Jesus through faithful discipleship (Luke 9:21-27, 57-62; Matt 10:1-15; 28:16-20). The reason why many (not all) of Jesus' fellow Jews, especially among the religious leadership, found his teachings so troubling is that Jesus pushed Jewish purity concerns and other legalities to the margins, even those that are inscribed in the law of Moses. In their place, Jesus offered the alternative, radical for many, of fulfilling torah by following his example and devoting themselves to his teaching and mission.

So how then are we to understand Jesus' statement earlier in the Sermon on the Mount that "until heaven and earth will pass away, not one letter, not one stroke of a letter, will pass from the law until all is accomplished" (Matt 5:18)? Scholars have struggled to discern Jesus' intention here as presented by Matthew. On the one hand, Jesus seems to be upholding the sacred and permanent nature of the law in all its detail: not one part of it is to be displaced. On the other hand, Jesus, as we have seen, so radically recasts certain elements of the Mosaic law that he essentially sets their original meaning and intention aside. In my view, the answer to this conundrum lies in recognizing that for Jesus the whole of torah, the whole of God's instruction, is contained in what he sees as its irreducible essence:

> "You shall love the Lord your God with all your heart, with all your soul, and with all your mind. This is the first and greatest commandment. And a second is like it. You shall love your neighbor as yourself. *On these two commandments hang all the law and the prophets.*" (Matt 22:37-40, italics added)

This, for Jesus, is what constitutes the law in both its particularity and totality: right relationship with God and one another, for "on these two commandments hang all the law and the prophets." These two commandments are the root and stem that gives every branch, twig, and leaf of law its meaning and purpose. Thus, if there are any laws that in a new time and place, or as a result of a greater depth of insight into God's will, no longer bear witness to what it means to be rightly related to God and one another (such as the purity codes and dietary restrictions), they are to be pruned away, for they no longer function as instruction for God's people. They are no longer torah. New branches, twigs, and leaves will take their place.

There is still the phrase, "Therefore, whoever breaks one of the least of these commandments, and teaches others to do the same, will be called least in the kingdom of heaven" (Matt 5:19) to consider, which sounds as though Jesus stood against any marginalization of the torah commands. The simplest and best solution, I think, is to understand "these commandments" as referring to the commandments and instruction offered by Jesus in the remainder of the sermon (5:21–7:27) and throughout the Gospel. It is the teaching *Jesus* provides that upholds the purpose and essence of the law more fully than what was given in the past ("You have heard it was said . . . but I say to you . . ."). In sum, it is not the law as proclaimed and practiced by the Pharisees and scribes (who claim to attend to every stroke and letter) that leads to true righteousness (v. 20), but the law as now redefined by Jesus. This explanation also fits well with the parable Jesus tells to conclude the sermon: "Everyone who hears my words and acts on them will be like a wise man who builds his house on rock" (7:24).

Paul's letters and Acts depict early believers taking their lead from Jesus' teaching and provide additional examples of the dynamic development of God's instruction by which some elements of Old Testament law are recast or set aside. Galatians, and the Jerusalem conference reported in Acts 15, make it clear that circumcision is no longer required of Gentile converts, despite the command given to Abraham that any male member of his extended household, including any foreigner, was to be circumcised (Gen 17:9-14). At the Jerusalem conference, Gentile Christians are simply instructed to "abstain from things polluted by idols and from fornication and from whatever has been strangled and from blood" (Acts 15:20). This represents a far less rigorous attitude regarding adherence to purity codes than that found in the Old Testament legal traditions. Not surprisingly (as discussed above in chapter 2), Paul seems to overlook even these limited dietary restrictions in his discussion of the "weak" and the "strong" in Romans 14 (see also 1 Cor 8:1-3, 10:14-22). Paul's understanding of the role of the law is no simple matter, and we will have the occasion to address it more fully in chapter 4. Yet it seems to me that the reason he came to set aside elements of the written law is that he considered the Spirit, coupled with Jesus' love command (Matt 22:37-40; Mark 12:30-31), to be first and foremost the sources of God's instruction of what it means to live as God's people (see, for example, Galatians 3-5; Rom 7:1–8:17; 1 Cor 6:12-20; Phil 3:2-11). For example, as Paul states in Rom 8:1-4 concerning the role of the Spirit,

> There is therefore now no condemnation for those who are in Christ Jesus. For the law of the Spirit of life in Christ Jesus has set you free from the law of sin and of death. For God has done what the law, weakened by the flesh, could not do: by sending his own Son in the likeness of sinful flesh, and to deal with sin, he condemned sin in the flesh, so that the just requirement of the law might be fulfilled in us, who walk not according to the flesh but according to the Spirit.

In Rom 13:8-10, Paul speaks to this "just requirement of the law" which the ongoing ministries of Jesus and the Spirit enable believers to fulfill. He exhorts the church,

> Owe no one anything, except to love one another; for the one who loves another has fulfilled the law. The commandments, "You shall not commit adultery; You shall not murder; You shall not steal; You shall not covet"; and any other commandment, are summed up in this word, "Love your neighbor as yourself." Love does no wrong to a neighbor; therefore, love is the fulfilling of the law.

In Galatians 3-5, Paul commands the Galatian church to reject those demanding that Gentile converts be circumcised. Paul beseeches them to set aside these commands of the law and to live by the guidance of the Spirit. He then states in Gal 5:5-6:

> For through the Spirit, by faith, we eagerly wait for the hope of righteousness. For in Christ Jesus neither circumcision or nor uncircumcision counts for anything; the only thing that matters is faith working through love.

Later, he adds in 5:13-14:

> For you were called to freedom, brothers and sisters; only do not use your freedom as an opportunity for self-indulgence, but through love become slaves to one another. For the whole law is summed up in a single commandment, "You shall love your neighbor as yourself."

This focus on the Spirit and Jesus' love command did not mean for Paul a dismissal of the law. Instead, as with Jesus, it meant an understanding of torah that allowed for a recasting, even a setting aside of particular torah stipulations, in order that the *purpose* of God's law might now be more fully realized among God's people. As stated well by New Testament scholar James D. G. Dunn:

> (For Paul), faith operating through love is how the commandments are to be kept—including the necessity or otherwise of circumcision! In other words, the love command fulfills the whole law because it fulfills the spirit of the law and, in the given situation of loving the neighbour, indicates what things really matter and what can be treated as non-essentials (*adiaphora*). [3]

Indeed, the essential calling to love God and one another had always been the heart of torah. We see it embodied in the Ten Commandments and other commands, and even long before then we find that such right relatedness was inscribed in the very foundation of creation, as the source of blessing God intended for all creatures (see chapter 7). But Jesus, and after him, Paul, brought the heart of the torah front and center and used it as the crucible by which the value of all law was to be tested and all human behavior judged. Again, this did not mean for them an eschewal of piety and moral rigor. Quite the contrary—can anything be more pious and ethically rigorous than the two chief commands Jesus proclaimed and Paul echoed, to love God with all one has and to love neighbor as self? What it meant is that precepts leading people to value the means of law more so than its end goal of right relationship, the commands to which many pointed as markers of their own self-righteousness at the expense of their humility, the laws drawing boundaries that kept people on the outside rather than inviting them to come in from the dark and cold of this world and into God's kingdom, all these are to be set aside or transformed into instruction that is truly Spirit formed and life giving.

Stepping back and viewing Jesus' and Paul's recasting of God's torah against the backdrop of the entire canon lead us to see it as dramatic examples of what Terence Fretheim calls "a canonical witness to the process of unfolding law." Within Scripture's narrative, how humanity is to live out its calling as God's people develops throughout the history of the relationship between God and God's people, which climaxes in the life, death, and resurrection of Jesus. This ongoing development of the law is thus presented as part of God's unfolding plan to bring humans back into right relationship with God, one another, and creation. In other words, one of the ways God accomplishes this saving purpose is through such continuing and reforming instruction on what it means to be God's people: to live rightly with God and one another.

## The Crux of the Issue: Just How Dynamic Is God's Instruction?

I think that most Christians would find the notion of God's instruction as dynamic and reforming uncontroversial. After all, as Christians, our sense of ethics, conduct, church membership, and worship is heavily dependent on this very notion. Not many of us refrain from trimming our sideburns (Lev 19:27), abstain from eating pork and shellfish (Leviticus 11; 17), offer animal sacrifices, or avoid wearing clothes with two different types of fabric (Lev 19:19). Not many of us require circumcision for church membership or continue to observe the Sabbath or celebrate Passover, at least not in the traditional sense. For us, the way Jesus, Paul, and the writers of the New Testament reshaped our understanding of torah has become normative.

Many Christians, I think, would also find uncontroversial the notion that Jesus continues to instruct and guide believers. Christians commonly hold the conviction that the Holy Spirit deepens our understanding of God's will in new times and places, through Scripture, prayer, and shared reflection on our experiences as people of faith. Such continuing instruction is needed since—to use Paul's words—"we now see as in a mirror, dimly" and "know only in part" (1 Cor 13:12). The notion of God's ongoing instruction through the ministry of the Holy Spirit is firmly rooted in the New Testament. We have seen this already in the teachings of Paul cited above. According to the Fourth Gospel, Jesus himself tells his disciples that he has not finished revealing to them everything they need to know, for time and their lack of maturity have not allowed it. Yet after him will come the Spirit who will "guide you into all the truth" (John 14:15-17, 25-26; 16:13-14). The notion also holds a central place in Christian theological tradition. Commonly referred to as "illumination by the Spirit," it is generally understood as God's gift of helping believers to embrace within their own lives of faith the good news of God's grace as revealed in Scripture.

But now we come to a crucial issue, with which we move from a matter of widespread consensus to a matter of contentious dispute: can God's ongoing instruction lead us to view an issue differently from the writers of the New Testament? This also raises the question of what exactly is canonical, or authoritative, about Scripture. Is it simply its content? Or should the *ongoing development of God's instruction centering on Jesus' love command*—as portrayed in Scripture itself—also be received as normative and paradigmatic? To what extent is the continuing re-formation of the law "canonical," or "biblical," as Fretheim suggests?

As discussed at some length already, basic to the approach introduced here is taking the way Scripture itself shapes its traditions as instructive for our own reading of Scripture. Consequently, this approach views Scripture's portrayal of God's instruction as dynamic and reforming as an important tenet of our faith that is to be drawn upon in our own engagement with the biblical traditions. To put it simply, the Bible shows us that our grasp of what it means to be God's people has undergone significant development, even to the point that previously given laws may be set aside. In light of this observation, why would we assume that this could no longer happen? Why would we reject a priori the notion that the Spirit might lead us to recast or set aside elements of New Testament instruction, and to reach a deeper understanding of what God wills for human relationships?

### The Example of Homosexuality

This very point has often been debated in connection with the church's struggle over homosexuality. Because of this, it may be helpful to turn our discussion to that issue as a means of illustrating the relevance of this point for the church today. The New Testament injunctions against homosexual activity are rather straightforward (see 1 Cor 6:9-10, 1 Tim 1:10, Rom 1:26-27), and recent attempts by some scholars to limit the original purview of these statements to the particular practice of pederasty (adult males using male minors for sexual gratification) or male prostitution have not been convincing.[4] Yet many Christians are now sensing that committed, consensual homosexual relationships, like the best of heterosexual relationships, bear witness to the love, mutuality, and respect God intends for all human relationships. In short, homosexual relationships—in the eyes of many—serve as a source of blessing for the partners involved as well as for others, and in doing so glorify God.

But is this a biblically faithful position? This brings us back to the question at hand: would God lead us to an understanding of an issue that conflicts with what New Testament writers themselves state on that same issue?

Some do not believe so. Paul Achtemeier represents the view of many in arguing that the canonization of the scriptural texts serves an important *limiting function* that effectively puts a hold on their further development. In Achtemeier's view, this limiting role of the canon also preserves as abidingly normative the New Testament writers' specific injunctions against certain behaviors, including homosexuality. Thus, he claims that to deem homosexuality an acceptable lifestyle is to transgress the limits on behavior prescribed by Scripture.

The attempt to legitimate homoerotic sexual contact as an acceptable Christian "lifestyle" is another such attempt [to circumvent the limiting function of the canon], this time within the confessing Christian community. . . . In this instance, the limitations imposed by the canonical witness on certain ways of conducting a life in accord with the foundational Christian witness are themselves negated, and in that way actions can be declared acceptable which do in fact fall outside the hermeneutical limitation imposed by the canon.[5]

I truly appreciate Achtemeier's interest in rooting our reading of the New Testament in a canon-centered approach, one that is attentive to how the canon itself shapes our understanding and embrace of sacred tradition. However, I wonder how this "hermeneutical limitation" imposed by the canon is to be applied to other specific activities addressed by Scripture, such as slavery, the limitation of the role of women in the Christian community, the requirement of head-coverings in worship, and the practice of greeting one another with a holy kiss, all of which many Christians now see much differently than the New Testament writers did.

### Precedents: Slavery and the Role of Women in Christian Community

Indeed, those who advocate accepting homosexual relationships have pointed to changed perceptions among Christians on slavery and the role of women in the Christian community as analogues to how the church could be led to an understanding of an issue that differs from that of the New Testament writers. They argue that if many Christian believers today can be rightly led to understand the institution of slavery and the role of women in the church community differently from how they are regarded by some New Testament texts, then perhaps one should not rule out the possibility that the same might also rightly take place with respect to our understanding of homosexual relationships. Let us pause to examine the New Testament's teachings on slavery and the role of women in the Christian community as a means of clarifying how most Christians have come to view these issues much differently.

Some modern scholars, understandably, are reluctant to admit that Scripture affirms slavery. Several have argued that the New Testament writers merely tolerate it as an unavoidable part of the social fabric of the ancient world.[6] But it seems to me that the New Testament household codes addressing the slave–master relationship reflect an attitude toward slavery that goes well beyond resigned toleration (see Eph 6:5-9; Col 3:22–4:1; 1 Tim 6:1-2).[7] Consider, for example, Eph 6:5-9:

Slaves, obey your earthly masters with fear and trembling, in single-ness of heart, as you obey Christ; not only while being watched, and in order to please them, but as slaves of Christ, doing the will of God from the heart. Render service with enthusiasm, as to the Lord and not to men and women, knowing that whatever good we do, we will receive the same again from the Lord, whether we are slaves or free. And, masters, do the same to them. Stop threatening them, for you know that both of you have the same Master in heaven, and with him there is no partiality.

To be sure, the writer of this text is not simply echoing the dominant Greco-Roman sentiments about slavery but seeks to shape the practice of the institution in a way that is consistent with the core Christian ethic upholding the integrity of all people. Yet at the very same time, he urges that the slave–master relationship be maintained with an extraordinary degree of devotion on the part of the slave, beyond what would otherwise be typical: "obey your earthly masters with fear and trembling, in single-ness of heart, as you obey Christ" (v. 5). In fact, a Christian slave's service to his or her earthly master was considered part of his or her service and devotion to Christ and to God (vv. 5-6). The author believes that in God's future kingdom the distinction between master and slave will ultimately vanish (v. 9). Yet remarkably, the hope in God's eternal blessing is cited as *motivation for the proper exercise of the practice of slavery* by both master and slave, *not* the cessation of it (vv. 8-9). The tone and content of this and other passages addressing slavery go beyond simple tolera-tion (see especially 1 Tim 6:1-2). The institution of slavery is fastidiously maintained and affirmed as consistent with the Christian life.

A number of scholars, however, have pointed to Paul's letter to Phi-lemon as an example of the New Testament writings challenging the practice of slavery. But in requesting the release of the slave Onesimus, Paul is doing nothing to challenge slavery as a social institution. Paul clearly recognizes that Philemon has a claim on Onesimus (vv. 8-10, vv. 18-20). Moreover, in the first-century Mediterranean world, the release of slaves was not uncommon but could occur in several ways, including the adoption of a slave by another and payment for his or her freedom. Note Paul's description of his relationship with the slave in v. 10: "I am now appealing to you for my child, Onesimus, whose father I have become during my imprisonment." Paul then goes on to say that any outstanding debt resulting from Onesimus's release should be charged to Paul's account, while slyly adding, "I say nothing about your owing me even your own self" (v. 19). Paul is simply requesting the release of a particular slave who has become dear to him, and he does so in a manner that follows the customs governing the practice of slavery in his time.

Similarly, there are several New Testament texts that, if followed, would prevent women from taking leadership positions in Christian communities. Consider 1 Tim 2:8-15:

> I desire, then, that in every place the men should pray, lifting up holy hands without anger or argument; also that the women should dress themselves modestly and decently in suitable clothing, not with their hair braided, or with gold, pearls, or expensive clothes, but with good works, as is proper for women who profess reverence for God. Let a woman learn in silence with full submission. I permit no woman to teach or to have authority over a man; she is to keep silent. For Adam was formed first, then Eve; and Adam was not deceived, but the woman was deceived and became a transgressor. Yet she will be saved through childbearing, provided they continue in faith and love and holiness, with modesty.

We also find a very similar perspective expressed by Paul in 1 Cor 14:33b-36.

> As in all the churches of the saints, women should be silent in the churches. For they are not permitted to speak, but should be subordinate, as the law also says. If there is anything they desire to know, let them ask their husbands at home. For it is shameful for a woman to speak in church. Or did the word of God originate with you? Or are you the only ones it has reached?

There have been numerous attempts to soften these injunctions severely limiting the participation of women in Christian communities. Various theories have been offered in terms of what was taking place in these communities to warrant such a harsh response on the part of the epistle writer. Most of the suggestions play off the hypothesis that in some fashion the women were acting up and disturbing worship, perhaps through the overzealous practice of spiritual gifts, and needed to be reined in. Some thus maintain that these commands should be seen as applying only to these particular communities at this particular time. Yet the absolute and universal character of the instructions is not so easily overcome: "I permit *no* woman to teach or have authority over a man." "It is *shameful* for a woman to speak in church." "As in *all the churches of the saints*, women should be silent in the churches." Moreover, in 1 Timothy the rationale for this prohibition is grounded in the narrative of Genesis: "For Adam was formed first, then Eve; and Adam was not deceived, but the woman was deceived and became a transgressor" (1 Tim 2:14). Others have argued that what we need to do with these difficult passages is to look for some underlying principle that transcends their particular historical and cultural context, such as "be orderly and respectful in worship." But this is far from dealing with the text in terms of its plain meaning.

If we honestly appraise these texts, we cannot avoid the conclusion that many of us now view the role of women in the church community much differently than how it was viewed by these writers of the New Testament. Similarly, we now view the institution of slavery much differently than did nearly all the writers of the New Testament who address the issue. We no longer consider their specific instructions on these issues as binding for us today. We no longer consider these texts faithful instruction on what it means to be God's people.

But why is this? If, as Achtemeier and others maintain, the canonization of our sacred traditions imposes a hermeneutical limitation that preserves the New Testament writers' instruction to us as fixed and unchanging, why do so many Christians tolerate such a clear and obvious divergence from the Bible on these issues? What justifies our understanding of God's will on these matters if it so sharply contrasts with what the New Testament writers themselves held?

Some have argued that with respect to these two issues in particular, the Bible does not speak with one voice but represents a diversity of perspectives.[8] In addition to these texts that call for the subordination of women to men, deny women authority within the faith community, and require women to learn in silence with full submission (1 Tim 2:8-15; 1 Cor 14:34-35; see also 1 Cor 11:2-16), other writings affirm the important role of women in the history of God's relationship with Israel (Miriam, Deborah, Huldah, Esther), in Jesus' ministry (for example, Luke 8:1-3), and in the early church (Romans 16). Similarly, in addition to those texts in the New Testament that legitimate the practice of slavery (such as Eph 6:5-8; Col 3:22–4:1; 1 Tim 6:1-2), there are other texts that at least suggest that slavery is not in accord with God's ultimate plans for humanity (Gal 3:28). Thus, as the argument goes, it follows that the passages offering a positive portrayal of women in ministry and possibly in leadership positions and others that seem to move us to a view of human relations beyond institutionalized slavery provide the cue (and permission) for our own development of thought on these specific issues. In short, Scripture reflects mixed opinions on these matters. Because of this, we are free to regard as authoritative those portions of Scripture which cohere with our emerging views of the issue, when those views have been affirmed through much prayer, reflection, and discussion.

I find much to commend in this approach. Note how dialogical it is! The realization that Scripture—even the New Testament—may not always speak with one voice on a particular issue, as we saw in chapter 2, is an important step in recognizing Scripture's diverse and dialogical character. Likewise, the conviction that in such cases we need to engage in careful, prayerful reflection and dialogue also points to the conversational character of interpretation.

Nevertheless, these same scholars argue that one does not find such diversity in the Bible when it comes to the issue of homosexuality. There are no verses that positively regard same-gender sexual relations. Consequently, they argue, we are not justified in claiming that God would now have us regard same-sex relations differently than the biblical writers.

I agree that Scripture nowhere affirms same-gender couples. However, I disagree with the notion that a dialogical engagement of Scripture is to be practiced only when addressing matters on which Scripture itself seems unclear. *Rather, the struggle to understand God's will, as reflected in the contrasting views we see within the biblical tradition on slavery, the role of women, and other issues reveals that Scripture does not always provide the final answer to specific issues that vex us as God's people.* The Bible did not provide a final answer to the issue of slavery or—for many Christians at least—the role of women in the Christian community. More than that, its dominant tendencies are in contrast to what many Christians now perceive is God's will on these matters. Galatians 3:28 may give us pause when it comes to slavery. But it is a far cry from a clear protest against the practice, especially when later texts such as Ephesians 6 have no trouble with the notion that slave and free are equal in God's sight while unequivocally enjoining slaves to devote themselves to their masters. Some passages do indeed hold in high regard women's contributions to ministry. However, the clearest and most direct New Testament statements on the issue, and what New Testament as a whole says about it, indicate that such ministry is to take place in very narrowly defined boundaries: women can play an active, important role in the church's ministry, as long as they are subordinate to men, silent in worship, do not ask questions of anyone (except their husbands in the quiet and comfort their own patriarchal homes), and make babies! (1 Tim 2:11-15). In short, Christ had some things yet to teach us that were in stark contrast to what most of the New Testament writers addressing these issues and the New Testament as a whole had to say. That, I think, is the really important point to appreciate.

To say that such revising of biblical instruction must be limited to those matters on which Scripture itself is not unanimous strikes me as special pleading and artificial. It is special pleading because, as we have seen, the dominant tendencies and corporate witness of the New Testament on two such matters—slavery and the role of women in Christian communities—are actually very different from how we now commonly regard these issues. It is artificial because, as we have also seen in this chapter, there have been developments in God's instruction on a variety of matters throughout Scripture. Why would we now be willing to entertain development on only these two? We must also note that the changes in God's instruction which Jesus introduced rest solely in his (and, Jesus claimed, God's) authority; they are consistent, in a broad sense, with preceding tradition (that is, the essence of God's law) but do not require any specific precedents. On the contrary, some were outright radical. If as Christians we truly believe that Jesus is among us still, guiding us to proclaim faithfully and live into God's saving reign, then on what basis might we claim that Jesus could never lead us to understand the issue of homosexuality differently from the New Testament writers?

### Allowing Scripture and Jesus to Guide the Way

To build on this point, the confluence of two observations we have already discussed suggests a way of engaging biblical instruction that better appreciates the Bible's witness to God's will and the Bible's canonical function within the life of the Christian community. First, there is Scripture's own testimony to the ongoing revision of God's instruction concerning what it means to be God's faithful people. The dynamic and reforming nature of this instruction reveals that God does not simply want our adherence to a fixed set of laws. Instead, God desires that we continually open ourselves to God's Spirit and to one another to discern anew how the essential purpose of God's instruction as defined by Jesus—to love God and one another—can be more fully lived out among us. As stated well by I. Howard Marshall,

> Since we may be led to conclude that some teachings of Scripture need to be understood and applied differently from in the first century, it follows that such reconsideration is a task that involves considerable risk, but also great is the risk of misleading the church by dwelling in the first century and refusing to go beyond the letter of Scripture. We must beware of the danger of failing to understand what God is saying to his people today and muzzling his voice. Scripture itself constrains us to the task of ongoing theological development.[9]

Second, although the unfolding drama of salvation history reaches its culmination in Jesus, the New Testament texts themselves indicate that Jesus' instruction of believers will continue through the ongoing ministry of the Spirit (see John 14:15-17; 16:13-14; Rom 8:1-11; 1 Cor 2:12; 7:25-40; Gal 5:16-26). The reason this must be so is that, as Paul says, we yet "see as in a mirror, dimly" and "know only in part" (1 Cor 13:12). The blessed, yet still deeply troubled human characters of the unfolding drama of God's salvation necessitate a continuing path of illumination, a path that was also treaded—and magnificently so—by Paul and the other inspired writers of the New Testament.

In light of this, it is a crucial fact that Scripture itself provides no indication that the dynamic nature of God's instruction is suddenly to cease. To insist, as some do, that all of the specific injunctions of the New Testament concerning particular behaviors must stand for all time *is to assign to biblical instruction a role that it has never before performed.* In other words, the hermeneutical limitation Achtemeier and others believe the canon imposes on our sacred traditions actually leads us to read against the grain of what the canon as a whole has to teach us about our reception of God's instruction. It treats our perception of God's instruction as fixed and static, when so much in our biblical and ecclesial tradition points to the reality that our grasp of God's will is dynamic and reforming. Again, to argue as others do that our understanding of particular issues can develop beyond the New Testament witness only when Scripture itself displays some uncertainty on those issues also neglects the larger lesson the canon provides about the dynamic nature of God's instruction. The reformation of God's instruction taking place within the canon is much broader and more dynamic than such a perspective appreciates. Equally troubling, this perspective also fails to embrace the full implications of Jesus' sovereignty as resurrected Lord and Savior, the Living Word, who continues to unveil to us God's will and purpose for our lives.

In contrast, the approach presented here finds Scripture embodying and advocating a different way of reading and reflecting on sacred tradition. The hermeneutic to which Scripture bears witness is, first of all, one in which the sacred stories of God's people are continually retold and celebrated as one, great, overarching history, culminating in God's act of salvation in Jesus (more on this in chapters 6 and 7). Second, it bears witness to the need for those who embrace this great story as their own to reflect continually, together with Scripture, other believers, and with hearts open to Jesus' *ongoing* instruction on what it means to live as those who are transformed by this story.

All of this, of course, does not necessitate the view that homosexual relationships are in accord with the will of God. This is where the struggle to understand God's will marked by prayer, reading of Scripture, discernment, humility, and a willingness to listen to the stories of others comes into play. But Scripture, and our history as God's people, should lead us to be open to this possibility. Scripture, and our history as God's people, allows—even calls—for us at least to consider that Jesus may be leading us once again to new understandings of faithfulness. This does not mean, in my view, that we have progressed beyond the instruction offered in Scripture, as though we have outgrown it. Far from it! The instructions guiding behavior given in both testaments, when viewed in their narrative contexts and especially through the lens of Jesus' own instruction, are the starting point for discerning how we are to live as Christ's disciples. But in some cases it may just be that through the Spirit, Jesus—the Living Word—comes to us and once again says, "You have heard it was said . . . , but I tell you . . ." and so calls us to discover more deeply what it means to live out the essence of God's torah, and to be God's people.

## Implications: Being Attentive to Jesus' Ongoing Instruction

As I have emphasized in this chapter, taking the Bible and its own example seriously leads us to see that God may teach us new things in new times and places, even things that conflict with God's instruction as previously understood. Accordingly, to be open to the possibility that Jesus may be leading us to a different understanding of homosexuality is—in my view—a thoroughly biblical position. This way of reading Scripture, however, is certainly not without its share of sticky challenges. As pointed out in the introduction, the dialogical approach poses the challenge of ambiguity. For instance, in the case of homosexuality, how are we to know if those believers who sense Jesus moving them to a position of accepting same-gender unions are perceiving God's direction correctly? The monological approach has the advantage of pointing to the biblical text and finding instructions spelled out in black and white. The approach to Scripture as sacred dialogue must engage in the more difficult task of *discernment*. It calls us to bring into conversation Scripture, one another, our experiences, and our reasoning faculties, with hearts open to the guidance of God's Spirit.

Yet what is said (or revealed) in those conversations is not always a straightforward matter. Different folks hear the Spirit saying different things, as our debate over this and other issues testifies. The dialogical approach also faces the challenge of defining standards and boundaries. Others might reasonably ask, if now, after all these years and in contrast to both the Old and New Testament traditions, homosexuality is to be viewed as an acceptable Christian lifestyle, what's next? Where and how do we "draw the line"? In addition, if we come to a position on an issue that has no clear precedent in Scripture, how is it that we can claim that Scripture is one of our dialogue partners? Allow me to offer a brief word in response to these concerns.

First, no way of reading Scripture is without a healthy share of ambiguity. Even someone adopting a position of biblical inerrancy—holding to the view that every single word of Scripture is the word of God without error—faces the challenge of translating the biblical texts from their original languages into a modern tongue, interpreting the intended meaning of those passages in their original context, relating that passage to the broader witness of the canon, and applying that meaning or story in a way that is faithful for our time and place. In many cases, uncertainty plagues each of those steps, especially the latter two. Even if the biblical text itself is infallible, we still have fallible human beings translating, interpreting, and proclaiming it. In addition, as more and more scholars themselves have come to realize, biblical interpretation is more an art than an exact science. As with art, it deals more with ideas, impressions, exemplary characters, inspiring portrayals, and the difficult task of translating these sometimes slippery, polyvalent entanglements with the biblical texts into a particular culture than with hard-and-fast, black-and-white units of meaning that easily transfer wholly intact from one realm to the next (see chapter 5). This is not to say that the biblical story lacks basic, fundamental truths that we can solidly grasp. It certainly does: the reality and destructiveness of human sin, God's forgiveness and love made known in Jesus, and our undeserved welcome into God's saving realm, among others. But when it comes to discerning how we are to live into those basic truths as God's people in our time and place and in response to all of the issues and trials we face, we enter a domain of our faith that is far less straightforward, as the diversity and disagreement among the biblical traditions themselves reveal (chapter 2).

Second, many are likely concerned that to engage Scripture as recommended here places one on the proverbial "slippery slope." For example, if homosexuality is no longer sinful, then what else will we accept? Well, a whole host of things really, starting with harboring runaway slaves, women taking on leadership positions in Christian communities and not wearing head-coverings in worship, men having long hair, the wearing of clothes with two different types of fabric, neglecting to greet one another with a holy kiss . . . I could go on, but I trust that the point is clear. As I have stressed in this chapter, Scripture itself often reworks and reprioritizes elements of God's instruction, even to the point that some laws and prohibitions are essentially set aside. The upshot of this is that *Scripture itself places us on that slippery slope, by its own example.* And in varying degrees, all Christians follow the Bible's lead. Note that Jesus, Paul, and the other writers of the New Testament never tell us to set aside all of the purity codes, or many of the other (sometimes downright obscure) commands contained in biblical books such as Leviticus and Numbers. Yet Christians freely regard most of these instructions as nonbinding, as well as others from the New Testament that we have already noted. How did this slippage in legal rectitude come about? Not in a moment of instantaneous clarity but through years of debate, prayer, and discernment among Christians. The issue is not whether we are on the slippery slope—all of us are. The issue is, at what point will we have slid too far, and what strategies and dispositions for reflecting on Scripture should we embrace to keep us from reaching that point?

Still other readers may fear that I am proposing a method of reading Scripture that does not allow for any boundaries in matters theological or ethical. But this too is not the case. I definitely think there are boundaries, but they are ones that emerge from our prayerful reflection on the whole of the story as we read it through what I take, with many Christians, to be its essential core—Jesus' teaching, example, and self-sacrifice—in dialogue with God and one another. It is just this Spirit-led discernment and conversation that provide us with the footholds and helping hands we need to keep climbing—even though precariously at times—on the path that God has granted us to tread.

Third, if we come to a position on an issue that has no clear precedent in Scripture (as with the acceptance of homosexuality), how is it that we can claim that Scripture is one of our dialogue partners? It is true that Scripture nowhere specifically endorses homoerotic relationships. However, to say that Scripture has nothing to say about human relatedness that might closely parallel the positive elements of committed homosexual relationships is another matter. For as we read through the biblical traditions, we find that Scripture does provide us with a rather clear conception of God's intentions for human relationships: mutual edification, rearing and instruction of children, protection, security, hospitality, and so on. Scripture also unveils features of human relatedness that lead to blessing: interdependence, mutuality, respect, intimacy, loyalty (see chapter 7). If there are homosexual couples that exhibit those features of blessed human relatedness and largely fulfill God's intentions for human relationships, shouldn't that give us pause when denouncing the sexual intimacy that is also an important part of, and even a resource for, the blessing those couples share with one another? The Bible may not endorse homosexuality per se, but it does say a lot about the kind of relatedness that leads us more deeply into God's intentions for humanity. It also teaches us to be careful about identifying certain persons and lifestyles as intractably opposed to the will of God, especially when the standards for doing so reside on the periphery of our faith and may be transcended by later God-given insight and instruction. Remember Ezra and Nehemiah's concerns about Israelite marriage and the drastic, exclusive, unwelcoming, yet torah-approved steps they took to restore the purity of that institution (see chapter 1). Remember the Second Isaiah's radical proclamation (in response to Ezra's policies) that God's house is big enough for those foreigners and that they too will participate fully and faithfully in God's restored community. As we enter into dialogue with Scripture, God, and one another on this issue, the challenge facing us is to discern how our response to homosexuality best fits those patterns of the biblical story that are most closely aligned with Jesus' own teaching and example. In short, would Jesus have us respond to homosexual couples as though we were Ezra and Nehemiah or as though we were Isaiah?

# Theologizing in the Thick of Things

## chapter four

*"I urge you, brothers and sisters . . ."*
*(Rom 16:17)*

**Here is a paraphrase of some of the more** impassioned moments in Paul's letter to the Galatians.

> *I am astonished! You are doing nothing less than deserting God. He called you by the grace of Christ, and here you are, turning to a different gospel! Not that there really is another gospel, but you've been fooled into thinking so by those who pervert the good news of Christ. Hear me clearly now. If we ourselves, or even an angel from heaven, proclaim a gospel to you that is different from what we set before you, let him be damned to hell. I'll say it again! If we ourselves, or even an angel from heaven, proclaim a gospel to you that is different from what we originally set before you, let him be damned to hell!*
>
> *You foolish Galatians! Who has bewitched you? I wish those who unsettle you would castrate themselves!*

Paul's letters are never boring. They are a bit dense in style and their meaning is difficult to untangle at times, but never boring. As we find in this paraphrase of select verses from Galatians and many other segments of his letters, controversy and passion abound. In his letters we get glimpses of church life that bears more resemblance to a soap opera or a "reality TV" series than the blissful harmony we might have expected. Even in a letter as friendly in tone as Philippians we hear Paul emphatically caution, "Beware of the dogs, beware of the evil workers, beware of those who mutilate the flesh!" (Phil 3:2). But there is another side of Paul, too. Even in a letter as caustic in tone as Galatians, we hear Paul gently say, "My little children, for whom I am again in the pain of childbirth until Christ is formed in you, I wish I were present with you now and could change my tone, for I am perplexed about you" (4:19-20).

## The Occasional and Conversational Character of Paul's Letters

What gives Paul's letters their energy and focus is the very reason for their existence. They are letters written to encourage, instruct, warn, rebuke, and express thanks to Christian communities that Paul himself established or with whom he wished to develop a relationship (such as the church at Rome). His letters are, as scholars put it, *occasional* documents, meaning that much of their focus is on particular occasions or situations, affecting the communities to whom he is writing.

As I noted in the preceding chapter, many scholars argue that some of the thirteen letters attributed to Paul were likely written by followers of Paul some time after he was martyred. Seven of his letters are considered by nearly all to have been written or dictated by Paul: Romans, 1 and 2 Corinthians, Galatians, Philippians, 1 Thessalonians, and Philemon. Scholars debate the authenticity of the remaining six: Colossians, Ephesians, 2 Thessalonians, 1 and 2 Timothy, Titus. Still, nearly all of the thirteen letters are occasional in that they address a set of specific concerns, even though some were likely not written with a particular community in mind (see Ephesians, 1 and 2 Timothy, Titus). Moreover, the canon's inclusion and attribution of all thirteen letter to Paul would justify our use of any or all of them in our attempt to pursue the character of the "canonical Paul." However, for the sake of brevity and in deference to those for whom the undisputed Paulines represent a distinct (even sacrosanct?) collection, my discussion in this chapter will draw heavily from the undisputed Paulines, and also from Colossians and Ephesians which, if not written by Paul, are commonly judged as heavily influenced by Paul's thought.

The occasional character of Paul's letters poses challenges both for interpreting them and for using them for Christian theology. When reading the letters, interpreters must do their best to reconstruct the situation or concerns Paul is addressing. No sources for reconstructing the specifics of any given situation exist apart from the letter itself, and so with great care scholars must "read between the lines" of Paul's instruction to figure out what was likely going on in the community to which he is speaking and fill out that picture with more general information about the first-century Mediterranean world. Further complicating this task is the fact that in Paul's letters we have what amounts to one part of an *ongoing conversation*. Thus scholars must also discern what information Paul might have received from or about the community to which he is writing in order to understand fully his response. For instance, in 1 Corinthians, Paul not only responds to questions the Corinthian church sent to Paul in a letter (see 7:1ff.), he also cites slogans that were popular among some members of the Corinthian community (6:12; 8:1, 14) and addresses other matters of contention that were likely relayed to Paul by his associates (3:1-23; 5:1–6:11). Over the last century especially, scholars and theologians have been careful to mind the occasional character of the letters and take into account that much of Paul's discussion is in response to particular concerns or situations. This has helped many appreciate the "context-bound" character of Paul's deliberations and better understand some of the variation in thought we find in Paul's letters.[1]

Still, while our recognition of the letters' occasional and conversational character has greatly assisted our attempts to explore Paul's thought, most scholars tend to treat the contextual and occasional character of the letters as an obstacle that needs to be overcome before Paul's theology can be discerned and used as a source of edification for believers today. David J. Lull speaks for many Pauline scholars when he says,

> The attempt to sketch a "synthesis" of the "theology" in Paul's letters must take into account the *ad hoc* character of Paul's letters. These letters do not present Paul's thought in a systematic form. Instead, they present his thought as practical reflections on the concrete issues of faith and life in the Christian communities founded by Paul. This fact poses two problems for our task: How are "Paul's theology" and particular arguments in his letters related? And how should a "synthesis" deal with differences among the letters?[2]

On the one hand, taking stock of the letters' occasional character and the challenges it poses for interpretation is entirely appropriate and helpful, since appreciating the contextual nature of the letters leads us to a better understanding of why Paul shaped them the way that he did and rightly cautions us against facile and superficial appropriation of his teachings in the church. On the other hand, the context-bound character of the letters is not simply a feature we must try to transcend in our use of Paul's instruction. This is an important point to appreciate. Scholars commonly treat Paul's letters as if their abiding value has little or nothing to do with their occasional and dialogical character, as if their nature as practical and impassioned discourse is a detriment to their use and not in itself a source of edification. However, *not only is the content of Paul's letters instructive for us, so also are their form and function as dynamic conversation.*

## Paul: Conversing with His Communities

What we find going on in Paul's letters is theological reflection deeply immersed in the lives of the Christian communities for whom he lived and died. In his letters we see the religious rubber of the gospel hitting the road. We encounter practical theology dynamically engaged, in which the claims of the gospel and lived experience are knit into dynamic exchange. The occasion at hand sets the agenda, and Paul responds by casting Israel's Scriptures and the proclamation of God's salvation in Jesus to meet the needs of the moment. As J. Christiaan Beker states, Paul's "heremeneutic consists in the constant interaction between the coherent center of the gospel and its contingent interpretation."[3]

The dynamic reflection in Paul's letters is also cast in the form and function of conversation, one piece of an ongoing dialogue between Paul and those to whom he wrote. In them are preserved exchanges that were likely not uncommon within the Christian community during its infancy and early development. And in them are some of the clearest examples of the conversational character of Scripture. What we see modeled by Paul's part in this dialogue is conversation marked by passion, anxiety, hope, and ingenuity, spurred on by an unrelenting commitment to proclaim the gospel and its manifold implications in response to the matters of the day.

In all of this we may have something to learn about anxious, passionate, yet faithful dialogue in contentious times. But it entails asking questions of Paul's letters that go beyond simply a concern with the *content* of Paul's theology. Instead, *we must also ask how Paul's understanding of God, God's will, and God's ways of salvation provided resources for and directed his engagement with and conversation about the challenges he and his communities faced.* In doing so, we are fighting the current of much scholarly discussion about Paul.[4] Many interpreters begin with Paul's contextualized conversations and seek to whittle away all of their occasional elements in the attempt to get back to his "pure" theology. The following discussion works in reverse. I identify what seem to me prevailing elements of Paul's thought and explore how they direct and pattern his conversation in response to the crises at hand. Thus, I cherish both Paul's theology *and* the tendencies of his context-driven discourse as essential to the instruction Paul continues to provide us. Again, this is a different sort of pursuit from that often undertaken with Paul's letters. But it is an equally important pursuit for those who see his letters as wonderfully edifying examples of sacred dialogue. What can we learn from both Paul the theologian *and* Paul the shepherd, who engaged his flock and their troubles in passionate discussion and debate? What can we learn from both Paul's theology *and* his modeling of faithful conversation?

To get at this question, we will examine five prevailing tendencies in Paul's shaping and proclamation of the good news in response to the concerns facing the communities to whom he wrote. Again, the objective here will be to explore how Paul's conversation is grounded in and guided by essential features of his thought. Next, we will consider some potential implications of these tendencies for those who may be inclined to use Paul's example of sacred dialogue as a model for their own faithful conversation.

### Prevailing Tendencies of Paul's Theologizing
### 1. Grounded in Sacred Tradition and Sacred Story

As we shall see in what follows, Paul radically reconceptualizes traditional Jewish understandings of God's will and what it means to be God's people. However, Paul never leaves behind the Scriptures or the story they proclaim, which nourished his own faith as a Pharisaic Jew. On the contrary, his letter to the Romans opens with the statement "Paul, a servant of Jesus Christ, called to be an apostle, set apart for the gospel of God, which he promised beforehand through the prophets in the holy scriptures . . ." (Rom 1:1-2) and all his letters are filled with reference after reference to the Scriptures he claims as his own. As James D. G. Dunn points out, "Paul's theological language was, by and large, the language of scripture. Scripture formed the 'substructure of his theology.'"[5] Or as helpfully described by Richard B. Hays,

> In Paul we encounter a first-century Jewish thinker who, while undergoing a profound disjuncture with his own religious tradition, grappled his way through a vigorous and theologically generative reappropriation of Israel's Scriptures. However great the tensions between his heritage and his new Christian convictions, he insistently sought to show that his proclamation of the gospel was grounded in the witness of Israel's sacred texts.[6]

Throughout his letters, Paul's attempt to ground his proclamation of Jesus in the Jewish Scriptures takes on a variety of forms. He frequently employs Old Testament passages to show how various features of Jesus' ministry and the salvation he achieved were rooted in the story of God's relationship with Israel using the formula "as it is written" (see Rom 1:17; 3:4; 4:17; 9:33; 15:9; 1 Cor 1:19; 2:9; 14:21; 15:45; 2 Cor 4:13; 9:9; Gal 3:10, 27). With greater subtlety, Paul also weaves biblical language and allusions into his discourse, inviting his readers to hear the echoes of the biblical story in and through his writing and to see God's act of salvation in Jesus as its fulfillment.[7] Perhaps the most well known and discussed tendency of Paul's use of the Jewish Scriptures is his proclivity toward recasting Old Testament passages to mean something quite different from what they meant in their original context in order that his readers might see how the good news of God's salvation is rooted in the story the Old Testament traditions collectively tell. Consider, for instance, Gal 4:21-31:

> Tell me, you who desire to be subject to the law, will you not listen to the law? For it is written that Abraham had two sons, one by a slave woman and the other by a free woman. One, the child of the slave, was born according to the flesh; the other, the child of the free woman, was born through the promise. Now this is an allegory: these women are two covenants. One woman, in fact, is Hagar, from Mount Sinai, bearing children for slavery. Now Hagar is Mount Sinai in Arabia and corresponds to the present Jerusalem, for she is in slavery with her children. But the other woman corresponds to the Jerusalem above; she is free, and she is our mother. For it is written,
>
> "Rejoice, you childless one, you who bear no children,
>> burst into song and shout, you who endure no birth pangs;
> for the children of the desolate woman are more numerous
>> than the children of the one who is married."
>
> Now you, my friends, are children of the promise, like Isaac. But just as at that time the child who was born according to the flesh persecuted the child who was born according to the Spirit, so it is now also. But what does the scripture say?" Drive out the slave and her child; for the child of the slave will not share the inheritance with the child of the free woman." So then, friends, we are children, not of the slave but of the free woman.

As vv. 24-26 make clear, Paul is here using the story of Sarah and Hagar from Genesis 21 as an allegory to speak to the topic dominating his letter to the Galatians: the role of the Mosaic law now that Christ has come. Through his creative shaping of the passage, Paul has Hagar represent those who still trace their spiritual heritage back to Mount Sinai; that is, Paul's fellow Jews (and some among his fellow Jewish Christians) who insist that keeping the commands of the torah is necessary for attaining righteousness and salvation, even for Gentile converts to Christianity. Those who require law obedience are the descendants of the slave woman Hagar, who, with their mother, still live as those enslaved to the law (v. 25). They, like Hagar, will be driven out and will not partake of the promised inheritance (v. 30). The other woman, Sarah, is free (v. 22) and bears children who are born through the promise and heirs of the promise (v. 23). Theirs is the promise of righteousness that comes through entrusting themselves to God's gift of salvation in Jesus, not to the works of the law (see Gal 3:1-29).[8]

Many interpreters have pointed out that Paul's dynamic methods of interpreting Old Testament texts parallel Jewish exegetical techniques commonly employed during and long after Paul's time, including, among others, allegorical interpretation, typology (Gal 3:8-9), focusing on a particular word and enlarging its meaning (for example, Gal 3:16), analogy (Rom 9:14-18), linking texts together by virtue of a catchword (Rom 9:32-33), and inference from the lesser to the greater (Gal 4:1-7; Rom 5:12).[9] This helps us to understand that Paul is using the Jewish Scriptures in ways that would not be completely foreign to his historical milieu. At the same time, there is a "madness" behind Paul's method leading him to readings of sacred tradition that would have likely sounded very strange to many of his fellow Jews.

## 2. The Defining Center: God's Act of Salvation in Jesus Christ Crucified and Risen

Paul's conviction that in the cross and resurrection of Jesus Christ God has accomplished the salvation of all who believe serves as the basic datum of reality that orients all of Paul's thought.

> For I am not ashamed of the gospel; it is the power of God for salvation to everyone who has faith, to the Jew first and also to the Greek. (Rom 1:16)

> Now I would remind you, brothers and sisters, of the good news that I proclaimed to you, which you in turn received, in which also you stand, through which also you are being saved, if you hold firmly to the message that I proclaimed to you—unless you have come to believe in vain. For I handed on to you as of first importance what I in turn had received: that Christ died for our sins in accordance with the scriptures, and that he was buried, and that he was raised on the third day in accordance with the scriptures. (1 Cor 15:1-4; see also 1 Cor 4:17, 11:23)

Leander Keck points out that the message Paul presented in order to elicit faith included a variety of themes such as monotheism, Scripture, and the coming judgment, yet "the core was the particular interpretation of the Jesus-event, and its focal point was the cross and resurrection."[10] This is the "madness" behind Paul's method of engaging sacred tradition and that which above all else directs and empowers his conversation.

What we see repeatedly expressed in Paul's letters is that *all commitments and beliefs must be subordinated to and recast into alignment with the good news of God's salvation in the cross and resurrection of*

*Jesus.* For Paul himself, this entailed setting aside all the defining markers of his life before Christ as "rubbish" in order that he may "gain Christ and be found in him" (Phil 3:7-9a). It led him to redefine what it meant to be rightly related to God, "not having a righteousness of my own that comes from the law, but one that comes from faith in Christ, the righteousness from God based on faith" (Phil 3:9b). In his conversation with his Christian communities, Paul repeatedly calls them back to the basic gospel he preached, urging them to put away any allegiances or desires distancing them from the foundation on which their faith stands. And so, in response to some in the Corinthian community who thought themselves wiser and more gifted than others and were "puffed up" with their own knowledge, Paul emphasizes that the wisdom that they should cherish is not what they themselves have obtained but only what God has revealed through Jesus.

> For the message about the cross is foolishness to those who are perishing, but to us who are being saved it is the power of God. For it is written,
>     "I will destroy the wisdom of the wise,
>     and the discernment of the discerning I will thwart."
> Where is the one who is wise? Where is the scribe? Where is the debater of this age? Has not God made foolish the wisdom of the world? For since, in the wisdom of God, the world did not know God through wisdom, God decided, through the foolishness of our proclamation, to save those who believe (1 Cor 1:18-21).

Likewise, for his engagement with sacred tradition, Paul's "hermeneutical foundation" is "the conviction that the Law and the Prophets bear witness to the gospel of God's righteousness, now definitively disclosed in the death and resurrection of Jesus Messiah."[11] With that hermeneutical lens in place, Paul turns to his sacred tradition and reads it in ways that bear witness to this fundamental truth while addressing the needs of the communities with whom he conversed.

One clear example of how Paul's commitment to the universality of God's salvation in Jesus crucified and risen steers him to recast sacred tradition in response to the concerns of his day is his conversation concerning the written law. As conveyed throughout the Old Testament (and as we will emphasize in chapters 6 and 7 below), the written torah was understood to have come from God and to have been mediated through Moses in order to lead the people into right relationship with God and one another. An Old Testament scene that may help us to capture the essence of the written law's crucial significance is one described in Deuteronomy. Moses stands before the Israelites right before they are about to enter the promised land, repeating to them all of the commands of God's law. He urges them to entrust themselves to God by obeying these covenant laws with every ounce of effort they have so that they may live long and blessed lives in the land that God is giving to them. For Moses, and for those attending to his exhortation throughout the centuries, following God's law is a matter of life and death (see Deut 30:11-20).

Paul, however, believed that God's act of salvation in Jesus precipitated nothing less than a turn of the ages, accomplishing what the written torah could not and relegating it to a bygone era. Motivating his revisionist reading of the torah was the occasion at hand. Some of Paul's fellow Jewish Christians challenged Paul's understanding of the gospel and did so among those he had converted to the faith. They maintained that the Gentile converts needed to abide by at least some of the Jewish laws, including circumcision and dietary restrictions. This crisis has center stage in Paul's letter to the Galatians but spills over into Romans, Philippians, and the Corinthian correspondence. In response, Paul unveils a rereading of Jewish tradition that upholds trust (faith) in God's salvation apart from the works of the law as that which alone leads to "justification"—the return to covenantal relatedness with God.

> We ourselves are Jews by birth and not Gentile sinners; yet we know that a person is justified not by the works of the law but through faith in Jesus Christ. And we have come to believe in Christ Jesus, so that we might be justified by faith in Christ, and not by doing the works of the law, because no one will be justified by the works of the law. (Gal 2:15-16)

There is scant mention in Galatians of the historical role of the law in guiding God's people into right relationship with God and one another. Instead, Paul views the written law primarily in negative terms and sees it as a temporary stopgap measure that God provides as a check against human sin. Paul argues that we were imprisoned and guarded under the law until the superior covenant mediated through trust in God would be revealed. The law served as a temporary disciplinarian, mediated through angels, but it is unable to provide life (Gal 3:19-23). In contesting the claims of those who argue that obedience to the law is necessary for salvation, Paul counters that all who rely on the works of the law are under a curse, since they have enslaved themselves to a law that they are unable to keep. Moreover, if one chooses to be circumcised in order to find righteousness from the law, he is obliged to obey the entire law and has cut himself off from Christ (Gal 5:2-5). How does he justify this extraordinary, revisionist treatment of God's torah? He argues from the Scriptures that the promise given to Abraham was nothing other than the gospel of grace in Christ (Gal 3:7-8). This gospel is and always has been based on trust in God, not on law, for "Abraham 'believed God and it was reckoned to him as righteousness,'" (Gal 3:6; cf. Gen 15:6). Coming 430 years before the law of Moses, God's covenant with Abraham based on trust takes precedent over the Mosaic covenant. Because the prior covenant also indicated that Gentiles would one day receive the promise, they too are heirs to the promise—a promise that they, like Abraham, are granted through trust in God alone (Gal 3:6-18).

Paul's discussion of the written law is a bit less negative in Romans, but still reflects a drastically revised account of its continuing role in the lives of God's people. Paul grants that the law is good and was meant to produce life, and we are right to delight in it (see Rom 7:9, 12, 16, 22). What the law fundamentally requires is that which God calls forth from all believers: a heart devoted to serving God and one another (Rom 2:15, 25-29; 6:17-18). However, under the power of sin, the commands of the law were turned into irresistible temptations (Rom 7:7-13). Therefore, no one can be made right with God through outward deeds of conformity to the law, because all fall short of living out the commandments of God (Rom 7:14-24; 3:19-20). The law itself cannot save; it only makes us more aware of our sin and our accountability to God's judgment (Rom 3:20; 5:12-13). A person can return to covenantal relationship with God only by trusting in God's gift of mercy in Jesus, not by faithfully performing the works of the law (Rom 3:21-26). Yet by living in this trust and guided by the Spirit, the basic purpose of the law—to lead God's people to trust in God alone as the source of blessing and to live in right relationship with one another—is upheld and fulfilled (Rom 3:27-31; 9:30—10:4; 16:26) As he did in Galatians, Paul again turns to Abraham to show how the gospel of grace in Christ was anticipated by the Scriptures (Rom 4:1-25). Here Paul emphasizes that Abraham—because he trusted in God—was reckoned as righteous by God before he was circumcised. Circumcision only served as a sign of the righteousness that he had already received. Because his righteousness came from trusting in God and not the law, Abraham became "the ancestor of all who believe without being circumcised and who thus have righteousness reckoned to them, and likewise the ancestor of the circumcised who are not only circumcised but who also follow the example of faith" (Rom 4:11-12).

Had some among Paul's fellow Jewish Christians not opposed his understanding of the gospel and tried to force Gentiles to follow the written law, I would likely not be turning to these passages in Galatians and Romans to illustrate the centrality of Jesus Christ crucified and risen in Paul's thought. These passages, perhaps all of Galatians, and significant portions of Romans wouldn't exist! Another crisis may have taken its place. But, for us, these passages and others like them exist as a testimony to how Paul, in facing the concerns of his day, was uncompromising in the pervasive relevance of God's salvation in Jesus' death, resurrection, and ongoing ministry. God's gift of grace was now made available to all who trust in God apart from law obedience, religious heritage, ethnicity, gender, and social status (Gal 3:23). And all things, including the composition of God's people, the teachings on torah, and even the way in which the Scriptures are read, needed to be reframed in order to reflect faithfully the fundamental and unconquerable reality of God's gift of love and mercy in Jesus Christ.

> What then are we to say about these things? If God is for us, who is against us? He who did not withhold his own Son, but gave him up for all of us, will he not with him also give us everything else? Who will bring any charge against God's elect? It is God who justifies. Who is to condemn? It is Christ Jesus, who died, yes, who was raised, who is at the right hand of God, who indeed intercedes for us. Who will separate us from the love of Christ? Will hardship, or distress, or persecution, or famine, or nakedness, or peril, or sword? As it is written,
>
> > "For your sake we are being killed all day long;
> > we are accounted as sheep to be slaughtered."
>
> No, in all these things we are more than conquerors through him who loved us. For I am convinced that neither death, nor life, nor angels, nor rulers, nor things present, nor things to come, nor powers, nor height, nor depth, nor anything else in all creation, will be able to separate us from the love of God in Christ Jesus our Lord. (Rom 8:31-39)

### 3. The Ministry of the Holy Spirit

Basic to Paul's conversation was the conviction that Scripture and the Christian community exist as a witness to the gospel of Jesus Christ. Accompanying these claims and also shaping Paul's discourse with the churches to whom he wrote is Paul's belief that the Holy Spirit enables and empowers that witness, in both Scripture and the Christian community. Faithful interpretation, discernment, testimony, service, and conversation were all Spirit-formed activities.

The early Christian controversy over the written law also serves as the context for much of Paul's discussion on the role of the Spirit. In Galatians and Romans Paul emphasizes that our freedom from the written law is to lead to a way of life governed by the Spirit.

> But now we are discharged from the law, dead to that which held us captive, so that we are slaves not under the old written code but in the new life of the Spirit. (Rom 7:6)

Paul also claims that under the ministry of the Spirit, our ability to discern what it means to live in accord with God's ways is enhanced far beyond the direction provided by the written law. Consider the often-cited passage of 2 Cor 3:7-18:

> Now if the ministry of death, chiseled in letters on stone tablets, came in glory so that the people of Israel could not gaze at Moses' face because of the glory of his face, a glory now set aside, how much more will the ministry of the Spirit come in glory? For if there was glory in the ministry of condemnation, much more does the ministry of justification abound in glory! Indeed, what once had glory has lost its glory because of the greater glory; for if what was set aside came through glory, much more has the permanent come in glory! Since, then, we have such a hope, we act with great boldness, not like Moses, who put a veil over his face to keep the people of Israel from gazing at the end of the glory that was being set aside. But their minds were hardened. Indeed, to this very day, when they hear the reading of the old covenant, that same veil is still there, since only in Christ is it set aside. Indeed, to this very day whenever Moses is read, a veil lies over their minds; but when one turns to the Lord, the veil is removed. Now the Lord is the Spirit, and where the Spirit of the Lord is, there is freedom. And all of us, with unveiled faces, seeing the glory of the Lord as though reflected in a mirror, are being transformed into the same image from one degree of glory to another; for this comes from the Lord, the Spirit. (2 Cor 3:7-18)

The issue at hand within the broader context of this passage is not the law per se. Rather, in this section of 2 Corinthians, Paul is defending his ministry against those who have attempted to undermine it among the believers in Corinth by questioning his sincerity and his calling as an apostle. Paul begins by contrasting himself with his accusers, who came to Corinth bearing letters of commendation (2 Cor 3:1). In contrast, Paul claims that the Corinthians themselves are his letter of recommendation, "a letter of Christ, prepared by us, written not with ink but with the Spirit of the living God, not on tablets of stones but on tablets of human hearts" (2 Cor 3:2-3). The point that Paul seems to be making in his defense is that *his* ministry is attested to and affirmed by the ministry of the Spirit. Consequently, the proof of Paul's character and faithfulness is none other than the Spirit of God at work in their hearts (see also Gal 3:1-5). Then, as means of further distancing himself from his opponents, he associates their reliance on written commendation with the inferior glory of the written law, and his ministry with the superior glory that is made known through the Spirit.

It is just this figurative shift from written letters to the analogy of written tablets that leads to the passage cited above. Here we have another example of the creativity Paul employs in reframing Old Testament traditions. Paul has in view Exod 34:10-35, a covenantal renewal ceremony following the tragic golden calf affair. So vile was the people's act of betrayal and so damaging to the covenant relationship between God and Israel that a new moment of covenant making was needed in order to reestablish their commitment to one another. Moses presents the commandments (re)written on two tablets of stone to the people. Yet the people recoil in fear. Moses has been in the presence of God, and his face shines with God's glory. In the context of the Exodus account, it is clear that the reason Moses wears the veil is not to hide the end of the written torah's glory, which, according to Paul, God was already "setting aside" (2 Cor 3:13). Instead, Moses wears the veil out of concern for the people, who fear the glory of God manifest in his face (Exod 34:29-30) and takes it off when teaching them in order to signal that the words he mediates are none other than the words of Yahweh (Exod 34:33-35).

Yet Paul engages in the interpretive venture of 1 Cor 3:7-18 to point out that the ministry of the Spirit is far superior to that of the written law. Those who rely on tablets of stone are those who have veiled their minds and hearts from recognizing that the glory of the Mosaic law has faded and is now transcended by a greater glory. Consequently, they have failed to recognize the new way God has provided: the ministry of the Spirit, which enables them to be transformed into the very likeness of Christ (2 Cor 3:14-18). Accordingly, the Corinthians need to reassess their own criteria for discerning the presence of faithful service in their midst. It resides not in written words of commendation but in the testimony and transforming work of the Spirit in and through that service among them. Paul is calling them to cultivate hearts that recognize and receive ministry that truly mediates the Spirit.

Perhaps it was because of some prior conversation with the Corinthians that he thought the contrast between the written law and the instruction of the Spirit might serve as a helpful analogy to address the differences between himself and his opponents and to call the Corinthians to greater faithfulness. For our purposes, however, the passage helps us to grasp the tremendous gulf Paul sees between the efficacy of the written law and the ministry of the Spirit. The fundamental purpose of each is the same: to lead believers into right relationship with God and one another. This why the written law also bears the glory of God, even if only for a time. But the Spirit is able to achieve what the written law ultimately cannot:

> There is therefore now no condemnation for those who are in Christ Jesus. For the law of the Spirit of life in Christ Jesus has set you free from the law of sin and of death. For God has done what the law,

weakened by the flesh, could not do: by sending his own Son in the likeness of sinful flesh, and to deal with sin, he condemned sin in the flesh, so that the just requirement of the law might be fulfilled in us, who walk not according to the flesh but according to the Spirit. For those who live according to the flesh set their minds on the things of the flesh, but those who live according to the Spirit set their minds on the things of the Spirit. To set the mind on the flesh is death, but to set the mind on the Spirit is life and peace. For this reason the mind that is set on the flesh is hostile to God; it does not submit to God's law—indeed it cannot, and those who are in the flesh cannot please God. But you are not in the flesh; you are in the Spirit, since the Spirit of God dwells in you. (Rom 8:2-9)

It is because Paul sees the ministry of the Spirit as that which enables believers to be transformed into the image of Christ that he repeatedly portrays the Spirit as empowering and directing all faithful activity on the part of believers. This new life in the Spirit enables Christians to live out the "just requirement of the law" and walk not according to the flesh but in accord with the will of God, a way of life characterized by "faith working through love" (Gal 5:6; see also Rom 7:6). The Spirit affirms the truth of the gospel and grants believers the assurance that they are held in God's keeping (see Rom 5:5; 8:16; 2 Cor 1:22; 5:5; Eph 1:13). The Spirit empowers gifts of worship and witness, equipping Christian communities with the abilities they need to care for their members and reach beyond themselves to share the good news with others (see 1 Cor 2:6-16; 12:1-11; Eph 3:5; 1 Thess 1:5-6).

## 4. The Blessedness of Christian Community

Another major feature of Paul's conversation is his repeated concern for the maintenance and blessedness of Christian community. In part, this is necessitated by the fact that many of the crises Paul addressed threatened the faithful witness and unity of these communities. However, Paul speaks to the needs, function, and maintenance of community life so extensively that one cannot help but recognize it as a crucial parameter to the way he understands Christian faith and shapes his dialogue with others. While the individual believer has an important place in his understanding of God's salvation, Paul's conception of Christian life is that of a covenanted community.

If faithfulness to the gospel of God's grace in Christ was Paul's top priority, the maintenance and nurturing of the Christian community ran a close second. Paul was unwilling to sacrifice allegiance to the gospel in order to maintain an artificial peace in the community. Any proclamation that struck against the heart of the gospel were "fighting words" for Paul, and in response to such attacks on the gospel Paul came out swinging (as we saw, for example, in Galatians). Yet even the harshest of Paul's rhetoric is balanced by a "motherly" concern for the well-being of the community (recall Gal 4:19-20; see also 5:15–6:4). In fact, any dichotomy we might presume between Paul's dedication to the gospel and his dedication to the community is a false one. For Paul, his dedication to both were one in the same. The community needed the gospel in order to take part in and serve as stewards of God's gift of salvation. Without it, they could not become or remain the new, redeemed people that God was fashioning from all the peoples of the earth. And the gospel needed the community to embody the blessings of God's salvation and to share the good news with others.

At the risk of serious oversimplification, I am going to identify and briefly describe two features of Christian community that in my view prevail throughout much of Paul's thought. These two ideas emerge repeatedly in his conversation and guide his response to the situations facing the churches under his care. First, Paul sees Christian communities as a base of operations for ongoing mission to those outside of the church. The proclamation of the gospel originates in and moves outward from the fellowship, gifts, and resources of gathered believers, and Paul frequently cites the church's mission to spread the message of God's love in Christ (Rom 10:14-15; 1 Cor 14:15-17; Eph 4:11; 1 Thess 1:6-8). He commends the faithful witness of others (Rom 16:7; 2 Cor 8:16-24; Phil 2:22, 25-30; Col 1:7; 4:7-17; 1 Thess 2:13-14; 3:1-2) and asks for (Rom 15:23-24) or thanks churches and individuals (Rom 16:1-2; Phil 1:7, 19-20; 4:10-20) for the assistance they provide for his ministry.

Second, Paul repeatedly exhorts the churches to whom he writes to serve as vehicles of God's instruction, care, and love. It is by the Spirit of Christ, working through the gifts it has granted, that believers are called to work together for the common good of the community (1 Cor 12:4-11). At that key transitional moment in Paul's letter to the Romans, when he switches from proclaiming God's act of salvation in Jesus to exhorting believers to respond faithfully, Paul calls on believers to "offer your bodies as living sacrifices" and to "be transformed by the renewing of your minds, so that you may discern what is the will of God—what is good and acceptable and perfect" (Rom 12:1-2). As a direct application of this exhortation, Paul then immediately launches into an extended discussion of how believers are to minister to one another in the Christian community.

> For by the grace given to me I say to everyone among you not to think
> of yourself more highly than you ought to think, but to think with
> sober judgment, each according to the measure of faith that God has

assigned. For as in one body we have many members, and not all the members have the same function, so we, who are many, are one body in Christ, and individually we are members one of another. We have gifts that differ according to the grace given to us: prophecy, in proportion to faith; ministry, in ministering; the teacher, in teaching; the exhorter, in exhortation; the giver, in generosity; the leader, in diligence; the compassionate, in cheerfulness.

Let love be genuine; hate what is evil, hold fast to what is good; love one another with mutual affection; outdo one another in showing honor. Do not lag in zeal, be ardent in spirit, serve the Lord. Rejoice in hope, be patient in suffering, persevere in prayer. Contribute to the needs of the saints; extend hospitality to strangers. (Rom 12:3-13)

Living together in loving, caring, mutually up-building and out-reaching community that provides fertile ground for the ongoing work of the Spirit is a hallmark of Paul's exhortation, especially in the face of crisis and division. While we most often encounter the movingly eloquent words of 1 Corinthians 13 at weddings, Paul did not write them for a husband and wife (even though they are very useful words for couples!). He penned them for the deeply divided community of Corinth, suffering from various forms of factionalism. For all their giftedness, the Corinthian Christians had forgotten the most important gift they had to share: their love for one another. Moreover, on matters Paul deemed peripheral to the Christian faith, he was content to let disagreement stand if pursuing unity of thought threatened the unity of the community. And so (as we saw in chapter 3) in Romans 14 Paul urges both the "weak" and the "strong" to put aside their differences on matters of food and holy days. He calls them to recognize that "the kingdom of God is not food and drink but righteousness and peace and joy in the Holy Spirit" and to "pursue what makes for peace and mutual up-building" (Rom 14:17, 19; see also 1 Cor 8:1-13). The unity of the Roman community was more important to Paul than their unanimity on every matter of faith.

As a helpful summary of Paul's frequent instructions of living together in Christian community, let us turn to the exhortation he gives to the church at Colossae. In that letter Paul emphasizes that the renewal made possible in believers through the ongoing work of Christ (Col 3:1-11) is to be marked and facilitated by blessed life in community:

As God's chosen ones, holy and beloved, clothe yourselves with compassion, kindness, humility, meekness, and patience. Bear with one another and, if anyone has a complaint against another, forgive each other; just as the Lord has forgiven you, so you also must forgive. Above all, clothe yourselves with love, which binds everything together in perfect harmony. And let the peace of Christ rule in your hearts, to which indeed you were called in the one body. And be thankful. Let the word of Christ dwell in you richly; teach and admonish one another in all wisdom; and with gratitude in your hearts sing psalms, hymns, and spiritual songs to God. And whatever you do, in word or deed, do everything in the name of the Lord Jesus, giving thanks to God the Father through him. (Col 3:12-17)

## 5. Cultivating Trust, Wisdom, and Transformation

With all of the passionate angst and criticism Paul expresses in his letters (especially in Galatians and the Corinthian correspondence), some may be inclined to view Paul as driven by the obsessive need to have his minions in Christ slavishly devoted to every detail of his teaching. To be sure, it is undeniable that Paul believed that the gospel he proclaimed to the communities he founded and others to whom he wrote was of utmost significance. "I handed on to you as of first importance what I in turn had received" he tells the Corinthians, and then goes on to review for them the basic story of the gospel (1 Cor 15:3). In his view, the gospel he proclaims is the means by which humanity can hear God's call for them to return to God and trust in the blessings God now provides in Christ. In addition, he repeatedly holds himself out as an example for others to follow (see Phil 3:17; Gal 4:12).

There are two currents in Paul's teaching, however, that counter any inclination to view him as a stodgy dogmatist. First, as I noted above, Paul recognized that there was a center and a periphery to the gospel, and with matters on the periphery he was content to let disagreement and diversity stand in order to preserve the unity of the community. Second, Paul repeatedly speaks of believers' trust, knowledge, and wisdom as that which undergoes ongoing cultivation and growth, nourished by the ministry of Christ through the Spirit (see Rom 8:1-11). This reveals Paul's recognition that spiritual maturity is Spirit-formed and ever evolving, and is certainly not limited to his own instruction.

In his discussion of what it means to be "baptized in Christ," he tells believers that they have been buried with Christ in his death, "so that, just as Christ was raised from the dead by the glory of the Father, *so we too might walk in newness of life*" (Rom 6:4). Therefore, he instructs them to "consider yourselves dead to sin and alive to God in Christ Jesus" (Rom 6:11; see also vv. 12-23). Believers are, Paul emphasizes, "new creations in Christ":

From now on, therefore, we regard no one from a human point of view; even though we once knew Christ from a human point of view, we know him no longer in that way. So if anyone is in Christ, there is a new creation: everything old has passed away; see, everything has become new! All this is from God, who reconciled us to himself through Christ, and has given us the ministry of reconciliation. (2 Cor 5:16-18)

In short, both reconciliation *and* re-creation are the saving work of Christ. Throughout his letters Paul repeatedly calls his dialogue partners to grow in their faith in Christ and in their understanding of God's ways. Here are a few additional examples out of many.

Do not be conformed to this world, but be transformed by the renewing of your minds, that you may discern what is the will of God—what is good and acceptable and perfect. (Rom 12:2)

Besides this, you know what time it is, how it is now the moment for you to wake from sleep. For salvation is nearer to us now than when we became believers; the night is far gone, the day is near. Let us then lay aside the works of darkness and put on the armor of light; let us live honorably as in the day, not in reveling and drunkenness, not in debauchery and licentiousness, not in quarreling and jealousy. Instead, put on the Lord Jesus Christ, and make no provision for the flesh, to gratify its desires. (Rom 13:11-14)

Those who are unspiritual do not receive the gifts of God's Spirit, for they are foolishness to them, and they are unable to understand them because they are spiritually discerned. Those who are spiritual discern all things, and they are themselves subject to no one else's scrutiny. "For who has known the mind of the Lord so as to instruct him?" But we have the mind of Christ. And so, brothers and sisters, I could not speak to you as spiritual people, but rather as people of the flesh, as infants in Christ. I fed you with milk, not solid food, for you were not ready for solid food. Even now you are still not ready, for you are still of the flesh. (1 Cor 2:14–3:2)

And all of us, with unveiled faces, seeing the glory of the Lord as though reflected in a mirror, are being transformed into the same image from one degree of glory to another; for this comes from the Lord, the Spirit. (2 Cor 3:18)

. . . and this is my prayer, that your love may overflow more and more with knowledge and full insight to help you determine what is best. (Phil 1:9-10)

I know that I will remain and continue with you for your progress and joy in faith. (Phil 1:25)

Therefore, my beloved, just as you have always obeyed me, not only in my presence but much more now in my absence, work out your own salvation with fear and trembling, for it is God who is at work in you, enabling you both to will and to work for his good pleasure. (Phil 2:12-13)

. . . to equip the saints for the work of ministry, for building up the body of Christ, until all of us come to the unity of the faith and of the knowledge of the Son of God. (Eph 4:12-13)

You were taught to put away your former way of life, your old self, corrupt and deluded by its lusts, and to be renewed in the spirit of your minds, and to clothe yourselves with the new self, created according to the likeness of God in true righteousness and holiness. (Eph 4:22-24)

. . . be filled in the knowledge of God's will in all spiritual wisdom and understanding . . . as you grow in the knowledge of God. (Col 1:9, 10)

. . . admonish one another in all wisdom . . . (Col 3:16)

Finally, brothers and sisters, we ask and urge you in the Lord Jesus that, as you learned from us how you ought to live and to please God (as, in fact, you are doing), you should do so more and more. . . . May the God of peace himself sanctify you entirely; and may your spirit and soul and body be kept sound and blameless at the coming of our Lord Jesus Christ. (1 Thess 4:1; 5:23)

Paul is also quite honest about the fact that he himself has not attained all he seeks to know and understand about faith in Christ. He includes himself among those who "now see in a mirror, dimly" and "know only in part" (1 Cor 13:12). For him, knowing Christ and receiving the blessings of new life in him are an ongoing journey of devotion and discovery, a race he presses on to run.

I want to know Christ and the power of his resurrection and the sharing of his sufferings by becoming like him in his death, if somehow I may attain the resurrection from the dead. Not that I have already obtained this or have already reached the goal; but I press on to make it my own, because Christ Jesus has made me his own. Beloved, I do not consider that I have made it my own; but this one thing I do: forgetting what

lies behind and straining forward to what lies ahead, I press on toward
the goal for the prize of the heavenly call of God in Christ Jesus. (Phil
3:10-14)

## *Summary*

In the above review, I have attempted to elucidate five dimensions
of Paul's theological vision that play a major role in patterning his conversation with the church communities to which he wrote. To be sure,
there are many other elements of Paul's thought that could have been
discussed to help us fill out our understanding of how Paul's theology
guides his conversation. But the goal of the above discussion is illustrative rather than exhaustive. Moreover, if we were to survey Paul's
thought from letter to letter, we would see that certain elements get
more attention depending on the particular situation Paul is addressing.
Still, on the whole, these five serve as the poles around which Paul's discourse often revolves. They provide the foundation on which Paul stands
and the cues for his conversation as he addresses the various concerns
and crises facing the early Christian community. The following summary
statements attempt to capture the essence of the preceding discussion.

1.  Paul emphasizes that God's work in Jesus Christ is the fulfillment
    of the story told by the Jewish Scriptures of God's undying effort to
    redeem all of humanity. Therefore, when properly interpreted, the
    Scriptures anticipate Christ's salvation and bear witness to the gift
    of God's righteousness through trust.

2.  The good news of God's salvation in the crucifixion, resurrection,
    and ongoing ministry of Jesus as a gift of grace for all who trust
    is the cornerstone of Paul's worldview. It is the lens through which
    Paul reads Scripture, leading to creative and dynamic engagement
    with his sacred tradition. It is the fundamental center from which he
    speaks to his fellow Christians and engages the crises of his time.

3.  Paul repeatedly upholds the ministry of the Spirit as the source for
    faithful living and discernment. It is no longer our adherence to the
    written code that leads us to covenantal relatedness with God and
    one another, but the ongoing ministry of the Spirit at work within us
    and among the community of God's people.

4.  Despite its chronic dysfunctionality and manifold struggles, the
    Christian community is regarded by Paul as a precious entity, the
    unity of which he fights hard to maintain. The church is constituted
    by Christ and empowered by the Spirit to serve as a source of blessing

for its members and for all those whom it reaches out to serve with God's steadfast love, kindness, forgiveness, care, and instruction.

5. Christian faith is an ongoing process of transformation. Setting aside the patterns of this world, persevering through the struggles and persecution it sets before us, and entrusting ourselves to the ongoing work of the Spirit among us, we are to become new creations in Christ.

### Implications: Faithful, Practical, and Imaginative Conversation

If we look to Paul's conversation as a model after which we might pattern our own, I believe several necessities present themselves. First, our conversation must first and foremost seek to help ourselves and others celebrate the gift of God's forgiving grace most fully made known in Jesus for all of humanity. This is much easier said than done. As Paul's letters indicate, the Christian community has, since its inception, struggled to appreciate the rich implications of that fundamental truth for their daily walk of faith. All claims, all allegiances, all "sacred cows," all patterns and practices of faith and life must serve this fundamental truth or be set aside as "rubbish"! This is as daunting a calling for the church today as it has been since its early days. And in our time especially, with the modern emphasis on individual autonomy, self-control, and self-gratification through consumption, Paul's call to respond to this good news by offering oneself as a "living sacrifice" to God (Rom 12:1) is often a tough sell. But to speak as Paul speaks is to be utterly uncompromising in the proclamation of God's provision made known in Jesus' death, resurrection, and ongoing ministry and the need to embrace it above anything else.

Second, the form and function of Paul's letters as dialogue centered on proclaiming the gospel in and through the circumstances and struggles facing his communities call Christians to take note of the contextual, the "real-life rooted," *and* "conversational" character of both biblical revelation and the reflection it invites among believers. Theology of and for believing communities is not created through sterile, erudite reflection uninfected by the exigencies of daily life. Rather, Spirit-driven speech emerges from the give-and-take exchange between the gospel, the Scriptures, the needs of the moment, and, at times, contentiously competing claims among believers. *As much as they teach anything else, Paul's letters teach that faithful testimony is composed in and through the messiness of lived experience. As Christians dialogue with one another, with their sacred tradition, and with the Holy Spirit, they are to discern what it means to live out the good news in their present time and place.*

Third, Christians' discourse with one another must always serve the mission of the community, seeking to shape it into a place of faithful witness and ministry. Paul bemoaned controversy in the church not simply because it often meant some of its members misunderstood the essence or implications of God's salvation in Jesus but also because it threatened the unity of the community and thus subverted its ministry. It is through the body of Christ that the Spirit moves to proclaim the good news of God's forgiveness and to transform believers into the image of Jesus. It is through the body that the Spirit calls others into Christ's saving ministry. When the community is fractured by pride, jealousy, and a divisive spirit, its ability to serve as a steward of God's blessings is severely degraded. Before speaking to fellow believers, I think Paul would have each Christian ask him- or herself, "Is what I am about to say going to build up or tear down, do good or do harm? Will these words call the community to greater faithfulness? Can they be used by God's Spirit as a source of transformation, or will they be used for evil as a source of destruction?"

Finally, we find in Paul's reflection and conversation a dynamic tension between his commitment to Israel's Scriptures and his rereading of those Scriptures so that they bear witness to God's salvation in Jesus. We see in Paul both a conserving and a revising tendency in his engagement with sacred tradition. While Paul, as we shall note in chapters 6 and 7, re-presents the broad contours of the biblical story, portions of that story are reread and even rewritten in order that they might faithfully testify to Christ's work of salvation in ways that makes sense for his communities in their time and place. Even beyond that, Paul so greatly reworks elements of the story that their function in directing the lives of God's people are radically altered: for example, the written law recast as a temporary guardian and replaced by the "law of the Spirit." As helpfully put by Richard Hays,

> Because God has acted in Jesus Christ to initiate the turn of the ages, everything past must be read with new eyes. Scripture, of course, is not exempt from this eschatological reassessment; Paul insists, as we have seen, that his privileged position in the climactic chapter of the story of God's dealings with Israel allows him to perceive patterns—both unities and ironies—that were hidden from previous actors and readers. Consequently, the eschatological perspective becomes the hermeneutical warrant for major shifts and revisions in the reading of Scripture.[12]

Hays goes on to claim that the same sort of interpretive freedom that Paul employed in his recasting of Scripture is to be embraced by believers today as they converse with their sacred tradition, God, one another, and their lived experience. The community of faith is called to read Scripture, guided by the Spirit, in order to discern the ways in which the Bible is speaking anew about God's salvation in Jesus and what it means to be God's people in this time and place: "Only when our interpreters and preachers read with an imaginative freedom analogous to Paul's will Scripture's voice be heard in the church. We are children of the Word, not prisoners."[13] Or, as stated by J. Christiaan Beker, "for Paul, tradition is always interpreted tradition that is executed in the freedom of the Spirit."[14]

Thus, to not embrace the imaginative freedom Paul employed in his reading of Scripture, argues Hays, leads to a way of reading Scripture that is contrary to the nature of Scripture itself:

> The attempt to separate Paul's hermeneutical freedom from ours cuts off the word at its roots. It is ironically unfaithful, in the most fundamental way, to the teaching of the apostle who insisted that "the word is near you, in your mouth and in your heart." Those who would be faithful to Paul's word must take the risks of interpretive freedom. Those who do not take and acknowledge such risks will either stifle the word of God by parroting fixed formulas or turn the notions of inspiration and revelation into a smokescreen for self-deception, because they will in fact continue to generate their own transformative readings of Scripture while pretending not to do so.[15]

What does such interpretive freedom entail? Using Paul as our paradigm, it entails being faithful to our story by consistently rehearsing the broad contours of what it proclaims about God's undying attempt to reclaim humanity and seeing that story fulfilled in Jesus Christ. It entails remaining open to the new and surprising ways the Spirit is guiding believers to recast sacred tradition in order that they too might faithfully converse with one another in response to God's ongoing instruction and the concerns of the present day. Like Jesus (as we saw in chapter 3), Paul also teaches through his radical revision of his own tradition that not even ancient, established norms of what it meant to be God's people are impervious to this generative conversation. For as Jesus transforms Christians more and more into his image, the Spirit is leading them to imagine new ways of proclaiming and living as God's faithful people.

# God's Word
# in Many Voices

## chapter five

"He began to be in need . . ." (Luke 15:14)

**A seminary student from Russia reflects on** the criticism his exegetical essay on the Parable of the prodigal son received from his American professor:

*I have come to think of myself as a good student of the Bible. My religion professor at the University in St. Petersburg, Russia, often praised me for my insight into the Scriptural texts. But now I am studying here in America, and I am not so sure. My seminary professor did not care for my interpretive essay on Luke's parable of the prodigal son. He said I focused much too much on the famine as the cause of the son's need. The parable, he said, emphasizes the son's sinful squandering of his father's wealth. That is the primary reason for his neediness when the famine arrives. It is that of which he repents and is forgiven when he returns home and is welcomed by his father. I should have known he would think this. All of the American commentaries I read said the same: the story is about one who sins against his father and heaven by "squandering" his father's wealth in "dissolute living," then, inspired by his need, he repents of his mistake, and returns home to his father's welcome. Most of the commentaries didn't even mention the famine.*

*But this makes no sense to me. Yes, he was careless with the money he had received. But in times of famine even the wealthy can go hungry. Their wealth soon disappears and then they are at a disadvantage, for they are not used to meeting their basic needs with so little. And yes, the son should not have spurned his family. But it is the fact that he is now alone that is more important; for in times of famine it is those who are alone who are in the greatest*

*danger. In Russia, we know this. We remember. I think the mean-*
*ing of the parable is God's gift of salvation for all of us in our times*
*of need, especially the foolish, the alone, the sinful. It is about God*
*joyously calling the lost and famished into God's eternal kingdom,*
*where they will be reunited with God and never hunger again. My*
*professor back home in Russia would have praised this paper.*

## The Reality of Polyvalence in Our Reading of Scripture

In much of his recent work, New Testament scholar Mark Allan Powell has investigated, catalogued, and reported on differences in the ways readers understand scriptural passages. The fictional illustration I provide above is inspired by a study Powell conducted on Luke's parable of the prodigal son (Luke 15:11-32).[1] In the study, he asked one hundred Americans of diverse gender, race, age, economic status, and religious affiliation to read the parable carefully, close their Bibles, and then recount the parable as completely as possible. All of the American respondents (100 percent) remembered the detail of the son squandering his father's wealth. Only a small fraction (6 percent) were able to recall the detail of the famine. He conducted the same study with fifty diverse respondents in St. Petersburg, Russia. In sharp contrast to their American counterparts, 84 percent of the Russian respondents remembered the detail of the famine and only 34 percent recalled the son squandering his father's wealth.

Powell presumes, rightly, I think, that the reason the Americans surveyed remembered the detail of the squandering and did not (except for a few) recall the famine is that they understood the son's squandering of his father's wealth as the only, or primary, cause of the son's plight. In other words, the narrative function of the squandering was just too essential to ignore, whereas the famine was regarded as an ancillary detail that could be easily forgotten. In contrast, the vast majority of the Russian respondents did not consider the detail of the famine superfluous, but essential to understanding why the son was in need. This raises the question of why the American readers would focus on the son's squandering and the Russian readers on the famine. Powell explains,

> One probably does not need to look too far for a social or psychological explanation for this data. In 1941, the German army laid siege to the city of St. Petersburg (then Leningrad) and subjected its inhabitants to what was in effect a 900-day famine. During that time, 670,000 people died of starvation. Some of the current inhabitants of the city are survivors of that horror; more are descendants of survivors. . . .

In modern St. Petersburg, typical social issues (abortion, care of the elderly, imprisonment of lawbreakers, socialized medicine, and so on) are often considered through the lens of an important question: *but what if there is not enough food?* . . . It is, I think, not surprising that in *this* social location, more than four-fifths of the persons who read Luke's story of "the Prodigal Son" and then repeat it from memory do not forget that there was a famine.[2]

Reading the parable through a lens shaped in part by their experience and historical memory, Russian readers find it speaks to dimensions of God's character and provision in ways that differ from how their American counterparts understand it. As Powell explains, most American readers he surveyed, including a good number of American commentators (most of whom do not even mention the famine), understand the parable to be emphasizing the moral depravity of the son's squandering, the licentiousness of his pleasure-seeking lifestyle, and his repentance from his sinful ways. In contrast, when the detail of the famine is not forgotten but emphasized, as it is by Russian readers, the son's squandering and repentance need not function as the primary focus of the parable. Instead, for those who regard the famine as the primary cause of the son's suffering and attach less importance to the son's spending habits, the parable might be viewed as emphasizing God's gracious provision for and welcome of all the lost, alone, and famished into God's eternal kingdom. In this reading, it is God's rescue of the needy *from matters beyond their control* rather than their moral transformation that takes center stage.[3] In Russia (and perhaps also in first-century Palestine, where famine was an all-too-common occurrence), it makes sense that this reading of the parable would be far more common than in America, where resources are far more abundant for many and perhaps also more frequently squandered.

Lest we quickly dismiss the reading of the parable favored by the Russian students as overly tendentious, Powell notes that several features of the parable as it appears in Luke's Gospel could be marshaled to support it. He points out that the Greek terms that are commonly rendered "squandering," "dissolute," "riotous," "loose," and "reckless" in our English Bibles could just as easily be translated in a far less pejorative sense, identifying the son not as "prodigal" ("recklessly wasteful") but more along the lines of "carefree spendthrift." He also argues that viewing the primary focus of the parable as God's salvation of the wayward and needy actually fits better with the two parables preceding it. Taken together, these three parables form a triad in response to the grumbling of the scribes and Pharisees (Luke 15:2) and portray "repentance," not so much as the moral transformation of the sinner, but as God's gracious act of welcoming home or "finding" those who would otherwise be lost (see Luke 15:32).[4]

Some time later, Powell had the opportunity to conduct a similar study on the parable with Tanzanian seminary students, in which he specifically asked them why it was that the prodigal son found himself in need. He eagerly awaited the results, wondering which of the two reasons held in opposition by the American and Russian students (squandering and famine, respectively) would be favored by the Tanzanians. The answer: neither! The majority of the responses, from a people who highly value the virtue of hospitality, identified as the chief cause of the son's hunger the fact that no one gave him anything to eat (see Luke 15:16).[5]

Powell's efforts to catalogue the different responses of readers to the parable of the "prodigal son" and other biblical texts helpfully illustrate for us the reality of polyvalence in our reading of Scripture.[6] *Polyvalence* is a fancy term scholars in several fields use to refer to the multiple (poly) meanings (valence) that may emerge in any attempt at communication. Spouses are, of course, familiar with the reality of polyvalence. "No, that's not what I said! How could you think I meant *that*?" So too are all of us who regularly engage in interpersonal communication. Some of us have also been part of book discussion groups or literature courses or casual conversations about politics where there seem to be as many interpretations of texts and events as there are participants. Often the variation is not all that extreme, but it happens frequently enough for us to realize that the construction of meaning is a complex process, and different people frequently construct meaning differently.

While polyvalence is a common if somewhat annoying phenomenon in our daily lives, the reality of polyvalence in our reading of Scripture presents us with a rather uncomfortable conundrum. So much of our talk and treatment of Scripture presume that there is one, and only one, right meaning to a biblical passage. Major developments and rifts in the history of Christianity have been driven by this presumption. Contemporary debates among Christians often follow suit, with each side defending its reading of the text as the one right way. Much of modern biblical scholarship still produces volumes of work pursing the agenda of determining the one right interpretation of what a biblical author or editors (in cases where texts were likely edited before reaching their final form) intended to convey. Traditionally and still today, Christians have responded to the reality of polyvalence by resisting it and have in turn insisted that while multiple interpretations of a passage may exist, there is only one interpretation that faithfully renders the passage's meaning as God's word. But the conundrum in which we find ourselves is this: how, then, do we know which interpretation is the one right interpretation? Perhaps another way of framing the issue is more helpful: are we sure that the biblical authors, and God, always intended there to be only one right way of understanding the meaning or significance of their words?

## Characteristics of Biblical Narrative that Lead to Polyvalence

### The Meaning of "Meaning"

Before we go any further, I think it important at this point to clarify what I and others mean when we talk about the "meaning" of a passage. This clarification will help us in our discussion of polyvalence and biblical narrative to follow. When folk ask "What does this passage *mean*?" they commonly blend together two senses of the expression. On the one hand, they are interested in what the passage means on its own terms. To use more scholarly jargon, they are interested in its "authorial intent," what the author or editor(s) of the passage intended it to convey. At the same time, these folk are also likely interested in what the text means *for them* as Christians. Can the text offer instruction on how to be more faithful? How can it expand one's understanding of God and/or Jesus? Many biblical theologians find it important to hold these two senses of "meaning" separate. For them, the "meaning" of the text is that which the original authors/editors intended to communicate, or at least the meaning that the text conveys when certain methods of interpretation are applied to it. In contrast, the "application" or "actualization" or "living out" of the text is the exercise of discerning how a text's apparent meaning can serve as edifying instruction for believers here and now. Others argue that these two senses of "meaning" cannot be separated out so neatly, and they invite readers to collapse the two categories in their reading of Scripture. I will address this later. For now, let me say that while I think distinguishing what a text means on its own terms from what it means for us today is in some ways simplistic and problematic, it is still generally useful. Thus, for the sake of more clearly presenting the points I want to emphasize in this chapter, I will distinguish between these two senses of the word "meaning." This distinction can help us identify certain characteristics of biblical narrative that may contribute to the prevalence of polyvalence in our reading of Scripture.

### Factors Complicating "What the Text Means"

There are several features of biblical narrative challenging our ability to discern what a passage or story means on its own terms. First, because of our distance from the time and place in which these biblical texts were written, we may be unfamiliar with some of the cultural norms and perspectives they reflect. If we are not careful, this alone has the potential to derail our grasp of the author's intended meaning. In addition, our interpretive endeavors are complicated by the fact that the Scriptures are written in ancient languages that we must translate into our own. Our most recent critical translations make use of the best manuscripts and linguistic resources available and, on the whole, likely capture very well the essential meaning of the original texts. But as a brief perusal of any commentary on a biblical book will reveal, scholars often quibble over the best way to render the original Hebrew or Greek into modern tongues, and decisions on such matters can at times significantly affect the interpretation of a passage.

Another feature of biblical narrative that poses challenges for us is its characteristic *reticence*. Typically, biblical narrative is reluctant to state explicitly what it would have us think about the events and characters depicted. To be sure, the biblical authors usually craft the narrative in such a way as to lead us to a conclusion about a character or event. This often becomes clear when we read individual passages in close relationship to their wider, narrative context. For example, when the disciples argue among themselves about which of them will be greatest in the kingdom (Mark 9:33-34), right after Jesus has called them to a ministry of service (8:34-35) and told them that he will be laying down his life on the cross (8:31; 9:36-32), it is quite apparent that we are to view this passage as illustrating the incredible thick-headedness of the disciples (see also Mark 10:32-45). Or when we come to Jacob's earnest prayer to God in Gen 32:9-12, after he has just learned that Esau is coming to greet him with four hundred men, the wording of the prayer, the author's depiction of Jacob's character up to this point, as well as his actions immediately following the prayer, would certainly justify our wondering about the sincerity of Jacob's feigned trust in God. Effective storytellers know that narrative is more engaging and powerful when readers have the sense of discerning and discovering the truth it seeks to convey, rather than when the narrator drops obvious hints every step of the way. Having to recognize the truth of the matter draws readers more deeply into the narrative. Concerning the story of Jephthah from Judges 10–11, Robert Alter writes,

> The narrator's extreme reticence in telling us what we should think about all these conflicts and questions is extraordinary, and, more than any other single feature, it may explain the greatness of these narratives. Is Jephthah a hero or villain, a tragic figure or an impetuously self-destructive fool? There are bound to be disagreements among readers, but the writer draws us into a process of intricate, tentative judgment by forcing us to negotiate on our own among such terms, making whatever use we can of the narrative data he has provided.[7]

This reticence, while drawing us more deeply into the narrative, may at times also complicate our understanding of what the author intends to communicate about the character of God and God's will. For instance, the account of the rape of Dinah and the vengeful response of her brothers in Genesis 34 lacks any reference to divine action or commentary, and we are left to wonder about God's regard of the situation. Similarly, when Moses comes down from his meeting with God atop Mount Sinai and sees the Israelites worshiping the golden calf (Exodus 32), he calls those remaining who are faithful to the LORD to kill those partaking in the revelry, and three thousand are slain. But we are not told whether this action was in accord with God's will or not.

I believe that in many cases, with careful study, what the author or editor of a passage intended us to get out of it can be reliably discerned. But it is far from an exact science, and our cultural distance from these texts, the challenges of translation, and the reticence Scripture often displays are such that readers will frequently disagree on what these passages intend to convey about God and God's will and their function in relation to the larger narrative in which they reside.

Beyond this, there is still another feature of biblical narrative, and of biblical tradition in general, that complicates our interpretation and leads to polyvalence. The biblical traditions offer us a testimony to the character of God and God's ways that is "polyphonic" or "polyvocal;" that is, characterized by many different "tones" (phonic) or "voices" (vocal). We have already had the opportunity to explore diverse understandings presented in Scripture of what it means to live as God's people, and the ongoing and reforming character of God's instruction (chapters 2 and 3). Here we will briefly pause to consider Scripture's polyphonic testimony to God.

Walter Brueggemann will serve as our guide on this matter, since his magisterial *Theology of the Old Testament* devotes a significant amount of attention to the rich and varied portrayal of Yahweh's character in the Old Testament.[8] His survey rehearses many of the commonly recognized activities and attributes assigned to God by the Old Testament. For instance, God is one who creates, promises, delivers, steadfastly loves, forgives, commands, and leads. God is portrayed as king, father, judge, one who is incomparably holy, powerful, faithful, and sovereign. To these common images, Brueggemann adds others, such as healer, artist, gardener-vinedresser, mother, and shepherd.[9] Yet there are still other images or attributes to consider; ones that might be regarded as less positive. Yahweh is also portrayed as fiercely jealous, defined by Brueggemann as "Yahweh's strong emotional response to any affront against Yahweh's prerogative, privilege, ascendancy or sovereignty" (see, for example, Exod 20:5; 34:14; Deut 4:24; 5:9; Josh 24:19-20).[10] Yahweh is also a warrior, a "man of war who acts in fierce and violent ways on behalf of Israel" (Exod 15:1-18; Isa 40:10; Psa 24:8, 10).[11] As we saw in preceding chapters, God's violence exclusively construed is manifested in the directive for Israel to annihilate all peoples inhabiting the promised land during the conquest (Joshua 11). Moreover, and signaling for Brueggemann a deep disjunction in Yahweh's character, Yahweh is self-professed not only as merciful and gracious, slow to anger and abounding in steadfast love and faithfulness, but also sovereign Lord who by no means clears the guilty but visits the iniquity of the parents "upon the children, and the children's children to the third and fourth generation" (Exod 34:6-7; see also Num 14:18-24, Nahum 1-2).

> This disjunction, so fully articulated in Exodus 34:6-7 and so oddly enacted in Numbers 14:18-24, states what is most crucial about Yahweh. And what is most crucial, I submit, is that Yahweh's capacity for solidarity and sovereignty is the primary reality that Israel finds in the character of Yahweh. This means that Israel's relationship with Yahweh is one of heavily freighted possibility. Yahweh may act in any circumstance in gracious fidelity, and often does. And Yahweh may act in any circumstance in ferocious sovereignty, and sometimes does, sometimes on behalf of Israel and sometimes against Israel. The affirmation of Yahweh's sovereignty is endlessly unsettling and problematic. . . . This second half of the formulation bears witness to something potentially wild, unruly and dangerous in Yahweh's life.[12]

Readers respond to the polyphonic testimony to God's character in various ways. Some are attracted to certain images of God and give them priority in their engagement with Scripture, often to the exclusion of others. Other interpreters may seek in varying degrees to integrate these disparate images and reshape the apparent contradiction in Yahweh's character into some sort of coherence (see, for instance, my discussion of God's judgment in chapter 7). There are fewer commentators like Brueggemann who so intently emphasize the distinct voices of the Old Testament witness in order to honor the unsettled diversity and the disjunction integral to the portrayal of Yahweh as one who is both graciously merciful and yet also free to respond to human sin with "ferocious sovereignty." The varied ways in which scholars and other readers address this challenging feature of the text ensure a multiplicity of readings. Not only does the construal of God's composite character take varying forms among readers, but the different understandings of God are likely to condition and guarantee readers' different responses to many individual passages.

## Factors Complicating "What the Text Means for Us"

The use of narrative form in Scripture also poses a significant challenge for discerning what the text *means for us*, how we are to actualize its meaning in our walks of faith. Narratives do not consist of straightforward, easily restated, propositional truth claims about the character of God or the nature of reality. Narratives do not *describe* God in concrete terms as much as they *portray* God; and as we just noted, they portray God with a polyphonic array of images and activities. Nor do the biblical stories come out and specifically state how the events and interactions between characters portrayed are to inform one's daily walk of faith. The stories of Scripture present events and characters and then invite readers to discern how the depictions may help them better understand and more faithfully pursue their own relationship with God. Consequently, translating narrative episodes into easily digestible "lessons for faith" is no easy matter. It involves switching from one medium of expression to another, from narrative to propositional truth, from story to didactic exhortation. It also runs the risk of being reductive. When we seek to turn a biblical story into a religious truth claim or lesson for faith, we may be simplifying it to the point that other ways in which narratives engage us can be lost. Some of what we experience when we immerse ourselves in stories is just plain difficult to put into words, such as our emotional and imaginative involvement with the text, which often leads us to identify with certain characters or experience a sense of connection with God or Jesus through the telling of the story.

Moreover, when we engage a biblical text as Scripture, we are naturally led to understand it within the larger context of the canon. The claim made by the very existence of the canon as well as by its shaping (see chapter 6) is that all of its constituent elements together comprise a witness to God, God's will, and what it means to be God's people. The proclamation of each passage, in other words, is to be held in conversation with the witness of the whole. So, for example, when we encounter God's invitation for Israel to become God's "treasured possession" in Exod 19:5, it may seem to us at first that God is playing favorites. But if we read this passage within its broader biblical context in conversation with the creation narratives and God's covenant with Abraham (see Gen 12:3; 22:18), we see instead that God's election of Abraham's descendants is not simply for their own sake, but for the sake of all of humanity. While texts are often relatively straightforward, reading them within their wider, canonical context can at times be a complex affair. As illustrated and discussed in chapters 2 through 4, the canon contains diverse perspectives and developments in thought on what it means to be God's people at different points in time. Reading backwards from the teachings of Jesus, let alone the ongoing ministry of the Spirit, leads to varied formulations of how believers are to respond to those perspectives in the present time and place. As noted above, choices also need to be made on how to handle Scripture's polyphonic testimony to God's character. When conflicting portraits of God or God's will seem to be present, it may not always be clear how best to integrate those opposing perspectives or honor the integrity of each, so different readers will do this differently.

Throughout its history, the church has dealt with the difficulty of translating biblical stories into spiritual truths in various ways. Figurative interpretation, including allegorical interpretation, was widely employed from the earliest days of the church well into the medieval period. Allegorical interpretation treats the biblical texts as allegories, or symbolic tales, in which each element of a biblical story is viewed as symbolizing a particular reality beyond its narrative context (for a clear, biblical example of allegory, see the explanation of the parable of the sower in Mark 4:13-20). Practitioners of allegorical interpretation include the apostle Paul (for example, Gal 4:21-31; 1 Cor 5:6-8), Clement of Alexandria, Irenaeus, Origen, Tertullian, Augustine, Gregory the Great, and Thomas Aquinas, among many others. While these interpreters often sought to address the literal meaning of biblical texts, they also held that certain texts were best understood in an allegorical sense (and some held that biblical texts can have multiple senses, including an allegorical or "spiritual sense"). Allegorical interpretation was frequently employed to wring edifying instruction from passages that did not seem to fit with the revelation of God in Jesus (such as the meaning of the Old Testament law codes for Christians). It was used to shape biblical passages in ways that would directly respond to heretical teachings of the day. It was also employed to cast biblical stories into lessons of moral instruction for believers. Consider this example from the writings of Origen, whose allegorical reading of the story of the Hebrew midwives first explains the significance of their names as symbolizing the Old and New Testaments and then turns the tale into a lesson of edification for the faithful.

> For one midwife is like a sparrow who teaches lofty things and calls forth souls to fly to the heights on rational wings of instruction. The other, who is blushing or modest, is moral. She regulates morals, teaches modesty, and institutes integrity.
>
> It seems to me, however, since Scripture says of these women, "Because they feared God, they did not carry out the command of the king of Egypt," that the two midwives serve as a figure of the two Testaments. "Sephora," which is translated as sparrow, can be applied to the Law which "is spiritual." But "Phua," who is blushing or modest, indicates the Gospels which are red with the blood of Christ and glow

reddish through the whole world by the blood of His passion. The souls, therefore, which are born in the Church are attended by these Testaments as if by midwives, because the entire antidote of instruction is conferred on them from the reading of the Scriptures.

But let us apply these words also to ourselves. If you too fear God, you do not carry out the command of the king of Egypt. For he commands you to live in pleasure, to love the present world, to desire present things. If you fear God and perform the office of midwife for your own soul, if you desire to confer salvation on it, you do not do these things. You keep alive the male which is in you. You attend and assist your inner man and seek eternal life for him by good actions and understandings.[13]

Although not often utilized by biblical scholars today, vestiges of allegorical interpretation still can be commonly found in sermons and homilies. One advantage of this method is that texts become so malleable that they can be made to speak to nearly any type of situation. This method frees and invites the interpreter or preacher to engage the text through an imaginative reconfiguring of its elements, leading to theology and preaching that are often very dynamic as well as relevant to the concerns at hand. But the allegorical approach also has a serious disadvantage in that it often takes elements of the text (characters, settings, events, interactions, dialogue) as symbols of realities that have little or nothing to do with the text on its own terms in its literary and historical contexts. The text basically becomes a template for plugging in particular realities that stem from the concerns of the interpreter, leading us to wonder how much of the text itself is actually in focus. Nor does this method allow us to escape polyvalence. It eagerly invites it by greatly expanding the possible range of meanings one can glean from any particular passage.

A more common way of applying biblical stories to the life of faith in recent times has been to use the principle of analogy. This form of interpretation first explores the meaning of the text on its own terms. Then, in order to "apply" or "actualize" the meaning of the text in view, the interpreter looks for situations or realities in our time and place that are analogous to the situation described or addressed in the biblical text. Often the process occurs in reverse as well, as interpreters frequently have concerns about a particular issue or situation and then look for biblical passages that might meaningfully speak to it. In either case, however, the goal is to understand the text first in relation to its historical and literary context, and then in relation to our contemporary context. In his *Introduction to the Hebrew Bible*, John Collins offers a helpful description of this twofold engagement with the biblical text:

Placing the Bible in its historical context is not, however, an end in itself. For most readers of the Bible, this is not only a document of ancient history but also in some ways a guide for modern living. The responsible use of the Bible must begin by acknowledging that these books are not written with our modern situations in mind, and are informed by the assumptions of an ancient culture remote from our own. To understand the Bible in its historical context is first of all to appreciate what an alien book it is. But no great literature is completely alien. There are always analogies between the ancient world and our own. Within the biblical text itself we shall see how some paradigmatic episodes are recalled repeatedly to guide the understanding of new situations. The use of the exodus as a motif in the Prophets is an obvious case in point. Biblical laws and the prophetic preaching repeatedly raise issues that still confront us in modern society. The Bible does not provide ready answers to these problems, but it provides occasions and examples to enable us to think about them and grapple with them.[14]

The advantages of this method are many. It takes seriously the function and meaning of a passage within its own literary and historical context. It does not—at least in principle—allow the concerns of the present to override the importance of studying the text on its own terms. In doing so, it provides a "baseline" reading of the passage that guards against tendentiousness and undue relativism. By utilizing analogy, this method seeks to forge a recognizable, commonsense connection between the proclamation or exhortation of the text and situations in people's lives of faith that can be profitably informed by the biblical story. While still allowing room for imagination, creativity, and insight when discerning how a biblical story may guide lives of faith in the present, analogous reasoning guards against uses of the text that are unrelated or cut against the grain of the text itself. However, even with an approach that carefully applies the concept of analogy in its reading and proclaiming of Scripture, we encounter the inescapable reality of polyvalence. The complex, imaginative, and creative dimensions of discerning how the biblical text speaks to the challenges of our time, along with the widely varied settings in which Christian faith is lived, ensure that Christians will apply or actualize biblical texts in very different ways. Even if most Christians were to agree on what a text meant on its own terms, there would still be a plethora of views on what the text *means for us*, as Scripture, in our various times and places.

### Postmodern Challenges to "Meaning"
Relatively recently, an increasing number of interpreters—often labeled "postmodern" by themselves and others—have argued that no

text, nor any form of communication, contains a precise, fixed meaning. Meaning, they argue, is always in flux for at least two reasons. First, language itself is an unstable vehicle for meaning, containing inconsistencies and variations that continually subvert the linear transmission of information. Second, the communication of meaning is always subject to a host of variables that change from one recipient to another. All recipients, readers, or hearers of a text bring with them a set of experiences, intellectual abilities, predispositions, and commitments that leads them to engage and respond to information—to create meaning—differently. Thus, "meaning" does not reside in the text per se but is something that is created only in the interaction between a reader and the text, with the reader—not the author—being the agent that primarily and ultimately shapes how the text is going to be understood. Consequently, those holding to this perspective would challenge the claim that a distinction can be maintained between what the text means on its own terms and what it means for us. In their view, whenever we read a biblical story, we are always deeply engaged in what the text means for us, not on its own terms but on *our* terms.

I do not subscribe to some of the more tendentious elements of postmodern thought. While language does indeed have limitations and is at times problematic, I think that, overall, it functions rather well, and more often than not is able to convey information from a sender to a recipient. (As the author of this book, I'd like to think you are getting out of it at least *some* of what I intend to say.) I also don't believe that meaning is wholly reader/recipient-centered. Authors and speakers can pattern information in such a way that it will elicit (not always, but often) the intended response in terms of reader reaction and understanding. We share enough conventions of communication and perspectives on the nature of reality with one another that, in most cases, with texts that are well crafted and well read, a genuine transfer of information and meaning can take place.[15] Perhaps this transfer is not always perfect or complete, but it is good enough to make it worthwhile for us to keep talking with one another (and, I hope, for you to keep reading).

At the same time, the recognition that people come to texts with a various sets of experiences, intellectual abilities, predispositions, and commitments that may lead them to understand and apply the significance of a text differently than others is a valuable insight. It is one of several factors that help us to see why the biblical narratives elicit such diverse responses. It may also help us to consider that the biblical narratives may actually be designed to invite such diversity.

## How Biblical Narrative Invites Polyvalence

Polyvalence in our reading of biblical narrative is a reality. That much is clear. It also seems inevitable. Even if, as I and many other readers of Scripture maintain, it is often possible to discern meaning and direction from biblical texts that have a high degree of continuity with what the biblical authors or editors intended, the additional steps of then asking how this passage relates to the view of God and of faith expressed in the wider biblical canon, and how then one might seek to live out its teachings about God and faith in one's daily life, are going to yield diverse opinions. If we regard these writings as "the word of God," we might well ask: Why would God choose such a messy medium for instruction and edification? How can we call these texts the "word of God" if their meaning varies so widely for different people in different times and places?

### *The Narrative Form of Scripture*

The medium may be messy, but it is also exceptionally engaging. Although biblical narrative may be prone to polyvalence, it excels in applicability and relevance for life. The point of biblical narrative, as I have come to understand it, is not simply to convey timeless truths about the character of God and our calling as God's people. It does indeed do that through its recurring story lines and canonical shaping, as I will discuss in the following chapters. But in disclosing the character of God and the history of the relationship between God and God's people through the medium of *story*, biblical narrative invites readers/hearers to invest themselves in their encounter with the text to a degree that a dry recitation of prepositional truth claims could never achieve.

Narratives are powerful. When we take the time to read a good book or see a well-conceived play, we find ourselves getting "caught up in the story," identifying with certain characters, imagining what we might do if we were one of them. With really engaging narrative, we yearn for the stories to be real, so that we too might live in the world they describe, become friends with leading characters, and join them in their brave and noble cause against evil and injustice. Even if we pick up a book or go to a play or movie simply to be entertained, what often takes place in our encounter with the tale depicted—at least the better ones—is an encounter with a way of seeing the world. Storytelling is about creating meaning. In their depiction of characters, events, interactions, sorrows, triumphs, tragedies and blessings, stories provide us with a view of reality, a dramatic account of the ways of the world. Perhaps the plotless and artless shells of stories we often find on movie and television screens are an exception, but most often stories are nothing if not rhetorical, in the sense of promoting a perspective. One of the primary objectives of most worthwhile stories is to lead us to see something about the world or the human condition that the author wants us to see. And very often, if it is a compelling story, we soon find ourselves adopting certain perspectives of the story, perhaps even without realizing it. Narratives gather us, with subtlety and at times subversively, into their storied world and call us to dwell there for a while. The more deeply we invest ourselves in that narrative world, the more likely that world is going to rub off on us and lead us to see our own world differently.

The story that Scripture weaves, of course, is one of those stories that has deeply engaged and moved many of its hearers and readers. But here we come to a crucial point. That which enables stories to engage us and move us—their powerful ability to get their readers to inscribe themselves, intellectually and emotionally, into the story—is the very same thing that opens stories up to the inevitability of polyvalence. Stories—at least those good stories that we find compelling in their depictions of reality—entail such a significant investment of ourselves into their narrative world that the meaning we take from them is bound to reflect to some degree what we as groups and individuals bring to those stories. On this the postmodernists are at least partly right. The meaning of a story is not simply a linear transfer of information from author to text to receiver. As readers, we play a significant role in negotiating and discerning how a story moves us, how it compels us, how it leads us to a different view of the world and our place in it, what it means *for us*.

As noted earlier, many Christians consider polyvalent readings of Scripture a problem, a negative circumstance that we must find ways to overcome. But what if we suspend that judgment for a moment and entertain the notion that Scripture—at least to some degree—is supposed to be polyvalent? I realize that with those words, some of my readers may fear that I am heading toward an endorsement of a mind-numbing relativism in which any version of "what a text means for me" is to be regarded as lovely and edifying, at least for the person who utters it. That is not where I am headed, however, so bear with me a little longer. What if the drafters of Scripture, or if not them, then God, intended Scripture to be a work whose story and stories might mean different things for different believers in different times and places? I don't mean here differences on basic, core dimensions of the story. It seems to me that these are translatable across time, culture, and place, for they address basic dimensions of God's character and the human condition. But would Jesus find fault with Russian seminarians for failing to focus on the wastefulness of the prodigal son, and seeing the point of the parable as the generous provision of God? Would Jesus chastise those communities struggling against injustice for the tendency to read their own experience of oppression into the exodus story, or the beatitudes, and for not seeing them as simply referring to "spiritual" realities? Would God find problematic a Native American reading of the conquest narratives that sympathetically identifies with the Canaanites? Some of us who are Euro-Americans, living on the land that Native Americans used to inhabit, might be troubled by such a reading; but should we imagine that God shares our culturally conditioned discomfort?

As we consider whether, or to what extent, we should embrace polyvalence in our reading of Scripture, it may also be helpful to point out just a few examples of how various elements of Scripture either invite or model polyvalence.

## Polyvalence Embodied in Scripture
### The Psalms

As we noted in chapter 3, the psalms were shaped into such generalized language that their expressions to God could be claimed and echoed by believers in various times and places, and in response to all sorts of crises or moments of blessing. In other words, the psalms were deliberately composed to be polyvalent, for how the prayers specifically speak a word of God to each individual will differ depending on his or her situation. The polyvalent agility of the psalms is what has enabled them to serve for many as a powerful source of hope in trials of all kinds, and a faithful source of guidance in response to all manner of blessing.

Moreover, we find the psalms drawing from key moments of the biblical story in various ways, freely and at times creatively molding their remembrance of those narratives in a manner that addresses the need at hand. For example, in Psalm 77, the psalmist's desperate lament turns to praise as he remembers God's awesome deliverance of Israel during the exodus from Egypt. He uses that paradigmatic portrayal of Yahweh's power and faithfulness as a model for understanding the way in which Yahweh is present and at work in his current crisis, but with one significant alteration (note the emphasis added in this citation):

> *The crash of your thunder was in the whirlwind;*
> > *your lightnings lit up the world;*
> > *the earth trembled and shook.*
> *Your way was through the sea,*
> > *your path, through the mighty waters;*
> > yet your footprints were unseen. (Ps 77:18-19)

If we go back to the exodus traditions, we find that Yahweh's presence during their flight from Egypt was made known to the Israelites in obvious fashion: a cloud by day and a pillar of fire by night. Still, the psalmist takes the liberty of focusing on *the lack of God's footprints in the sand* as analogous to God's apparent absence, or "behind-the-scenes work" in the life of the psalmist! Recalling the exodus story through the lens of his present crisis (which involved for him the painful experience of God's absence [vv. 1-10]), he comes to remember God as one who is powerful and faithful but whose saving care is not always visible: "Here now as well, God must be present, even though I can't see God or God's footprints before me."

## 1 and 2 Chronicles

Attentive readers of 1 and 2 Chronicles often come to the realization that they have read much of the history it reports somewhere before. Indeed they may have, for the historical material in these books is a reworking of many of the same traditions presented in the books of Samuel and Kings. But it is not *exactly* the same material. What we find in 1 and 2 Chronicles is a recasting of Israel's history in response to the concerns facing the post-exilic Jewish community that had returned to Judah to rebuild Jerusalem and the temple. Whereas the books often labeled the "Deuteronomistic History" (Joshua through 2 Kings, excluding Ruth) and the works of the Chronicler both seek to explain why it was that Israel found itself in exile, 1 and 2 Chronicles are concerned with helping the post-exilic community reclaim its vocation and liturgical practice as God's people. Receiving much attention are David and Solomon as model kings (references to their failings are often omitted, such as David's affair with Bathsheba), their endorsement of the priesthood, the unity of the people in embracing the rule of the kings and priests (the power struggles surrounding their reigns are omitted), Solomon's building of the temple, the importance of worship for the people of Israel, and the celebration of the temple and the customs surrounding it. The Chronicler is, in effect, retelling the story in such a way that it speaks to the needs and concerns of post-exilic Jews in their time and place. Neither he nor the compilers of Scripture seem much concerned with the fact that he is telling the story in some ways quite different from the books of 1 and 2 Samuel and 1 and 2 Kings.

## Revelation

Readers of the Apocalypse (or Revelation) to John have long debated the question of how John's revelation is to be understood. Some have regarded it as offering a literal description of how the end-time events are going to take place, including beasts with multiple heads and the new Jerusalem actually descending from heaven. Others have seen it as a metaphorical depiction of the end-time or as a metaphorical commentary on the events of the first century. Still others have argued that it symbolically depicts the kinds of trials, adversity, and choices facing believers in every generation, while offering the proclamation that the ultimate fate of those who trust in God is not in doubt: they, with Jesus' help, will prevail over all evil. For many biblical theologians, including myself, the last option best captures the intent of the Apocalypse. If so, then here too we have an example of Scripture inviting readers to read their own experiences into the narrative. The text is intentionally made malleable enough to accommodate various settings and experiences of readers, with the result that the text is able to speak a word that helps readers better understand God's purpose and presence in the world in their time and place.

## Gospels

Scholars have long pointed out that each of the Gospels presents the life, death, and resurrection of Jesus somewhat differently. While they all agree on many basic details, each Gospel emphasizes particular dimensions of Jesus' ministry, either by adapting some of the stories the Gospels share or by including traditions not found in the other Gospels. The presumption of many scholars is that the Evangelists shaped their Gospels in a way that would most effectively speak to the situation of the communities they were addressing and/or concerns they themselves held. Matthew, for instance, emphasizes Jesus' role as a teacher of God's torah, or instruction, whose understanding of righteousness far exceeds that of the teachers of old and his contemporaries. Matthew also accentuates Jesus' criticism of the religious authorities, and composes sections of invective against the scribes and Pharisees unparalleled in length by the other Gospels (see Matthew 23). This has led many to suppose that Matthew was writing for a Jewish Christian community involved in a bitter dispute with an early form of rabbinic Judaism, which charged the Christian Jews with abandoning the proper observance of the law. Mark, on the other hand, is often seen as emphasizing Jesus' suffering and presenting Jesus' death on the cross as the climax of the Gospel. Many have argued that Mark was likely writing to a community facing severe persecution and becoming reticent in their proclamation of the good news. In response, Mark crafted his account to emphasize Jesus' repeated exhortations to the disciples to remain steadfast in the face of suffering. He provided numerous examples of the disciples' own failures in faithful following as a means of helping believers to understand that they are not the only ones who struggle with the demands of discipleship. He also abruptly ends the Gospel without any announcement of the good news of Jesus' resurrection (Mark 16:8). This abrupt ending serves as an invitation for his community to finish the Gospel story by boldly proclaiming God's defeat of death without regard for their fear. The situations and needs of the communities to whom Luke and John wrote have been more difficult for scholars to discern. Even so, Luke's emphasis on the plight of the poor, prayer, Jesus' fulfillment of the Old Testament story, the occurrence of key events (such as Jesus' birth and resurrection) in and around Jerusalem, and the connection between the ministry of Jesus and that of the early church are quite apparent. John's story of Jesus contains numerous traditions not found in Matthew, Mark, and Luke and lacks most of the traditions (miracles, parables, stories) common to the other three. Although similar to the others in its broad contours, John's portrayal of Jesus as the divine Son, the "Word" who brings salvation to all who recognize him as the one who descends from and fully reflects the glory of the Father, contains many distinct elements and emphases.

What the Gospels together represent, in effect, is the good news being told and engaged differently in different contexts. The basic dimensions of the story are solidly intact in each Gospel, and some scholars tend to overstate the differences between them. Yet there are differences, beyond the level of minor discrepancies in detail. The *meaning* of Jesus' mission and its significance is different for each of these contexts. The story of Jesus was reshaped to meet the needs that the Evangelists believed the story of Jesus could address in their respective times and places.

There is evidence that not all Christians in the early church were comfortable with four canonical versions of the gospel story. The second-century bishop of Lyons, Irenaeus, felt compelled to defend the canon, both from some Gnostic Christians, who wanted to add to the number of Gospels, and from those who thought there should be fewer.

> It is not possible that the Gospels can be either more or fewer in number than they are, since there are four directions of the world in which we are, and four principle winds. . . . The four living creatures [of Rev 4:9] symbolize the four gospels . . . and there are four principal covenants made with humanity, through Noah, Abraham, Moses and Christ. (Irenaeus, *Adversus haereses* 3.11.8)[16]

Shortly before Irenaeus offered this defense, Tatian, a student of Justin Martyr, combined the four Gospels into one harmonious account called the *Diatesseron,* which remained popular in some segments of the church for several centuries before falling into disuse. Yet the benefits of the fourfold Gospel witness, as many in the church came to appreciate, is that they provide us with four different vantage points from which to view and appreciate the story of Jesus. As a result, our understanding of Jesus and the significance of his ministry, death, and resurrection is enriched by these multiple perspectives.

These examples reveal that sacred traditions have often been employed by the biblical authors in different ways. To these examples, a multitude of others could be added. The New Testament authors, as we saw in the introduction and with Paul in chapter 4, frequently interpreted Old Testament traditions in ways that differed from what the narratives likely meant in their original, Old Testament contexts. At times, the same Old Testament tradition is employed differently by the New Testament authors (see, for example, two very different, though I think complementary, uses of the Abraham story in Romans 4 and James 2). The Old Testament writers (especially the prophets) also glean different lessons from preceding traditions, depending on the needs of the situation at hand.

What these examples demonstrate, in concert with the narrative form of Scripture, is that polyvalence has a central place in our heritage as God's people. The community of God's people—or, better, the *communities* of God's people—play a crucial role in negotiating the meaning of the biblical traditions in their particular times and places. This too affirms the dialogical character of both Scripture and biblical interpretation by people of faith. What is embodied in the Bible is not simply the timeless, unchanging word of God. What we also have are time-bound, polyvalent professions of faith by believers seeking to make sense of their own life-stories within the larger story of God's will and work on behalf of humanity.

## Implications: Hearing and Speaking God's Word in Many Voices

The heritage our forebears have bequeathed to us as sacred Scripture calls us to take up the biblical story as our own, not simply as a chronicle of our ancestors' interactions with God and one another, but as a living tale of which we ourselves are a part. To borrow the words of Joel Green, "Our task is to make our lodging the Genesis-to-Revelation narrative so that our modes of interpretation are conformed to the biblical narrative, so that this story decisively shapes our lives."[17] If we truly are to conform our modes of interpretation to those that are evident in and invited by the biblical narrative, then we cannot dismiss the appropriateness and *faithfulness* of polyvalence in our collective reading of Scripture and testimony to God's will. But let me conclude this chapter by offering some clarification of what I mean and do not mean by this.

As I noted above, I am not advocating a rampant relativism in our collective reading of Scripture. As I discuss in the next two chapters, I believe that there are central truths that Scripture conveys, dominant story lines that are foundational to the biblical story. Many of these are captured well in the historic creeds of the church and other statements of faith. If some of these central elements are pushed aside, or so radically reworked that they no longer resemble their articulation in

Scripture, then we run the risk of truncating our witness to God and to the divine will and ways in the world. To borrow a phrase from Mark Powell, we are called to "polyvalence within parameters."[18] Or, to use the long-standing maxim of the Evangelical and Reformed tradition, "In essentials unity, in non-essentials diversity, in all things charity." As indicated earlier, I am also not abandoning as an important goal of interpretive work the discernment of "authorial intent," even though this effort has been sharply criticized of late. Although challenging and uncertain at times, the pursuit of what the biblical authors or editors intended a text to convey remains, I believe, an important starting point for biblical interpretation.

Yet as our biblical heritage itself testifies, diverse, polyphonic conceptions of God and God's will abound in our sacred tradition. This serves as yet another witness to the character of Scripture as sacred dialogue: the Bible comprises a plethora of voices offering testimony to God's character and will. In parallel fashion, the narrative form of our tradition invites also from believers polyvalent understandings of what the text means as they deeply immerse themselves in the story Scripture proclaims, for there is a wide diversity of situations, needs, crises, and hopes directing different groups of Christians as they gather around that story. Therefore, when we truly honor the polyvalent testimony that Scripture both embodies and invites, it shapes our calling to conversation and mutual edification in at least three ways. First, readers are called to celebrate the reality of polyvalence as yet another manifestation of God seeking to engage and speak to believers in ways that make sense to them in their time and place. Such celebration further uplifts God's consistent practice of inviting humanity into conversation and discernment concerning God's activity in their lives and the world (see chapter 1). Second, readers are also called to a generous and humble spirit of openness when listening to the readings of others. Even, perhaps especially, in times of disagreement, readers are to be mindful that none of them, whether as individuals or as groups of believers, has exclusive access to or full comprehension of the potentiality of God's instruction in and through Scripture. No one so completely knows both the mind and heart of God. All believers, as Paul cautions, see the truth dimly, and thus are called to respond to one another humbly. Third, readers circumvent the fullness of what God may have to teach when they are not open to the readings of the story that others articulate. The lifeblood of ongoing dialogue and discernment is the community of faith gathered around the Scriptures, receptive to the various accounts of how that story has moved their lives, with hearts attentive to the witness of God's Spirit. The authors and compilers of the canon affirm that multiplicity of perspectives is a good and faithful thing and that there is more than one way to cast the significance of our heritage and relationship with God. Readers who respond to texts differently are invited to continue the very same conversation that the polyvalence of Scripture embodies, and thus help one another more deeply mine the various dimensions of a text and the story they share. Concerning the rich, dialogue-directed discernment to which readers are called, Allen Verhey eloquently states,

> Discernment is a complex but practical wisdom. It does not rely on the simple application of general principles (whether of hermeneutics or of ethics) to particular cases by neutral and rational individuals. There is no checklist for discernment, no flow chart for how to read and perform Scripture in "fitting" ways. Still, there is discernment. It is learned and exercised in the community gathered around the Scriptures, and it involves the diversity of gifts present in the congregation. Some, as we said, are gifted with the scholarly tools of historical, literary, and social investigation; others, with moral imagination or a passion for justice or with sweet reasonableness. But all are gifted with the Spirit that brings remembrance (John 14:26). Discernment requires a dialogue with the whole church gathered around the whole of Scripture; it requires reading Scripture with those whose experience is different from our own and whose experience of the authority of Scripture is different from our own. It requires a dialogue in which people listen to both Scripture and one another, muting neither Scripture nor one another. . . . Discernment enables us to see in the dialogue with Scripture and with saints and strangers that our readings of Scripture do not yet "fit" Scripture itself, and that our lives and our communities do not yet fit the story that we love to tell and long to live.[19]

Verhey captures well the polyvalent, conversational, communal, and humble character of the discernment that is to characterize the people of God. We have a long way to go before we find our lives fully inscribed in this story, as Verhey acknowledges. But because this same sort of dialogical discernment is embodied within Scripture itself, we can be assured that when we faithfully seek to do this we are already joining ourselves to the "story we love to tell and long to live."

# Coherence
# in the Conversation

---

## chapter six

*". . . for you are a gracious and merciful God."*
*(Nehemiah 9:31)*

**The High Priest Hilkiah rejoices in King**
Josiah's reforms, and decides to unveil the long forgotten book of the
law:

> For so long I have waited for this moment, for a king and a people
> who might care to remember who we are. The years have gone
> by with no memory of who we had been, and who we are called
> to be. The LORD's prophets have gone unheeded. God's torah has
> been unread. Our leaders' self-conceit, their self-fulfilling quest
> for wealth and glory has bred amnesia among us. For the things
> that truly matter, ignorance abounds. But now, the moment
> finally seems right! Josiah has given orders for repairs on the
> LORD's long-neglected temple to begin! My prayers for this young
> king have been answered. My years of gently prodding him to
> reclaim our faith, against the will of his other advisors, have now
> borne fruit. I will bring out the book of the law. The words of
> Moses will once again be heard among the people. The stories of
> our past will be recited and celebrated. We will remember who
> we are. Perhaps God will put away our many sins, and claim us
> as his own once more.

After an especially long tenure of kings who "did what was evil in
the sight of the LORD," Israel was on the verge of forgetting who and
whose it was. Under the reigns of Manasseh (fifty-five years) and Amon
(twenty-two years), idolatry was rampant, child sacrifice was practiced,
the temple was in disrepair, and "the book of the law" (likely an early,

written collection of laws and perhaps stories that later found their way into the Pentateuchal traditions) was collecting dust in some back room of the temple (2 Kings 21). Even the good king Josiah, eighteen years into his reign, did not know that this written collection of the sacred traditions existed. But after Josiah commissioned the restoration of the temple, the High Priest Hilkiah made sure that the book of the law received a hearing in the presence of the king (2 Kings 22). What a defining moment that was for Israel! Moved by the stories and instruction he heard, Josiah went on to institute widespread reforms throughout Israel (2 Kings 23).

Unfortunately, Josiah's reforms would not be taken up by subsequent kings, and Judah would soon fall into ruin. However, this time of remembrance under Josiah, coupled with the renewed knowledge of these traditions, provided a precedent that laid the groundwork for another time of remembrance, when Israel's very existence as a people hung by a thread. In 587 B.C.E. the Babylonian armies attacked Jerusalem, leveled the city, and carried the Israelites into exile. They were cast into a land that was not their own and tossed into a mix of people holding very different traditions than their own. The Babylonian Empire created a cultural melting pot fed with displaced peoples from throughout the Mediterranean world. It thrived on absorption and amnesia, melding together whatever cultural traditions mixed well into its syncretistic, polytheistic stew and skimming off the rest. One of the more remarkable developments in the history of the Jewish people is that at this extraordinarily tragic moment, when it would have been so easy for them to turn away from their past and their God, many of them chose to remember their story, reclaim their identity, and return to Yahweh.

## Harmony in the Midst of Cacophony

If, as the stories of Josiah and exiled Judah teach us, remembering the story of our faith is constitutive of identity—the lifeblood of our connectedness to God, one another, and God's will for us—then we do well to emphasize the importance of engaging this story. We also do well to explore how our remembrance and retelling of this story may best enable us to claim and reclaim our identity as God's people in our own time and place.

However, this may be easier said than credibly done. Many contributors to the field of biblical study over the last two centuries have resisted efforts to find in the biblical materials any overarching, coherent "meta-narrative" or other attempt to systematize its diverse elements into a unified theology. The interpretive program of "historical criticism," which dominated biblical study throughout much of the nineteenth and twentieth centuries and is still influential today, was often (though not always) uninterested in the literary and theological character of the text.[1] Instead, its chief goal has been to investigate the historical processes and socio-religious settings that contributed to the development of the biblical traditions. It has evolved an arsenal of critical tools (for example, source criticism, form criticism, redaction criticism, tradition history criticism) designed to peel back the various layers of a text's development and discern its function in the life of ancient Israel or early Christian communities. Those engaging in these disciplines routinely presume and discern in the biblical materials multiple sources, competing strains of tradition, and the recasting of sacred traditions in new times and places. In short, what most biblical scholars over the last two hundred years have spent much of their time examining are the various ways in which particular biblical traditions do not fit neatly together but instead represent the divergent and at times opposing concerns and beliefs of various parties in various contexts over the course of several hundred years. What is most basic to an educated view of Scripture, they would say, is not seeing the Bible as a unity but rather recognizing its multiform and multiperspectival character, betraying a dynamic and even contentious process of evolution.

More recently, many biblical scholars have moved beyond the historical-critical paradigm and have focused their investigation on the theological or literary character of the biblical texts. Yet a good number of them also find attempts to harmonize the biblical accounts into anything resembling a consistent "story" problematic. Some protest that the biblical materials are simply too diverse to allow for any meaningful degree of unity or coherence. At the very least, they argue, any such systematization needs to be viewed as an artificial construct imposed upon, not necessitated by, the text. Others trading in postmodern perspectives (as we noted in the previous chapter) argue in varying degrees that the same phenomena confounding the transfer of meaning in any communicative moment apply on a grand scale to the interpretation of ancient traditions. The only "story" that we may discern in our reading of the biblical traditions, they argue, is one not inherent to or necessitated by the texts themselves, but one composed by our own imaginative, contextually bound faculties and biases. Thus, any imposition of coherence on the biblical materials amounts to an agenda-driven, "totalizing" interpretation that construes the biblical materials according to only one of many possible perspectives.[2]

To some extent, I agree with these commonly raised challenges to the unity of the biblical materials. In preceding chapters, I have participated in the disciplines of historical criticism in order to show how the biblical texts preserve diverse, and even opposing, perspectives on certain crises at particular points in Israel's and the early church's history. Along with others who have emphasized the multivocal character of Scripture's testimony, I, too, have sought to show the diverse perspectives on God's character and will embodied in the biblical text and the text's dynamic, reforming representations of what it means to be God's people. I have emphasized that polyvalence is an inevitable and, in some senses, desirable element not only of biblical interpretation but also of Scripture itself. In sum, the persistent point underscored in the preceding chapters has been that it is crucial for us to attend to the diversity of the biblical traditions in order to appreciate Scripture's dynamic and conversational character. Just as important, Scripture's preservation of multiple voices serves as an invitation for us to join its sacred conversation. Scripture is diverse, even cacophonous at times, and that is a good thing!

My point here, however, is to draw attention to a strong, even if sometimes subtle, harmony that pulsates throughout Scripture's cacophonic conversation. In addition to its rich variegation, Scripture is also characterized by a consistent vision of God's will and ways in the world. To put it even more strongly, despite the diversity we find in Scripture, and despite the diverse ways people of faith interpret it, the Bible persistently rehearses central plotlines, broad movements, and characteristic claims disclosing (1) abiding features of God's character, (2) tendencies in God's engagement with an often wayward humanity, that is, engagement consistently oriented toward a desired end, and (3) essential elements of what it means to be God's faithful people. The Bible proclaims, in other words, a coherent *story*.

How can the traditions of Scripture be so diverse and yet also provide a coherent whole? Perhaps this analogy will help. Think of Scripture as a river. Anyone familiar with creeks or rivers knows that there are all sorts of currents, pools, obstructions, and inlets that affect the flow of the water. It is even quite common for there to be places where a current runs close to shore in the opposite direction of the main current. While some stretches of the stream flow easily with nary a disruption, other stretches are quite turbulent and treacherous. Yet despite all of the diverse ways in which water moves in that stream, despite all of the disruptions along the way, the water still flows—unequivocally—in a general direction. In a similar way, there is still a "flow" to Scripture, even though when we look at it up close we find that there are all sorts of eddies and countercurrents, and perhaps even some rapids and waterfalls. Despite these diversions, there is still a main "flow" that, with a bit of skill and a lot of grace, we can navigate—unless we get so caught up in the countercurrents that we simply spin in circles.

## Scripture's Movements Toward Unity

The notion that Scripture presents a coherent sacred story is not a construct that believers alone impose upon the text but one that the biblical traditions themselves presume and celebrate. There are several prominent features of Scripture that lead us to view its constituent elements as together forming a unified whole.

### *Summarizing the Story*

First, throughout Scripture we frequently encounter passages in which the author, or a character in the story, pauses to review events that have either already taken place, are yet to come, or both. Often these "biblical summaries" cast wide their purview over major segments of the story. They frequently occur at key moments in the life of Israel and function not unlike a soliloquy in a play: the action in the narrative stops, and a speaker steps forth to offer an explanation of how the critical moment at hand is to be understood in relation to the larger history of God's dealings with humanity and Israel. In non-narrative material, such as in the psalms or prophetic traditions, the summaries likewise serve the function of uniting the moment at hand with the overarching story of God's relationship with Israel. In this way, these summaries unite portions, sometimes vast portions, of the story as part of a larger, unified account. The summaries also consistently emphasize certain dimensions of God's character and will, indicating these as features basic to the biblical portrait of God. The following discussion provides some representative samples of biblical summaries.[3]

### God's Covenant with Abraham
### (Gen 12:1-3; 15:1-16; 17:1-22; 18:1-15)

God's covenant with Abram (Gen 12:1-3) comes on the heels of the opening chapters of Genesis.

> Now the LORD said to Abram, "Go from your country and your kindred and your father's house to the land that I will show you. I will make of you a great nation, and I will bless you, and make your name great, so that you will be a blessing. I will bless those who bless you, and the one who curses you I will curse; and in you all the families of the earth shall be blessed."

The elements of the promise may be listed as the following:

1. God calls Abram to trust in God and God's directive: "Go from your country and your kindred and your father's house . . ."

2. Promise of blessing: the repeated use of the verb "bless" reminds us of God's gift of blessing in the creation stories, and here consists of the promise of descendants, nationhood, land, and protection.

3. Yet Abram's descendants are not the only ones to be blessed. Rather, they are to be the means by which God brings blessing to all of humanity: "and all nations shall be blessed through you."

Additional details concerning the realization of the covenant promise are clarified over the next several chapters (Gen 15:1-16; 17:1-22; 18:1-15). The function of Gen 12:1-3 as an anticipatory summary of what is to come is made clear by the fact that the elements of the promise (trust in God, descendants, land, nationhood, and protection) are the abiding focus of the narrative as it continues through Genesis, the rest of the Pentateuch, and the books of Joshua and Judges. In these and later books, the promise is also frequently referenced as the moment that gave birth to Israel's existence and defines God's ongoing will for and commitment to Israel (see Gen 26:1-5, 23-24; 28:10-17; 35:9-15; 48:1-21; Exod 3:16; 6:2; 32:13; Lev 26:42; Num 32:11; Deut 6:10; Josh 24:2-3; 2 Kgs 2:23; 1 Chr 29:18; Ps 105:1; Isa 41:8; 51:2; Jer 33:25-26). Moreover, God's promise to Abraham establishes the major plotline of the biblical story: God's attempt to reclaim human beings and lead them back to blessing through a particular people, Israel. Thus, God's promise to Abraham reaches forward to unify the entire narrative to follow as the working out of this divine plan, the fulfillment of which, according to the writers of the New Testament, is accomplished in Jesus (Matt 1:17; Luke 1:55, 73; 19:9; John 8:31-47; Acts 3:25; Rom 4:1-25; Gal 3:6-18; Heb 6:13-15).

And Mary said,

*"My soul magnifies the Lord,*
　　*and my spirit rejoices in God my Savior,*
*for he has looked with favor on the lowliness of his servant.*
　　*Surely, from now on all generations will call me blessed;*
*for the Mighty One has done great things for me,*
　　*and holy is his name.*
*His mercy is for those who fear him*
　　*from generation to generation.*
*He has shown strength with his arm;*
　　*he has scattered the proud in the thoughts of their hearts.*
*He has brought down the powerful from their thrones,*
　　*and lifted up the lowly;*

*he has filled the hungry with good things,*
   *and sent the rich away empty.*
*He has helped his servant Israel,*
   *in remembrance of his mercy,*
*according to the promise he made to our ancestors,*
   *to Abraham and to his descendants forever."* (Luke 1:46-55)

### The Call of Moses (Exod 3:1-22; see also 6:1-8)

In the call of Moses and disclosure of God's plan to liberate Abraham's descendants from Egypt, God reveals the divine name, Y<small>HWH</small> (Yahweh), and embraces "the God of your ancestors, the God of Abraham, the God of Isaac, the God of Jacob" as "my name forever, and my title for all generations" (Exod 3:14-15). This twofold self-naming on the part of God emphasizes God's ongoing commitment to be in intimate relationship with Abraham's descendants and connects the exodus story with that of Genesis. It also affirms that such relatedness is essential to Yahweh's very character. Additionally, the call of Moses looks ahead as it summarizes the focus of God's activity for the rest of Exodus, the Pentateuch, and the book of Joshua: God will deliver the people from Egypt and lead them into the promised land. Throughout the rest of the Old Testament, the story of the exodus looms large and is constantly recited as a defining moment in the relationship between God and Israel.[4] Henceforth, God is known to Israel as Savior: one who will honor the covenant promises no matter who or what threatens the people. In essence, the exodus story reveals that Yahweh has both the will and the power to save Israel, and its remembrance throughout the biblical traditions serves as an ongoing testimony to Yahweh's fidelity to God's people and sovereignty over all of creation.

### The Call for Israel to Remember and Trust in God (Deut 1:1–3:29; see also 6:20-24, 26:5-9; Josh 24:2-13)

The book of Deuteronomy opens with Moses' lengthy summary of God's prior dealings with Israel. The purpose of the summary is to remind Israel of the many times Yahweh has provided for and forgiven the people through their forty-year journey in the wilderness. Moses also emphasizes the disobedience of the people during that journey, setting the stage for what will follow in the narrative: a second giving of the law, so that the Israelites may now truly follow God's ways and live abundantly in the land they have yet to receive. The summary in Josh 24:2-13 lists many examples of God's commitment to and provision for the people, beginning with Abraham, including the exodus and the conquest of the land, leading up to the present moment.

Then Joshua gathered all the tribes of Israel to Shechem, and summoned the elders, the heads, the judges, and the officers of Israel; and they presented themselves before God. And Joshua said to all the people, "Thus says the LORD, the God of Israel: Long ago your ancestors—Terah and his sons Abraham and Nahor—lived beyond the Euphrates and served other gods. Then I took your father Abraham from beyond the River and led him through all the land of Canaan and made his offspring many. I gave him Isaac; and to Isaac I gave Jacob and Esau. I gave Esau the hill country of Seir to possess, but Jacob and his children went down to Egypt. Then I sent Moses and Aaron, and I plagued Egypt with what I did in its midst; and afterwards I brought you out. When I brought your ancestors out of Egypt, you came to the sea; and the Egyptians pursued your ancestors with chariots and horsemen to the Red Sea. When they cried out to the LORD, he put darkness between you and the Egyptians, and made the sea come upon them and cover them; and your eyes saw what I did to Egypt. Afterwards you lived in the wilderness a long time. Then I brought you to the land of the Amorites, who lived on the other side of the Jordan; they fought with you, and I handed them over to you, and you took possession of their land, and I destroyed them before you. Then King Balak son of Zippor of Moab, set out to fight against Israel. He sent and invited Balaam son of Beor to curse you, but I would not listen to Balaam; therefore he blessed you; so I rescued you out of his hand. When you went over the Jordan and came to Jericho, the citizens of Jericho fought against you, and also the Amorites, the Perizzites, the Canaanites, the Hittites, the Girgashites, the Hivites, and the Jebusites; and I handed them over to you. I sent the hornet ahead of you, which drove out before you the two kings of the Amorites; it was not by your sword or by your bow. I gave you a land on which you had not labored, and towns that you had not built, and you live in them; you eat the fruit of vineyards and oliveyards that you did not plant.

The summary concludes with Joshua's exhortation for the people to devote themselves to Yahweh in the ages to follow, including Joshua's stirring testimony, "As for me and my household, we will serve the Lord!" (vv. 14-15).

### Predictions of Unrelenting Disobedience and Destruction (Lev 26:1-46; Deut 28:1-68)

At the conclusion of the two major bodies of legal tradition in the Old Testament, Moses exhorts the people to walk in God's ways by warning them of the potential consequences of their lack of trust. Yet these passages go beyond simple warning and actually predict Israel's unrelenting disobedience and the destruction that would come upon them at the hands of the Assyrians and Babylonians hundreds of years later. Thus, the consequences of Israel's sins at a much later time in their history are seen as fully consistent with the giving of the law and consequences enumerated by Moses. In other words, these distinct and widely separated portions of the story, one recounting the giving of the law as the people prepare for their entrance into the land and the other recounting the people's exit from the land hundreds of years later, are brought together in order to underscore a crucial, perennial issue facing the people of God: whether or not Israel will trust in Yahweh and follow Yahweh's ways.

### The Cycle of Sin, Judgment, and Redemption (Judg 2:11-23)

This concise yet dense passage provides an overview of Israel's history immediately following the conquest, thereby summarizing much of what takes places in the narrative of Judges to follow: the people betray Yahweh, Yahweh judges the people by giving them over to their enemies, the people cry out to God, God relents and raises up judges to deliver them, then the people betray Yahweh again and the cycle begins once more. This summary, however, applies not only to the narrative of Judges but to much of the rest of the Old Testament and reinforces what has already become apparent about Israel from the narrative preceding it, especially those portions that record the wilderness wanderings: the relationship between God and God's people will be a tumultuous one and will continue only because of Yahweh's mercy and steadfast resolve to stick it out with this people.

### The Davidic Covenant and the Building of the Temple
### (2 Sam 7:1-29; 1 Kgs 8:22-53; see also 1 Chr 17:1-15; 22:6-19)

In the narrative of 2 Samuel and its retelling in 1 Chronicles, God promises David that God will establish his dynasty forever. Known as the "Davidic covenant," this promise also included God's pledge for peace and security in the land, and indicated that the temple would be built by David's son, Solomon. Thus, these passages look ahead to the establishment and function of two major institutions in the history of Israel, the significance of which would be difficult to overstate. The Davidic dynasty, and more generally the monarchy, was to be the means by which Yahweh's faithful, providential, and just rule would be mediated and enjoyed by Israel. The temple was to serve as the center of Israel's religious life, housing the sacrifices that would enable Israel to return to Yahweh and the worship that would call Israel into Yahweh's very presence. Although scholars commonly point to tensions between the traditions portraying the Davidic dynasty and those focusing on the temple cult and sacrifice as examples of diversity in the Old Testament, Scripture in its final form gathers these major strands of the tradition and presents them together as *instigated and integrated* in a single act of divine intention, with far-reaching consequences (see 1 Kgs 8:22-53). Even when the Davidic dynasty fails and the temple is destroyed, these gifts of Yahweh's embodiment are not forgotten by the deity or the people. The prophets proclaim that Jerusalem and the temple will be rebuilt, possessing an unparalleled glory (see Isa 52:1-10; 60:1-22; Jer 33:10-11; Ezek 40–47; Hag 2:1-9), and one day a righteous Davidic heir will return to the throne to restore the fortunes of Israel (Isa 11:1-9; Jer 23:5-6; 33:14-22; Ezek 34:23-24; Zech 6:11-12; Hag 2:20-23). Of course, New Testament writers proclaim the renewal and fulfillment of the Davidic covenant in Jesus, and the final book of Scripture concludes with the new Jerusalem descending from heaven and the blessing of unhindered access to God (Rev 21:1-27).

### Prophetic Oracles of Judgment, Destruction, and Restoration (Jer 7:1−8:3; 30:1−31:40, for example)

Oracles such as these, which summarize the people's recent and distant past, predict Israel's/Judah's impending destruction, and announce a coming time of restoration, fill the prophetic books. I offer Jeremiah's temple sermon (7:1−8:3) and "Book of Consolation" (30:1−31:40) as representative examples. The temple sermon rehearses Yahweh's faithfulness to the people and Israel's sins and rejection of Yahweh and Yahweh's prophets throughout the ages; it presents the destruction to come at the hands of the Babylonians as Judah's long-deserved judgment.

> Thus says the LORD of hosts, the God of Israel: Add your burnt offerings to your sacrifices, and eat the flesh. For in the day that I brought your ancestors out of the land of Egypt, I did not speak to them or command them concerning burnt offerings and sacrifices. But this command I gave them, "Obey my voice, and I will be your God, and you shall be my people; and walk only in the way that I command you, so that it may be well with you." Yet they did not obey or incline their ear, but, in the stubbornness of their evil will, they walked in their own counsels, and looked backward rather than forward. From the day that your ancestors came out of the land of Egypt until this day, I have persistently sent all my servants the prophets to them, day after day; yet they did not listen to me, or pay attention, but they stiffened their necks. They did worse than their ancestors did. So you shall speak all these words to them, but they will not listen to you. You shall call to them, but they will not answer you.

Therefore, the days are surely coming, says the Lord, when it will no more be called Topheth, or the valley of the son of Hinnom, but the valley of Slaughter: for they will bury in Topheth until there is no more room. The corpses of this people will be food for the birds of the air, and for the animals of the earth; and no one will frighten them away. And I will bring to an end the sound of mirth and gladness, the voice of the bride and bridegroom in the cities of Judah and in the streets of Jerusalem; for the land shall become a waste. (Jer 7:21-27, 30-34)

The Book of Consolation provides several oracles announcing the restoration God will accomplish among the people: Israel's hurt will be healed, the land will once again be filled with people and abundance, Jerusalem and the temple will be rebuilt. And of chief importance for Jeremiah, the relationship between Yahweh and the people will be restored, and the people will embrace God's ways.

The days are surely coming, says the LORD, when I will make a new covenant with the house of Israel and the house of Judah. It will not be like the covenant that I made with their ancestors when I took them by the hand to bring them out of the land of Egypt—a covenant that they broke, though I was their husband, says the LORD. But this is the covenant that I will make with the house of Israel after those days, says the LORD: I will put my law within them, and I will write it on their hearts; and I will be their God, and they shall be my people. No longer shall they teach one another, or say to each other, "Know the LORD," for they shall all know me, from the least of them to the greatest, says the LORD; for I will forgive their iniquity, and remember their sin no more. (Jer 31:31-34)

These oracles, in concert with other prophetic texts, provide a view of Israel's history that is expansive, reaching out to both the distant past and distant future. As with most portions of the Old Testament that cast wide their purview, the prophetic view of Israel's history revolves around:

1. Yahweh's power, faithful provision, mercy, and steadfast love for Israel as demonstrated throughout their history,

2. Yahweh's gift of instruction so that Israel would walk in God's ways,

3. Israel's unrelenting unfaithfulness, as demonstrated throughout its history, interrupted by only momentary embrace of God and God's ways,

4.  Yahweh's attempt to lead the people back into right relationship through prophetic rebuke, warning, and judgment, finally leading to the last resort of destruction and exile, and

5.  Yahweh's steadfast love and mercy in calling the people back after the judgment of destruction and exile and restoring them.

### Looking Back as Israel Prepares for a New Future (Nehemiah 9)

One of the more notable biblical summaries is that found in Nehemiah 9. The setting for the book is post-exilic Jerusalem when some Jews who had been exiled by the Babylonians returned to rebuild the devastated city and the temple. Framed in the form of a prayer of confession, Ezra begins with the creation of the world and traces the history of Israel through nearly every major event up to the present moment. He laments Israel's unfaithfulness throughout the ages, culminating in the destruction of Jerusalem and the temple and exile. In this one chapter, we find a comprehensive and coherent recitation of nearly the entire Old Testament story, which shares the prophetic vision of God and Israel's history just listed above. The summary also makes a special point of emphasizing God's character as powerful creator and savior (vv. 6, 9-10, 24), faithful to the covenant (vv. 8, 23, 32), and above all else, forgiving, merciful, gracious, slow to anger, and abounding in steadfast love (vv. 16-17, 19, 27, 28, 31, 32).

### The Story as a Source for Praise, Thanksgiving, and Repentance (Pss 78; 105; 106; 135:8-12; 136)

Even though the psalms are hymns and prayers and not narrative, they are intimately connected to and expressive of the story of God's dealings with Israel and all creation. The psalms listed above recall major segments of the history of God's involvement with the people as motivation for the call to believers to praise and thank God or—in the case of Psalm 78—as motivation for repenting and returning to God. Together (and almost completely in Psalms 78 and 106), these summaries reflect the same motifs common to the prophetic texts and Nehemiah 9.

1.  God's faithful provision, mercy, and steadfast love for Israel, as demonstrated throughout their history (see Pss 78:9-21; 105:5-45; 106:6-23; 135:8-12; 136:1-26).

2.  God's gift of instruction so that Israel would walk in God's ways (Pss 78:5-8; 105:45)

3. Israel's unrelenting unfaithfulness, as demonstrated throughout their history, interrupted by only momentary embrace of God and God's ways (Pss 78:9-66; 106:6-39),

4. God's attempt to lead the people back into right relationship through prophetic rebuke, warning, and judgment, finally leading to the last resort of destruction and exile (Pss 78:9-66; 106:13-43), and

5. God's steadfast love and mercy in calling the people back after the judgment of destruction and exile and restoring them (Ps 106:44-47).

## The Kerygmatic Speeches in Acts
### (Acts 2:14-36; 3:12-26; 5:29-32; 10:34-43; see also 1 Cor 15:3-8)

*Kērygma* is a Greek word meaning "proclamation," and in the context of the Christian tradition it refers to the basic, core proclamation of early Christians about Jesus and his significance. The *kērygma*, in other words, is the essential story, or summary, that early Christians proclaimed about Jesus, and we find it represented in concise form in the speeches of Peter in Acts and also in what Paul says he passed on to the Corinthians "as of first importance" in 1 Cor 15:3-8. The *kērygma* also serves as a basic framework for the Gospel narratives, unifying various traditions about Jesus' ministry, death, and resurrection into one story and ensuring a common portrayal of Jesus' significance. Moreover, one of the basic elements of the *kērygma* is that Jesus' life, death, resurrection, and victory over sin and death on behalf of all believers took place in fulfillment of the Scriptures—a fundamental claim throughout the New Testament that inextricably intertwines the story of Jesus with the story of Israel. This element of the *kērygma* is well captured in a portion of Peter's speech from Acts 3:18-26:

> In this way God fulfilled what he had foretold through all the prophets, that his Messiah would suffer. Repent therefore, and turn to God so that your sins may be wiped out, so that times of refreshing may come from the presence of the Lord, and that he may send the Messiah appointed for you, that is, Jesus, who must remain in heaven until the time of universal restoration that God announced long ago through his holy prophets. Moses said, "The Lord your God will raise up for you from your own people a prophet like me. You must listen to whatever he tells you. And it will be that everyone who does not listen to that prophet will be utterly rooted out of the people." And all the prophets, as many as have spoken, from Samuel and those after him, also predicted these days. You are the descendants of the prophets and of the covenant that

God gave to your ancestors, saying to Abraham, "And in your descendants all the families of the earth shall be blessed." When God raised up his servant, he sent him first to you, to bless you by turning each of you from your wicked ways.

### Stephen's Speech and the Faithful Lot of Hebrews 11 (Acts 7:2-50; Heb 11:1-40)

We find another lengthy overview of the biblical story in Acts 7:2-50, which carefully traces the history of Israel from Abraham to Solomon, focusing on Israel's frequent rejection of God's messengers and prophets, and then concludes with Israel's rejection of Jesus. The intent of the summary is to show that the rejection of Jesus is fully consistent with the way in which God's people have responded to God's messengers in the past. The writer of Hebrews composes his well-known listing of the biblical heroes of old who served God "by faith" in order to emphasize the gift of blessing and life that God has now achieved for all believers through Jesus (Heb 11:1-40).

> Therefore, since we are surrounded by so great a cloud of witnesses, let us also lay aside every weight and the sin that clings so closely, and let us run with perseverance the race that is set before us, looking to Jesus the pioneer and perfecter of our faith, who for the sake of the joy that was set before him endured the cross, disregarding its shame, and has taken his seat at the right hand of the throne of God. (Heb 12:1-2)

### The Degradation of Humanity Overcome by Christ (Rom 1:18–3:20)

In the opening section of his letter to the Romans, Paul offers a lengthy account of humanity's fall into depravity. He describes how since the beginning of creation humankind has failed to honor God and walk in God's ways, leading him to the proclamation that both Jews and Gentiles are under the power of sin and that the law is powerless to change humanity's plunge toward self-destruction (Rom 3:9-20). Then comes the good news of God's mercy and forgiveness: "since all have sinned and fall short of the glory of God, they are now justified by his grace as a gift, through the redemption that is in Christ Jesus" (Rom 3:23-24). Paul joins with the other New Testament writers in casting wide their purview and proclaiming that God's age-old attempt to reclaim humanity has now come to fruition in the life, death, resurrection, and ongoing ministry of Jesus.

I hope that this brief perusal of biblical summaries provides a helpful illustration of what most readers of Scripture simply take for granted. Such summaries demonstrate that the biblical writers and the editors compiling the sacred traditions of the Old and New Testaments understood these traditions to be part of, and contributing to, the telling of a larger story about God and God's will for Israel and all of humanity. They help us to see that *the major elements of the biblical traditions are not presented in isolation from one another, but are expressly and repeatedly integrated into a largely consistent testimony to God's character and the history of humanity's relationship with God.*

### An Allusive, Not Elusive, Unity

A second feature of the biblical traditions that consistently gathers their various elements into a unified whole is the highly "allusive" nature of those traditions. The sacred traditions we encounter in Scripture are constantly referencing, or alluding to, key moments or developments in the history of the relationship between God and the people. In addition to the explicit and oftentimes lengthy summaries, briefer allusions both subtle and apparent within Old Testament narrative to other portions of Scripture abound. Allusions are especially prevalent in the psalms and prophets. The psalms frequently point to particular events, such as the exodus from Egypt, God's provision in the wilderness, the gift of God's torah, God's defeat of Israel's enemies (including specific battles), as those that inspire Israel to express thanksgiving and praise or to hope in Yahweh's continuing care. The prophetic writings also repeatedly reference events in the history of Israel's relationship with Yahweh in order to demonstrate Yahweh's justice and steadfast love (for example, Mic 6:3-5) and to interpret the significance of events that have taken place or are yet to come (see the use of exodus motifs in Isa 40:3-5). The image suggested by these bountiful allusions is the prophets and psalms—along with nearly all of the Old Testament works—weaving a tapestry of connections between various Old Testament traditions and presenting them as one integrated piece. To see this "intertextual connectedness" as simply resulting from the selective, isolated use of disparate sacred traditions by individual oracles or psalms (as some scholars do) is to narrow unnecessarily one's purview and to fail to take into account the cumulative witness of these connections as we move from psalm to psalm or oracle to oracle. As stated well by Luke Timothy Johnson,

> the world that Scripture produces (imagines) is not simply a haphazard collection of compositions written by various authors speaking from and for diverse communities over a period of centuries, but is also a complex network of literary interconnections established by the use and reuse of symbols that gain depth and richness by means of intricate and subtle allusion. Attention to these interconnections is justified, therefore, because together they create a world of metaphoric

structures within which humans can live in a distinctive manner, "worthy of God."[5]

Along with the summaries, the frequent and wide-ranging allusions found in the writings of the psalmists and the prophets indicate that the history of the relationship between God and Israel serves as the conceptual backdrop, or worldview, that guides their own expressions of praise, lament, rebuke, anguish, celebration, and pronouncements of doom or restoration. These and other biblical writers were, in essence, story-claimants and story-tellers, not simply scavengers of sacred trivia.

As we have already discussed in earlier chapters, the New Testament writings repeatedly and in manifold fashion also allude with great frequency to the Old Testament traditions in their portrayal of Jesus and his significance. Many allusions are subtle, containing simply a phrase or an echo of an Old Testament text; others are much more obvious, such as when authors tell us that a particular Old Testament passage has been fulfilled. By way of example, let us take a brief look at the manner in which each of the Evangelists begins his Gospel by connecting the story of Jesus with the Old Testament traditions (see chapter 4 for Paul's shaping of Old Testament tradition). The Gospel of Mark opens with "The beginning of the good news of Jesus Christ the Son of God, as written in the prophet Isaiah." A conflated citation of Mal 3:1 and Isa 40:3 then immediately follows to substantiate the prophetic fulfillment taking place in Jesus. The prologue of the Gospel (Mark 1:1-15) concludes with Jesus' proclamation, "The time is fulfilled, the kingdom of God has come near; repent, and believe in the good news" (v. 15), further signaling that the prophetic promises of restoration are now coming to pass. Matthew begins his Gospel with a genealogy (Matt 1:1-17). What appears on the surface to be a simple listing of descendants is actually dense with theological import. One of the several lessons the genealogy is composed to convey is the ancestral connection not only between Jesus and David (the messiah was to be of the house of David) but also between Jesus and Abraham. Along with Matthew's division of Israel's history into three epochs in v. 17 (from Abraham to David, from David to the Babylonian exile, from the exile to Jesus), the genealogy presents Jesus in connection with the whole history of Israel. In concert with numerous oracles of fulfillment throughout his infancy narrative (see 1:22-23; 2:5-6, 15, 17-18), Matthew proclaims Jesus as the culmination of that history.

The writer of Luke, more subtly but no less effectively, also opens his Gospel by making it clear that the story of Jesus is the continuation of what has come before. In his highly stylized prologue (Luke 1:1-4), the Gospel writer tips his hand about the significance of the events he is about to portray: they are the matters that have been "fulfilled among us" (v. 1). Then Luke goes on, beginning in v. 5, to tell us about the circumstances surrounding the births of John and Jesus. Since most readers of the Bible are not familiar with Greek, they are likely unaware of the fact that, with v. 5 and continuing through the infancy narrative, Luke switches to a literary style that would have reminded his readers of "biblical" Greek, the distinctive style of the language employed by Greek translations of the Hebrew Scriptures (as an analogy, think of these stories as being written in "King James English"). In this way, Luke signals to his readers that what he is setting out to record is nothing less than the continuation of the Old Testament story, as if this were its next chapter. In the stories that follow, Luke further cements this connection by having character after character come forth to proclaim the births of John and Jesus in songs and proclamations laden with Old Testament imagery and prophetic hopes for deliverance (Luke 1:47-55, 68-79; 2:10-14, 29-35), as in these words from Zechariah's canticle:

> Blessed be the Lord God of Israel,
>> for he has looked favorably on his people and redeemed them.
> He has raised up a mighty savior for us
>> in the house of his servant David,
> as he spoke through the mouth of his holy prophets from of old,
>> that we would be saved from our enemies and from the hand of all
>> who hate us.
> Thus he has shown the mercy promised to our ancestors,
>> and has remembered his holy covenant,
> the oath that he swore to our ancestor Abraham,
>> to grant us that we, being rescued from the hands of our enemies,
> might serve him without fear, in holiness and righteousness
>> before him all our days. (Luke 1:68-73)

In his own version of Jesus' genealogy in Luke 3, the evangelist traces Jesus' lineage back not only to Abraham but to Adam. From beginning to end, Luke makes it clear that the whole of the biblical story is in view, and all of it is fulfilled as God promised:

> Then he said to them, "These are my words that I spoke to you while I was still with you—that everything written about me in the law of Moses, the prophets, and the psalms must be fulfilled." Then he opened their minds to understand the scriptures, and he said to them, "Thus it is written, that the Messiah is to suffer and to rise from the dead on the third day, and that repentance and forgiveness of sins is to be

proclaimed in his name to all nations, beginning from Jerusalem. You are witnesses of these things. . . ." (Luke 24:44-48)

John pushes us back even further, calling us to see Jesus alongside of God, and as God, prior to the creation of the world (John 1:1-4):

In the beginning was the Word, and the Word was with God, and the Word was God. He was in the beginning with God. All things came into being through him, and without him not one thing came into being. What has come into being in him was life, and the life was the light of all people.

These examples, to which could be added scores of others, show that the Gospel writers begin and shape their stories of Jesus in order to present Jesus as the culmination of what Christians know as the Old Testament story. This leads us to the unavoidable conclusion that both the Evangelists and their readers held the notion that there is a coherent story, or history, which Jesus fulfills and to which the story of Jesus is inseparably connected. With great frequency and in manifold fashion, Scripture calls us to embrace all of its elements as part of one "salvation history," and to see Jesus as its fulfillment.

### Called Together into Canon

One other point should be briefly considered. While source criticism as a subdiscipline of historical criticism has often been employed by scholars to discern the various sources comprising our biblical traditions, and thus is one of those practices of reading used to "pull the text apart," it has also led us to see that Jews and Christians were interested in gathering texts together. The collection of Old Testament traditions in larger complexes is represented in the Pentateuch (Genesis through Deuteronomy), the Deuteronomistic History (Joshua through 2 Kings), the writings often attributed to the "Chronicler" (1 and 2 Chronicles, Ezra through Nehemiah), the Psalter, Proverbs, and each of the prophetic corpuses. These and the broader designations of Torah, Prophets, and Writings represent the effort and intention of Jews not only to preserve their sacred tradition but to claim some sort of coherence for the writings. On a grander scale, we see these same claims for coherence manifested in the formation of the Jewish Scriptures and later the Christian canon itself, in which the traditions emerging from the opening centuries of Christianity are joined with the Jewish Scriptures. The very activity of stitching these sacred writings together and regarding them as the holy tradition of God's people constitutes the conviction that together these traditions proclaim what is essential for us to know about God, God's will for humanity, and the history of the relationship between God and creation.

Of course, others are free to dispute the claim that these traditions hold together and present us with a coherent whole. To be sure, scholars will continue to debate whether and to what extent we can find coherence in this body of tradition, which is in many ways discordant. But *the claim for coherence is one made by the collection itself,* persistently set alongside its equally insistent embrace of diversity and dialogue. Remember the river—one filled with countercurrents and obstructions galore, but a river nonetheless, still winding toward its destination. For those attempting the ride, especially those who fixate on the obstructions and have trouble finding the main flow, it is easy to get caught up in a countercurrent, to be upended by a boulder, or to get stuck on a submerged log. Still, the river moves on. It has a story to tell.

## The Biblical Story in Summary

So what is the story that Scripture tells? To be sure, the true test that the Bible presents something like a coherent and unified account of God and the relationship between God and humanity is whether that story itself can be summarized in a manner that meets two criteria: (1) The summary itself presents a largely unified and coherent retelling, and (2) the summary closely parallels the biblical account and seeks to incorporate as many of its various elements as possible—that it isn't simply a forced reworking of hopelessly disjointed elements into a harmonious tale. The remainder of this chapter seeks to fulfill the first of these criteria as it offers a brief overview of the biblical story as a whole. The next chapter examines in greater detail several key story lines emerging from the summary in order to demonstrate that they are a persistent and integral part of the biblical traditions.

At the same time, I need to introduce what follows with a qualification. I do not pretend that the summary of the biblical story I provide below is necessarily the best way the story could be recited. In fact, it is not "The Story" at all, but a paraphrase that is unavoidably reductive and selective as conditioned both by space limitations and various idiosyncrasies affecting my psyche and soul. Still, it is my sincere attempt to offer a retelling that is faithful to the central plotline and core concerns of the biblical story as I understand them. That central plotline is God's undying attempt to redeem humanity through a particular people, Israel, culminating in the life, death, resurrection, and ongoing ministry of Jesus. Its core concern or purpose, as I see it, is to proclaim who God is, what God wills for humanity and all of creation, and what it means to be God's faithful people. I realize that there are many elements of the biblical story that are not presented here, or are given only brief mention. I also realize that others may retell the story slightly or very differently. My hope is that by sharing and comparing our summaries we could help one another to discern more clearly what is most essential to the story we love to tell and long to live.

### Part 1: God Creates a World of Blessing and Gives Humanity a Calling

In the beginning, God speaks into being a wonderful creation, teeming with life and provision. Human beings are part of this creation and are blessed with special capabilities and a special calling as those created in God's image. Human beings are relational creatures, and the "meaning of life" for them is to live in relationship with God, one another, and creation. With God, this is to be a relationship of intimacy, trust, dependence, and partnering in the ordering of a blessed creation. With one another—as illustrated in the first human couple—humanity is to pursue relationships of intimacy, interdependence, respect, and mutuality. With creation, humans are to care for creation so that it continues to fulfill the purpose for which God called it into being: to be a place of beauty, diversity, and abundant blessing for all creatures. In the very early stages of the story, we see God, humanity, and creation together participating in the wondrous blessings of God's new world.

### Part 2: Lack of Trust, Estrangement, and Destruction

Humanity's relationship with God was to be characterized by humanity's intimacy with God, trust in God, and dependence on God. God's command to humanity not to eat from the tree of the knowledge of good and evil is thus to be seen not as an arbitrary test of obedience, but as one that is designed to lead humans more deeply into the blessings God intends for them. But the serpent slithers its way into the Garden and puts before the woman and the man a most enticing temptation; to paraphrase: "Go ahead, eat the forbidden fruit! You won't die! God just wants to keep you stupid. God is hiding things from you! Eat it!" Then the serpent's final words fan the embers of temptation into a flame: "Eat it. And you will know everything God knows. In fact, you will be like God." The woman takes the fruit and eats. The man—standing by her the entire time—follows suit. Suddenly, the intimacy that was to be the foundation of this creation warps into estrangement. The man and the woman discover their nakedness and clothe themselves with shame. When the human pair hears God walking through the garden, they hide in fear. Adam blames his wife (and God) for their sin, and in sharp contrast to what God intended for human couples, Adam will now rule over his wife. Enmity will also curse the relations between the serpent and the children of Adam, representing the alienation that now exists between humanity and all creation. In return, creation becomes a far less abundant place than God intended. Adam will work hard, and the land will produce mostly thistles and thorns. What we see taking place here is the finely woven tapestry of creation beginning to unravel, along with its blessings. The question at hand is, how far will the unraveling go? To the complete destruction of creation? Or can the damage be repaired before it is too late?

Sadly, in the narrative that follows, we learn that humanity falls farther and farther away from God and the blessing God intended. Already in the next chapter of the story, Cain, in a fit of jealousy, murders his brother Abel. Lamech kills another and celebrates the act with a depraved boast (Gen 4:23-24). By chapter 6, we encounter some of the most tragic and heart-wrenching verses in all of Scripture. Things have gotten so bad, and humanity has gone so wrong, that God "was sorry that he had made humankind on the earth, and it grieved him to his heart. So the LORD said, 'I will blot out from the earth the human beings I have created—people together with the animals and creeping things and birds of he air, for I am sorry that I have made them'" (Gen 6:5-7). These opening chapters of Genesis introduce us to a fundamental truth of the biblical story: when we fail to trust in God as the source of blessing, and instead trust in ourselves or anything else as the source of blessing, we begin to tread a path that leads us into disobedience; estrangement from God, one another, and creation; and finally destruction. In essence, it is a path that leads us away from the source of blessing and life. And now, because nearly all of humanity has embraced this path and cast aside its calling as those created in God's image, creation is poised on the brink of annihilation.

### Part 3: God Preserves the Relationship and Seeks to Restore Humanity

Fortunately, there are other fundamental truths at work in the biblical story, and one that is most central is the truth of God's mercy and steadfast love. Yes, God was to bring destruction upon the earth in the form of a flood. "But Noah found favor in the sight of the LORD" (Gen 6:8). For the sake of one righteous man, God spares humanity, and what was supposed to be a story of calamitous judgment now becomes a story of deliverance through the waters and a new beginning for creation. In a covenant with Noah and all of creation, God promises never to bring such destruction on the earth again, indicating God's resolve to stick it out with the creation, come what may. This is good news for the rest of creation, but humanity fails to take advantage of the fresh start God provides. Immediately in Noah's own sons, humanity returns to its sinful ways, sowing consequences of corruption that reach far into the future. With the story of the tower of Babel we get a replay of the Fall. The tower of Babel represents yet another attempt on the part of humanity to be like God and to provide for its own blessing. In response, God confuses their language and scatters humanity about the earth, and the opening chapters of Genesis close on the familiar yet tragic note of pervasive estrangement between God and humanity, and of human beings with one another.

But God does not give up. God embarks on still another plan to reconnect with humanity and give humanity the chance to begin again. He chooses one man and woman, Abraham and Sarah, from whom he is going to birth a nation that will be God's people, Israel. They are to be a people who learn God's ways and enjoy God's tremendous provision. They are to show the rest of the world the abundant blessing that comes from living rightly with God, one another, and creation. This is, in short, what the rest of the biblical story is about. This is its main plotline: God's struggle, through a people that will be God's own, to teach humanity God's ways, to call humanity back to right relationship with God and one another, and to return human beings to the blessing God intended for them from the very beginning.

### Part 4: God and Israel, a Rocky Relationship

The rest of the Old Testament focuses on the history of the relationship between God and God's people, Israel. God's promise to Abraham to make him into a great nation, to protect him, and to give him an abundant land in which to dwell is passed on from generation to generation. We see God's promise to bless and protect Abraham's descendants repeatedly put to the test, and each time God is faithful. Most notably, God delivers Abraham's descendants from a severe famine by bringing them into the land of Egypt (the story of Joseph). Many years later, after the Egyptians had begun to enslave Abraham's descendants, Yahweh delivers them from the Egypt (the exodus story) and is henceforth known to them as Savior: one who has both the power and will to save. Now God continues the task of teaching them what it means to live rightly with God, one another, and creation. God makes a second covenant with Israel that in many ways mirrors the first: they will be God's people, a "treasured possession" out of all the nations of the earth, but also a "holy nation" and a "priestly kingdom"—a nation set apart (holy) to serve as mediators (priests) of God's instruction and blessing to the rest of humanity. They only need to trust God and walk in God's ways. God then gives them the torah, or instruction, beginning with the Ten Commandments. These are not so much laws the Israelites must follow so that they will be *rewarded* with blessing; they are laws that will lead the Israelites, in their time and place, into the kinds of relationships that will be for them a source of blessing. In following these commands, Israel will also bear witness to God and God's ways, and thus become a source of blessing for all the nations of the earth.

Yet the relationship between God and the people is a rocky one. Repeatedly, Israel fails to trust God's provision and instruction in the wilderness. In turn, God repeatedly corrects the wayward children. They return to God for a time, but then soon fall back into faithlessness. They are quick to turn to other gods. They set aside and even forget God's commands. God responds with judgment but also repeatedly forgives them, provides for them, and fulfills the promise to bring them into the promised land. God protects them and calls forth leaders for them, including a king. The temple is built and the divine presence dwells among them. Under the reigns of David and Solomon, God brings them into a period of tremendous prosperity. As those who are abundantly blessed, the Israelites now seem poised to fulfill their vocational calling, to serve as mediators of God's ways and blessings to the other families of the earth.

In the years that follow there are examples of faithful prophets, kings, and individuals. There are moments when the entire people rededicate themselves to God. But such moments are always short-lived. On the whole, the people and their leaders spurn God's ways. Early in the period of the monarchy there are indications that not all will be well. David, the most faithful of Israel's kings, commits adultery with Bathsheba and murders her husband, Uriah. As a consequence, we learn that the sword will ever threaten David's house, from within and without, and David's final words sadly reflect these dire consequences of his actions (1 Kgs 2:5-9). Solomon, whose wisdom is unparalleled, falls into the folly of idolatry and lust for possessions. His policies of enslaving his own people, when carried on by his son Rehoboam, split the nation into two far weaker nations: Israel in the north and Judah in the south. With few exceptions, the subsequent kings of both Israel and Judah are of lamentable character. They and the many priests and leading citizens who follow their example turn to other gods, oppress one another, neglect the poor, and pursue power and wealth above justice and mercy. God repeatedly sends prophets to rebuke them. When the people fail to listen, God threatens them with destruction. Yet the warnings go unheeded, and both nations find themselves on paths leading to annihilation. In 722, the northern kingdom rebels against Assyria and is destroyed. The southern kingdom survives a later Assyrian assault. God gives them time to turn away from their sins and turn back to God. Yet still the words of the prophets and warnings of impending doom go unheeded. And so, in 587 Judah is destroyed by invading armies, and the survivors are carried off into exile. Nearly all that has defined Israel as a people and nation is now gone: land, holy city, temple, king.

### Part 5: God's Promise for a New Beginning, and Waiting . . .

By now, we have come to know this God as a God of new beginnings. So even though destruction comes to God's people as a result of their unrelenting faithlessness, it does not surprise us that from the tattered remains of their relationship, God once again beckons Israel to start anew by returning to God and God's ways. God promises to restore Israel. Through the words of the prophets, God describes to them a future, glorious kingdom, a time of unparalleled intimacy with God that will be matched by their unparalleled faithfulness, and a king who will exceed all others in the righteousness of his rule. Some of the prophets—such as Isaiah—foretell that the coming restoration will also include Gentiles. It must have seemed to some Jews that the promised restoration of Israel was at hand when, under King Cyrus of Persia, the exiles were allowed to return to Judah and rebuild Jerusalem and the temple. But many did not return to rebuild the devastated city, and those who did strayed from God's ways. Life was hard, and other nations still ruled their fate. Yet the prophets continued to speak of a coming time of glory. So God's people continued to wait. Years, decades, centuries went by, and the people waited. It is with this promised hope in view, and God's people waiting for its fulfillment, that the Old Testament's portion of the story ends.

### Part 6: The Promised Fulfilled in Jesus, the Messiah

Central to the New Testament is the claim that God's promised restoration of Israel is accomplished in the life, death, resurrection, and ongoing ministry of Jesus Christ (Messiah). Even more than that, however, the New Testament proclaims that God's attempt to reclaim humanity through God's people Israel—the central plotline of the biblical story—also reaches its completion in Jesus' ministry. Long in coming, God's promise to Abraham that "all nations shall be blessed through you" (Gen 12:3) is now fulfilled in Jesus! It is through Jesus' teachings and example that his followers and generations of believers learn what it means to be God's faithful people, to live in right relationship with God and one another. God accepts Jesus' death on the cross as that final sacrifice, which once and for all proclaims to humanity the depth of God's mercy and forgiveness. Sacrifice is no longer needed in the temple. God's grace and presence in the Spirit are now freely given to all who repent and open their hearts to receiving it, including Gentiles. Jesus' resurrection signals God's defeat of death and announces the good news that Hades is not the end of the relationship between God and humanity. Like Jesus, all people can now be raised to unending blessedness with God and one another. The new kingdom that the prophets proclaimed is not a glorious, earthly Jerusalem rule by a mortal king, but

God's eternal kingdom ruled by Jesus Messiah, who sits on the throne of David forever. While believers await the full manifestation of the kingdom, they are called to make its blessings present among them: living as Jesus' disciples, enjoying life with God, one another, and creation, confronting evil and injustice, and doing all they can to share God's love with all people.

### Part 7: The End and Eternity

This is the part of the story that has yet to be written, but of which the biblical authors offer us a collage of images: the return of Jesus to gather the faithful, the final defeat of all that threatens humanity's relationship with God, vindication of the righteous and judgment of the wicked, eternal life with God and one another. Few state this vision of blessing as eloquently as the writer of Revelation:

> And I heard a loud voice from the throne saying,
>   *"See, the home of God is among mortals.*
>   *He will dwell with them;*
>   *they will be his peoples,*
>   *and God himself will be with them;*
>   *he will wipe every tear from their eyes.*
>   *Death will be no more;*
>   *mourning and crying and pain will be no more,*
>   *for the first things have passed away."* (Rev 21:3-4)

> Then the angel showed me the river of the water of life, bright as crystal, flowing from the throne of God and of the Lamb through the middle of the street of the city. On either side of the river is the tree of life with its twelve kinds of fruit, producing its fruit each month; and the leaves of the tree are for the healing of the nations. Nothing accursed will be found there any more. But the throne of God and of the Lamb will be in it, and his servants will worship him; they will see his face, and his name will be on their foreheads. And there will be no more night; they need no light of lamp or sun, for the Lord God will be their light, and they will reign forever and ever. (Rev 22:1-5)

Now, at last, humanity embraces the blessings God intended for them from the very beginning.

## Implications: Called to Live into the One Story

The goal of this book has been to elucidate the ways in which Scripture itself invites us to engage and reflect on the sacred traditions of Christian faith. Up to the present chapter, we have focused on the dialogical character of Scripture shaped in large measure by the diversity and dynamic tension between its various elements. In contrast, the goal of this chapter and of the one to follow is to show how Scripture also invites its readers to see its traditions as together composing one grand narrative, or sacred story. Moreover, a second tendency we discern from the frequent appearance of biblical summaries and Scripture's chronically allusive character is the practice of viewing any one moment of Israel's or the early church's history as part of this larger story of faith. The larger story, in other words, provides for the biblical writers the conceptual (narrative) framework for faithfully understanding and portraying any event or development within the history of God's people *and within their own lives.* The impression conveyed is of a people who—when at their most faithful—mold their understanding of life, purpose, and circumstance around the abiding features of the sacred story they recite and call their own.

If we embrace the tendencies of the biblical writers' engagement with sacred tradition as a normative guide for our own engagement with Scripture, then as previous chapters have shown, we must celebrate and honor the diversity that characterizes the biblical traditions and our reading them. At the same time, the diverse and dynamic tendencies evident in Scripture are to be held in tension with the Bible's often implicit yet always persistent claim that there is also an overarching story of faith that discloses consistent features of the character of God, God's will for creation, and God's undying attempt to lead a wayward creation back to blessing. *There is, in essence, a defining view of the world, or worldview, within which Scripture invites believers to gather their lives and around which believers are called to shape their conversation.*

Of course, the process of discerning the essential contours of that story and how it is to shape our view of the world is a matter of ongoing dialogue among and within communities of faith. But at the very least, those of us who view Scripture as foundational for the Christian theological tradition are called by Scripture to make the story it proclaims constitutive of our identity, our purpose, *and* our conversation as individuals and as communities of faith. Rooted in that place of unity, we can then celebrate our shared commitment to the one God and Savior Scripture proclaims and be well equipped to follow the good king Josiah and many other ancestors in the faithful yet difficult work of discerning what it means to serve this God and to live into our story in our time and place.

# Deep
# Harmony

*". . . the sacred writings that are able to instruct you for salvation . . ." (2 Tim 3:15)*

**This chapter joins with the previous one in** attempting to define the essential contours of the story Scripture tells. As I stated in the preceding chapter, I believe the central plotline of the biblical story is God's undying attempt to reclaim a wayward humanity through a particular people, Israel, and to restore to humanity the blessing God intended for them from the very beginning. Revolving around this central plot and interweaving throughout the narrative are numerous other story lines that contribute significantly to the biblical story's depth and unity. Drawing from the persistent elements found in the biblical summaries we reviewed in the previous chapter and many other scriptural traditions, the following survey identifies and examines in more detail five story lines that help tell the story of God and God's mission to restore humanity. It aims to fill out and affirm the overview of the biblical story provided in the previous chapter by demonstrating both the prevalence and the coherence of these motifs throughout the biblical traditions.

## 1. God Desires Abundant Life for God's Creatures

The opening chapters of Scripture do more than provide accounts of God's creation of the world (Genesis 1–2). They also disclose God's intentions for this world. From the character of the world God fashions and the commands God gives to its creatures we learn that God desires abundant life for creation. The account in Genesis 1 shows a creation that was thoughtfully composed, plotted out in deliberate fashion. The cadence of movement from one day to the next and the careful ordering of God's creative acts convey God's intentional designs. The realms of sky, sea, and a vegetation-laden land are first constructed (Gen 1:6-19). Then with measured symmetry, God calls into being entities to inhabit these three realms: heavenly bodies (including the sun and moon) to dwell in the sky and rule the night and day and birds to fly across the dome of the sky; sea creatures to swarm within the waters; and all manner of terrestrial creeping things, including humans, to inhabit the earth (vv. 20-30).

If we were forced to limit our description of God's creative acts to one phrase, "abundant provision" may be the best choice. All creatures are given a realm in which to dwell that is well suited to their kind. With obtrusive redundance, the biblical author emphasizes that God has populated the earth with a tremendous diversity of creatures (vv. 24-25, emphasis added; see also vv. 20-21):

> And God said, "Let the earth bring forth living creatures of *every kind*: cattle and creeping things and wild animals of the earth of *every kind*." And it was so. God made the wild animals of the earth of *every kind*, and the cattle of *every kind*, and *everything* that creeps upon the ground of *every kind*. And God saw that it was good.

Note too the expansive inclusiveness of God's provision: all creatures are provided with the sustenance they need (vv. 29-30).

> God said, "See, I have given you every plant yielding seed that is upon the face of all the earth, and every tree with seed in its fruit; you shall have them for food. And to every beast of the earth, and to every bird of the air, and to everything that creeps on the earth, everything that has the breath of life, I have given every green plant for food."

The divine design for such diversity and abundance also finds expression in God's call for the creatures to be "fruitful and multiply." This primal blessing is given not only to humanity (v. 28) but first also to other creatures (v. 22).

In sum, God wants creatures to be blessed, to have life and to have it abundantly. This, in essence, is the "good" that God celebrates throughout the process of calling creation into being (vv. 4, 10, 18, 25, 31). It is also the good that humanity is to nurture and ensure as those given the charge of dominion, or "lordship" over the earth (vv. 26-28).

The proclamation of God's desire for creation to have life and have it abundantly extends beyond the creation stories and courses through the biblical story. This primal blessing is given once again to Noah and his sons, the remnant of humanity delivered through the flood (Gen 9:1, 7). God's promise never to bring such destruction upon the earth again is given not only to humankind but to creation as well. Even though, in the wake of the Fall, enmity will continue to plague humanity's relationship with creation (9:2-8), creation itself will benefit from God's attempt to reclaim the world and bring it back to a state of abundant blessing (9:9-17).

The blessing of God's abundant care is spoken also to Abram at that pivotal moment in the biblical story when God calls out a particular people to be God's own (Gen 12:1-3; see also 15:1-6; 17:1-8). Note the repeated use of "bless"/"blessing," a word choice surely meant to link God's promise to Abram with the manifold blessing God bestowed on creation in Genesis 1-2.

> Now the LORD said to Abram, "Go from your country and your kindred and your father's house to the land that I will show you. I will make of you a great nation, and I will bless you, and make your name great, so that you will be a blessing. I will bless those who bless you, and the one who curses you I will curse; and in you all the families of the earth shall be blessed." (Gen 12:1-3)

As we noted in the preceding chapter, God's covenant with Abram includes the promise of land, numerous descendants ("great nation"), and protection from enemies. More specific details about the covenant blessings and responsibilities (and the change of Abram's and Sarai's names to "Abraham" and "Sarah") are spelled out in subsequent expressions of the covenant (Gen 15:1-6; 17:1-22; 18:1-15), including the miraculous birth of a son. This covenant of blessing is then passed on from generation to generation of Abraham's descendants (Gen 26:1-5, 23-24 [Isaac]; 28:10-17; 35:9-15 [Jacob]; 48:1-21 [Joseph and sons]). The genealogies throughout Genesis also function in part to affirm that God's promise of numerous descendants is being realized (Gen 11:10-26; 29:21–30:24; 36:1-43), as do references to Israel's fecundity throughout the Pentateuch, which echo the creational command to be fruitful and multiply (see Exod 1:9, 12, 20; Lev 26:8; Deut 6:3; 7:13; 13:17).

The story of the exodus revolves around Pharaoh's attempt to thwart the fulfillment of Yahweh's creational command for Israel. The story begins with the statement, "the Israelites were fruitful and prolific; they multiplied and grew exceedingly strong, so that the land was filled with them (Exod 1:7). As put well by Terence Fretheim,

> The point here is that God's intentions in creation are being realized in this family; what is happening is in tune with God's creational purposes. This is a microcosmic fulfillment of God's macrocosmic design for the world.[1]

On this score, Pharaoh emerges "not simply as a historical figure, but as a symbol for the anticreation forces of death which take on the God of life. . . . This is a life and death struggle in which the future of creation is at stake."[2] Yahweh's victory over Pharaoh stands as a paradigmatic proclamation of Yahweh's power over the forces of anticreation, and Yahweh's solidarity with both Israel and the world Yahweh yearns to once again call into being. Accordingly, the blessing of abundant provision is also framed in the description of the promised land as "flowing with milk and honey" (see Exod 3:8; 13:5; 33:3; Lev 20:24; Num 13:27; 16:14; Deut 6:3; 8:8; 26:15).

When the prophets look ahead to the deliverance of God's people from exile, their visions of the restored, abundant land echo the imagery of the creation stories (see Isa 32:15; Jer 31:10-14; 33:10-13), and other oracles promise abundant offspring (see Isa 44:3-4; Jer 23:3; Ezek 36:11). Ezekiel even goes so far as to describe the renewed land as "like the garden of Eden" (Ezek 36:33-36).

> Thus says the Lord God: On the day that I cleanse you from all your iniquities, I will cause the towns to be inhabited, and the waste places shall be rebuilt. The land that was desolate shall be tilled, instead of being the desolation that it was in the sight of all who passed by. And they will say, "This land that was desolate has become like the garden of Eden; and the waste and desolate and ruined towns are now inhabited and fortified." Then the nations that are left all around you shall know that I, the Lord, have rebuilt the ruined places, and replanted that which was desolate; I, the Lord, have spoken, and I will do it.

But God's blessing is not for Israel alone. From the very beginning, Abram's descendants, Israel, were constituted and blessed by God in order that through them God might bring blessing back to all of humanity: ". . . and in you all the families of the earth shall be blessed" (Gen 12:3; see also 18:18; 22:18). Instances of others blessed through Israel pepper the Old Testament. The Joseph story is one clear example, as Egypt and much of the Mediterranean world are spared from a seven-year drought as a result of Joseph's wise counsel and his ability to interpret dreams (Genesis 37–50). Non-Israelites are among those delivered from Egypt, and they take part in God's provision for the Israelites (see Exod 12:38; Lev 19:10, 33-34; 23:22; Deut 24:17-21). Moreover, the inclusion of non-Israelites in God's awaited restoration following the destruction of Jerusalem and the exile is celebrated in several prophetic oracles of salvation (see Isa 9:24-25; 56:1-8; Mic 4:1-3). For example, Isaiah proclaims:

*In days to come*
    *the mountain of the Lord's house*
*shall be established as the highest of the mountains,*
    *and shall be raised above the hills;*
*all the nations shall stream to it.*
    *Many peoples shall come and say,*
*"Come, let us go up to the mountain of the Lord,*
    *to the house of the God of Jacob;*
*that he may teach us his ways*
    *and that we may walk in his paths."*
*For out of Zion shall go forth instruction,*
    *and the word of the LORD from Jerusalem.*
*He shall judge between the nations,*
    *and shall arbitrate for many peoples;*
*they shall beat their swords into plowshares,*
    *and their spears into pruning hooks;*
*nation shall not lift up sword against nation,*
    *neither shall they learn war any more.* (Isa 2:2-4)

And Yahweh announces,

*"It is too light a thing that you should be my servant*
    *to raise up the tribes of Jacob*
    *and to restore the survivors of Israel;*
*I will give you as a light to the nations,*
    *that my salvation may reach to the end of the earth."* (Isa 49:6)

Such oracles served as a precedent for Jesus' own dispensing of blessing to Israelite and non-Israelite alike. Jesus performs miraculous healings and exorcisms on behalf of Gentiles (see Mark 5:1-20; 7:24-30; Matt 8:5-13), and sends out his disciples to proclaim the forgiveness of sins to all nations (see Mark 13:10; Luke 24:47-49; Matt 28:16-20; Acts 1:8). According to Paul, God's gift of restoration even extends beyond humanity to include creation. Even though some segments of Christian tradition envision the destruction of the current world order and the creation of a new world in which the righteous will dwell with God and one another, Paul speaks of creation yearning for redemption along with humanity: "creation itself will be set free from its bondage to decay and will obtain the freedom of the glory of the children of God" (Rom 8:21). The entire creation will be returned to a state of abundant blessing.

## 2. God Calls Humanity to Live in Right Relationship with God, One Another, and Creation

The Hebrew word *torah* is often rendered by our English translations of the Bible as "law." As such, it serves as a designation for several parts of the biblical tradition: (1) the "law"—the commands and statutes we find in the Old Testament, (2) the "law of Moses"—the Pentateuch (the first five books of the Old Testament), or (3) "law and prophets"—a phrase denoting the Old Testament as a whole. Another way of rendering *torah* promoted by a number of scholars is to translate it not as "law" but as "instruction." I prefer this as well. It better fits the narrative character of the first five books of the Old Testament, since most of the Pentateuch is comprised not of laws but of stories that are meant *to instruct* the faithful on the character of God, God's will for humanity, and what it means to be God's people. The term *instruction* also better conveys what God is up to when presenting statutes and commands to the people. For the statutes and commands God provides to Israel are not presented as ends in and of themselves. Rather, in the larger context of the biblical story, they are meant to lead Israel more deeply into the relationships God intends for humanity from the very beginning. They are meant to be instructive, pointing to a way of relating that, as we saw in chapter 3, ultimately transcends the laws themselves.

I think it is because Christians often fail to recognize the instructive purpose of God's commands that they tend to have a rather negative view of the laws and statutes found in the Old Testament traditions. To be sure, several of the laws we find in Exodus, Leviticus, Numbers, and Deuteronomy may strike us as rather arbitrary, odd, or even outrageous, such as forbidding the wearing of garments made from two different types of cloth (Lev 19:19) or guidelines for selling a daughter into slavery (Exod 21:7). Others regarding the practice of the sacrificial cult and purity restrictions may seem to us rather primitive, or at least as belonging to a bygone era. Walter Brueggemann, however, cautions against an easy dismissal of these laws. The concern for purity and order reflected in these statutes reflects a profound concern in the ancient world with the threat posed by impurity and disorder, fears exacerbated by the fragility of health and life, fears that we still hold in varying forms today.

> The remarkable thing about this trajectory of command is that the God of Sinai graciously attends to this enterprise and sanctions procedures, practices [such as sacrificial laws] and agents [the priesthood] by which an ordered, reliable, livable life is maintained and guaranteed. It will not do for us to regard this tradition of purity as primitive

and therefore obsolete, for the issues are still with us, even when we gather them around different sorts of threats.[3]

Understood in this context, laws such as these can be seen as helping Israel order their lives in ways that enable them to take hold of the abundant life Yahweh intends for them in their time and place. Moreover, the laws constituting the sacrificial cult and purity codes have a revelatory and relational dimension to them as well: "The sacrificial system of ancient Israel attests both to the generous availability of Yawheh to Israel and the ominous, unapproachable holiness of Yahweh."[4] Provided after the incident of the golden calf, the sacrificial laws both instruct Israel on the availability of Yahweh's forgiveness and also provide a concrete, sacramental ritual by which those who are truly repentant can be assured of Yahweh's grace. Yet the intimacy implied in Yahweh's mercy is not to detract from God's "otherness" and "holiness," elements safeguarded by the sacrificial laws circumscribing the priestly office, governing sacrificial offerings and implements, and restricting access to the realms of the temple in which Yahweh's presence dwells.

Moreover, there are parts of the Old Testament that, when taken out of context, suggest to some readers that God is interested only in enforcing a legalistic system of punishment and reward: obey me and you live; disobey me and you die (such as Deuteronomy 30). But as a whole, and when held against the backdrop of (1) the creation stories, (2) God's covenant relationship with Israel, and (3) God's ongoing attempt to reclaim humanity, God's laws do not present themselves as arbitrary tests of obedience. Instead, they are graciously given to help the Israelites discover, in their time a place, what it means to live in right relationship with God, one another, and creation. The laws are meant to help humans rediscover, in essence, what it means to live the blessed existence God intended for them from the very beginning.

### God's Instruction in the Creation Stories

We have already noted that in the first creation story humanity is created in the "image of God" (Gen 1:26-28). Over the centuries theologians have argued that God's image is reflected in certain capabilities humans possess, such as self-awareness, reason, communication, love. More recently, other theologians have stressed that our creation in God's image not only implies particular abilities but also a particular calling. Not only are we created *in God's image*, we are also called *to image God*, by virtue of how we live.[5] Genesis 1:26-28 offers us a first glimpse of this calling: we are called to have dominion, to rule, and subdue creation.

Then God said, "Let us make humankind in our image, according to our likeness; and let them have dominion over the fish of the sea, and over the birds of the air, and over the cattle, and over all the wild animals of the earth, and over every creeping thing that creeps upon the earth."

*So God created humankind in his image,*
*in the image of God he created them;*
*male and female he created them.*

God blessed them, and God said to them, "Be fruitful and multiply, and fill the earth and subdue it; and have dominion over the fish of the sea and over the birds of the air and over every living thing that moves upon the earth."

Much of our recent past is filled with painful examples of Christians taking these verses out of context and viewing them as a license to abuse creation. In the context of the creation stories, the call to have dominion over creation, *as those created in God's image*, can only mean to rule in a manner that enacts the divine will for all of creation. In this sense, dominion means *to rule as God would rule*. Since God's will in the creation stories is clearly for the diverse creation to have life and have it abundantly, this entails that humans are to order creation in a way that will sustain the blessing God intends for it. This is an essential dimension of our calling to live in God's image. We are, in essence, called to be caretakers of creation and not, as we have so often been since the Industrial Revolution, its undertakers.

The second creation story (Genesis 2) fills out additional dimensions of our calling to live in the image of God. This narrative celebrates the relationships into which God calls humanity, emphasizing humankind's relational nature. In Genesis 2, God's first creative act is to fashion humanity into existence (v. 7). Here we find a picture of God intimately engaged in the creative process. Down on hands and knees, God forms humanity out of the soil of the earth, and breathes God's very breath into this "earth creature" ("Adam" in Hebrew means "one from the ground/earth"). God then immediately fashions a garden of abundant provision and places Adam in its midst. Adam is given two charges. The first is to take care of the garden, to "till and keep it." This primeval charge reinforces what the context of the first creation story also makes clear: humanity's calling to be caretakers of creation's abundant blessing. But another charge follows: "You may freely eat of every tree of the garden, but of the tree of the knowledge of good and evil you shall not eat, for in the day that you eat of it you shall die" (Gen 2:16-17).

For millennia, readers of Scripture have debated the significance of "the tree of the knowledge of good and evil" and God's prohibition not to eat from it. Perhaps the writer's reference to the tree draws from some cultural element that has long been lost to us. Or perhaps it symbolizes the experiential knowledge of evil and lost good that comes when we choose not to trust in God's provision. This would make sense in light of the story of the Fall to follow. But whatever its particular significance, the tree, God's command not to eat from it, and the disastrous consequences that will commence if humanity disobeys make it clear that humanity's relationship with God is to be one in which humans recognize their dependence on God and trust God's instruction. Humanity's very existence depends on it.

There is, however, another dimension to humanity's relationship with God, and here we begin to get a fuller sense of God's care for humanity and the significance of this relationship for the rest of creation. God is concerned about the earth creature: "It is not good that the man should be alone. I will make him a helper as his partner" (Gen 2:18). In the process of searching for the appropriate partner for Adam, God fashions "every animal of the field and every bird of the air" (v. 19a). But Adam was not to stand idly by. He is called by God to take part in ordering creation: God brought the creatures to Adam "to see what he would call them, and whatever the man called every living creature, that was its name" (v. 19b). God's concern for Adam's well-being and contentment and God's involvement of Adam in the ordering of creation help to fill out our understanding of the relationship God intends between the divine and the human. The picture of God and humanity that emerges here is one of intimate partnership. God creates the garden, and Adam takes care of it. God forms the animals, and Adam provides them with an identity, thereby shaping their essence. Together God and Adam enact the divine life-giving will for creation. For humans, it is a blessed existence: to be creatures who are richly provided for and also to be those who provide richly for others. Humans are called to be receivers and givers of tremendous blessing. What a wondrous calling! But it is also an awesome responsibility, and it all hinges on humanity's trust in God.

In addition to humanity's relationship with God and the rest of creation, the story in Genesis 2 speaks to the nature of the relationships God intends among human beings. The search for an appropriate partner for Adam among the other creatures of the earth is not successful, and more drastic measures are taken. God performs creation's first surgery and fashions another earth creature from one of Adam's ribs (vv. 21-25).

> So the LORD God caused a deep sleep to fall upon the man, and he slept; then he took one of his ribs and closed up its place with flesh. And the rib that the LORD God had taken from the man he made into a woman and brought her to the man. Then the man said,

*"This at last is bone of my bones*
*and flesh of my flesh;*
*this one shall be called Woman,*
*for out of Man this one was taken."*

Therefore a man leaves his father and his mother and clings to his wife, and they become one flesh. And the man and his wife were both naked, and were not ashamed.

Throughout much of Judeo-Christian history, interpreters operating within a paradigm of patriarchy have exaggerated or misunderstood certain features of this text and neglected others. The designation of the woman as "helper" and the derivative nature of her origin (from man) have been and continue to be cited by readers in support of their views that woman, by nature, is to be subordinate to man. However, the Hebrew word commonly translated here as "helper" (*ezer*), is not used of a subordinate when it appears in the Old Testament, but of one who has the power to offer assistance. In fact, both verbal and noun forms of the word are most often used throughout the Old Testament in reference to God (for example, Gen 49:25; Exod 18:4; Deut 33:7, 29; Ps 10:14). Moreover, the derivative nature of the woman is not held up by the text as an indication of the woman's inferior stature. On the contrary! What Adam celebrates when the woman is brought to him is the *sameness* of their substance: "This *at last* [unlike the other creatures] is *bone of my bone and flesh of my flesh*; this one shall be called Woman [*ishah*], for out of Man [*ish*] she was taken" (v. 23). The concluding verses of the story reinforce the mutuality of their natures: "Therefore, a man leaves his father and mother and clings to his wife, and *they become one flesh*" (v. 24, emphasis added). The picture of human relations that emerges here, with the first human couple as a model, is that of intimacy, mutuality, and interdependence.

Thus, in the ideal world of the creation stories, we find that God's will for human beings, as relational creatures, is to image God and God's ways. Humanity is called to embrace God as Sovereign Provider, to trust God's guidance, and take up its commission to partner with God in ordering creation. Human beings are called to live in intimate, interdependent mutuality with one another, cherishing one another. Humanity is also called to serve the created world, so that it may be a place of blessed abundance for all of humanity and all of God's creatures. Basic to our existence, basic to our blessedness, is this call to right relationship with God, one another, and creation.

### God's Instruction for Covenant and Vocation

The creation stories provide the essential context for understanding the purpose of God's instruction throughout the biblical story: this instruction, or torah, defines and leads us more deeply into the relationships that are the source of God's blessing. For this reason, God's instruction is also central to Israel's call to serve as a source of blessing for others. In Exodus 19, we find the Israelites recently delivered from Egypt and now encamped at the foot of Mount Sinai. God speaks a new covenant to Moses that takes up the elements of God's covenant with Abraham and recasts them in light of this new stage in their history as God's people. God embraces the Hebrews as a "treasured possession" out of all the peoples of the earth (Exod 19:5), and calls them to be a "priestly kingdom" and "holy nation" (Exod 19:6). They are to be a nation set apart (holy) as a kingdom of priests: those who mediate God's will and ways to the rest of humanity. In so doing, they will fulfill God's earlier promises that "all nations will be blessed through you" (Gen 12:3). But in order for Israel to fulfill its vocation as a nation of priests, it must first embrace God's instruction: "If you obey my voice and keep my covenant, you shall be my treasured possession . . . a priestly kingdom and a holy nation" (Exod 19:5-6). It is only when Israel learns and embraces what it means to live in God's blessedness that it can be a source of blessing for others.

That the biblical laws are designed to teach these ways of right relatedness is reflected in the first major body of instruction that we encounter in the Old Testament: Exodus 20–23. The Ten Commandments, or Decalogue, which open this body of instruction, address what it means to live rightly with God and one another. The first four commands offer instruction on entrusting oneself to God as Sovereign Provider: recognize Yahweh alone as Savior and Lord; trust God alone (not idols) as the source of blessing; invoke my name alone, and not in concert with the names of other gods (see Exod 23:13); remember the Sabbath as a testimony to my work and will as Creator of all. The next six commands counter activities that destroy human community: honor father and mother; do not murder; do not commit adultery; do not steal; do not bear false witness, do not covet. The Decalogue appears again at the beginning of the restatement of these laws in Deuteronomy (Deut 5:6-21). Here at the forefront of God's instruction are laws that make explicit God's concern to guide human beings in living rightly with God and one another. As the basic principles of the Decalogue are worked out in the remainder of the law, we find that alongside the laws on purity and sacrifice are numerous commands calling for a social order that prioritizes justice. This concern dominates the "Book of the Covenant" (Exod 20:22–23:33), and laws ordering just social practice are interspersed throughout Deuteronomy (23:15-16, 19-20; 24:7, 10-13, 14-15, 17-18, 21-22; 25:1-3). Accordingly, Moses emphasizes:

You must not distort justice; you must not show partiality; and you must not accept bribes, for a bribe blinds the eyes of the wise and subverts the cause of those who are in the right. Justice, and only justice, you shall pursue, so that you may live and occupy the land that the LORD your God is giving you. (Deut 16:19-20)

Yahweh also provides laws for the proper treatment of creation so that under humanity's stewardship it continues to be a source of blessing. Domesticated animals are to receive care and protection (see Exod 23:4-5). The land is to lie fallow every seven years so that it may rest; whatever produce reseeds itself and grows during the Sabbath year is to be left for the poor and wild animals (see Exod 23:10-11). The Sabbath rest is for the Israelite, slave, animal, and resident alien alike (see Exod 23:12).

The dual concern for right relatedness with God and pursuing justice in relationship with others characterizes the warnings of the prophets. The prophetic texts rail against the Israelites for forsaking both Yahweh and Yahweh's ways, for both idolatry and mistreatment of one another. The prophetic catalogue of Israel's sins is lengthy and diverse, but repeated attention is given to the greed of the powerful and the injustice of scarcity that results (see Isa 1:1-31; 5:1-24; Hos 4:1-19; 6:4-6; Amos 5:1-24). In Micah, the Israelites cry out, "What does God want from us? What sacrifice will serve to vanquish our sin?" The prophet responds by calling the people instead to focus their hearts on the kind of offering that will lead them into right relationship with God and one another:

> He has told you, O mortal, what is good;
>    and what does the LORD require of you
> but to do justice, and to love kindness,
>    and to walk humbly with your God? (Mic 6:8)

Several hundred years later, another prophet taught a similar lesson in response to a similar question. "What does God want most from us?" a lawyer inquired. "Which command is the greatest?" Jesus replied,

"You shall love the Lord your God with all your heart, and with all your soul, and with all your mind." This is the greatest and first commandment. And a second is like it: "You shall love your neighbor as yourself." On these two commandments hang all the law and the prophets. (Matt 22:37-40)

Jesus repeatedly hammered home the point that people's relationships to one another are inextricably intertwined with their relationship to God (and on this basic point, the rest of the New Testament follows suit). Much of the Sermon on the Mount in Matthew (5:1–7:29), for instance, presumes or expressly underscores this connection. The beatitudes celebrate dispositions of humility, meekness, righteousness, and mercy and lift up those who live accordingly as blessed in God's sight (Matt 5:1-11). Offerings to God should be made only when one is in right relationship with others:

> So when you are offering your gift at the altar, if you remember that your brother or sister has something against you, leave your gift there before the altar and go; first be reconciled to your brother or sister, and then come and offer your gift. (Matt 5:23-24)

Jesus calls his disciples to love their enemies, "so that you may be children of your Father in heaven" (Matt 5:43-45), and instructs them that "if you forgive others their trespasses, your heavenly father will forgive you" (Matt 6:14). Later in the Gospel, Jesus concludes his lengthy apocalyptic discourse (Matt 24–25) with the parable of the sheep and the goats, in which we encounter the refrain, "just as you did it to one of the least of these who are members of my family, you did it to me" (25:40).

The biblical traditions also emphasize the interconnectedness between faithfulness to God and one another, and the abundance of creation. Time after time throughout the Pentateuch, the Israelites are exhorted to follow God and God's ways in order that they might live abundantly in the land. The provision of creation is either greatly enhanced or severely curbed depending on the state of the relationship between God and humanity, and the relationship of human beings to one another. Near the conclusion of his lengthy farewell discourse to the Israelites as they prepare to enter the promised land, Moses provides this description of the blessing that will be theirs if they follow in God's ways.

> If you will only obey the LORD your God, by diligently observing all his commandments that I am commanding you today, the LORD your God will set you high above all the nations of the earth; all these blessings shall come upon you and overtake you, if you obey the LORD your God:
> Blessed shall you be in the city, and blessed shall you be in the field.
> Blessed shall be the fruit of your womb, the fruit of your ground, and the fruit of your livestock, both the increase of your cattle and the issue of your flock.

Blessed shall be your basket and your kneading bowl.

Blessed shall you be when you come in, and blessed shall you be when you go out.

The LORD will cause your enemies who rise against you to be defeated before you; they shall come out against you one way, and flee before you seven ways. The LORD will command the blessing upon you in your barns, and in all that you undertake; he will bless you in the land that the LORD your God is giving you. The LORD will establish you as his holy people, as he has sworn to you, if you keep the commandments of the LORD your God and walk in his ways. All the peoples of the earth shall see that you are called by the name of the LORD, and they shall be afraid of you. The LORD will make you abound in prosperity, in the fruit of your womb, in the fruit of your livestock, and in the fruit of your ground in the land that the LORD swore to your ancestors to give you. (Deut 28:1-11)

This presumed connection between the state of the Israelites relationship with God and one another and the provision of creation continues in the prophetic books. Common to many prophetic oracles of judgment and restoration is the claim that Israel's sin not only disrupts the blessing God intends for all people but also results in the wasting or disorder of the land,

For the land is full of adulterers;
because of the curse the land mourns,
and the pastures of the wilderness are dried up.
Their course has been evil,
and their might is not right. (Jer 23:10)

and the suffering of its inhabitants:

Hear the word of the LORD, O people of Israel;
for the LORD has an indictment against the inhabitants of the land.
There is no faithfulness or loyalty,
and no knowledge of God in the land.
Swearing, lying, and murder,
and stealing and adultery break out;
bloodshed follows bloodshed.
Therefore the land mourns,
and all who live in it languish;
together with the wild animals
and the birds of the air,
even the fish of the sea are perishing. (Hos 4:1-3)

Conversely, as we saw in Ezekiel 36, the return of the Israelites into right relationship with God and one another will lead to a rebirth of the promised land: the land that was once desolate will become like the garden of Eden. Fruitfulness will overflow to all. The New Testament writers take up the prophetic vision of creation's rebirth into a land of abundant blessing, proclaiming it as the consequence of Jesus' victory over the sins of humankind and all evil. In some places, such as Romans 8, it is the current creation that will be renewed. In the apocalyptic visions of the kingdom, it is a new creation that emerges from the old (2 Pet 3:11-13; Rev 21:1-2, 9-27). Putting these two visions together, we might say that the new creation will be a transformation of the old, and that in a similar way believers will be transformed into "new creations" in Christ (2 Cor 5:17).

## 3. Humanity Fails to Trust God, and Creation Unravels

If only humanity had trusted God's provision and obeyed! Alas, one of the most painful developments of the biblical story is to go from the blessing and bliss of Genesis 1–2 to the beginning of creation's unraveling in Genesis 3. So much that once was good is now lost. It all began with human sin.

If you were to ask a group of Christians what led to the Fall of humanity as depicted in Genesis 3, my guess is most would answer that it was Eve's act of eating the forbidden apple. There are several problems with this response, however, some of which are more serious than others. On the trivial side, we are never told that the forbidden fruit was an apple. If you ask me, this undeservedly gives apples a bad rap; a sour passion fruit is the better candidate. On the more important side, it is not only the woman (later named "Eve") who eats of the fruit, but Adam as well. In fact, the text implies that Adam was by his wife's side during the whole twisted conversation with the serpent (see Gen 3:6: "and she gave some to her husband, *who was with her*, and he ate"). He too was duped, not by his own wife but by the serpent. Even more important, and essential to understanding the nature of sin, is that the Fall of humanity begins not with an act of disobedience, but with a lack of trust in God's provision. Note how the words of the serpent seek to undo the human couple's trust in God:

> Now the serpent was more crafty than any other wild animal that the LORD God had made. He said to the woman, "Did God say, 'You shall not eat from any tree in the garden'?" The woman said to the serpent, "We may eat of the fruit of the trees in the garden; but God said, 'You shall not eat of the fruit of the tree that is in the middle of the garden,

nor shall you touch it, or you shall die.'" But the serpent said to the woman, "You will not die; for God knows that when you eat of it your eyes will be opened, and you will be like God, knowing good and evil." (Gen 3:1-5)

The serpent says in effect, "God lied to you. God is keeping things from you. God doesn't want you to be like God. God is preventing you from being fully blessed!" Despite all indications to the contrary, Adam and the woman buy the lie. God is not to be trusted. God will not provide the full measure of blessing that could be theirs. They need to take it for themselves. They need to be their own master. It all begins with a lack of trust in God as the source of blessing and misplaced trust in something else. And so, "when the woman saw that the tree was good for food, and that it was a delight to the eyes, and that the tree was to be desired to make one wise," they grasped the fruit and ate.

The rest of the biblical story is filled with redundant tales of humanity's lack of trust in God and the painful consequences of this distrust for humanity's relationship with God and one another. That Scripture intends to present right relatedness as foundational to what God intended for humanity's blessed existence is further affirmed in what follows: the unraveling of creation begins with the unraveling of these very relationships. Upon eating the fruit, Adam and the woman are immediately shamed by their nakedness and hastily clothe themselves. When God arrives for his daily time of fellowship with the human pair, they both hide in fear. After they are found and found out by God, the blame game begins. Adam whines, blaming both God and his wife: "The *woman*, whom *you* gave to be with me, *she* gave me fruit from the tree, and I ate" (Gen 3:12). In turn, the woman feebly protests: "The serpent tricked me, and I ate" (v. 13).

The verses that follow are commonly regarded as the "curses" of the Fall, but perhaps are more helpfully viewed as the types of consequences that result when people's relationships with God and one another are compromised by lack of trust in God's provision and instruction (Gen 3:14-19). Coming on the heels of the wondrous description of creation in Genesis 1–2, the tarnishing of the created order that we witness here is hard to take. What was once a garden of harmony and rich abundance becomes a weed-infested realm of alienation, hard living, and scarcity. Enmity will now characterize the relationship between humanity and the rest of creation (vv. 14-15). The blessed joy of new life will be accompanied by the excruciating pain of labor. The mutuality that was to characterize human relatedness will give way to the prejudice of patriarchy, as the man will now rule over the woman (v. 16). Humanity will now have to wring provision from the land with arduous labor. Humans will no longer cultivate a garden rich with produce, but with toil and sweat will eke out their existence on an accursed land (vv. 17-20). And then, in the end, they will die. Adam and Eve are cast out of the garden. The path to tree of life is guarded against their trespass. To dust they shall return.

Genesis 3 introduces us to what went wrong and what continues to go wrong with humanity. The human problem is most fundamentally a lack of trust in God as the source of blessing, replaced by trust in ourselves (pride) or something else as the source of blessing (idolatry). It is, then, this lack of trust that quickly leads to blatant acts of disobedience, the breakdown in relationships (between God and humanity, among human beings, and between humanity and creation), and increasing states of corruption that finally lead to destruction. In the narrative that follows we see the consequences of the Fall played out in heartbreaking fashion. In the very next chapter of Genesis, the first murder is committed—by Cain against his brother—and Lamech boasts of his murder of another (4:23-24). By Genesis 6, the earth has become so depraved that God is sorry that God has brought this creation into being and plans to wipe all creatures off of the face of the earth. Note that here too the focus is not simply on human disobedience but more on human "wickedness," defined by the biblical author as the corruption of humanity's inner disposition: "every inclination of the thoughts of their hearts was only evil continually" (6:5). Already at this point in the biblical story creation has unraveled to the degree that it is on the brink of annihilation.

Much of the rest of the biblical story is one account after another of humanity's lack of trust in God as the source of blessing and the painful consequences of this faithlessness for human beings' relationship with God and one another. Indeed, there are numerous references to people simply disobeying God's commands, without any reference to a lack of trust in God and God's provision. However, the creation narratives, along with persistent reminders along the way, keep readers mindful of sin's fundamental, and (anti)relational, character, leading to the consistent call for trust in God in the prophetic and New Testament writings. Space does not permit a thorough survey of these reminders, but I offer a very brief review of representative examples instead, inviting the reader to turn to the passages I cite for further exploration of this central story line.

- Twice Abraham fails to trust in God's promise for protection and passes off Sarah as his sister (Gen 12:10-20; 20:1-18).

- Jacob repeatedly shows his lack of trust in God, stealing Esau's blessing, making conditional promises (28:20-22), offering insincere prayers (32:9-12), and trying on his own to weasel out of a confrontation with his brother (32:6-8, 13-22).

- One of basic purposes of the exodus was to help the Israelites realize that Yahweh is indeed Lord of all and that they must trust in Yahweh's will and ability to care for them (see Exod 4:30-31; 6:7; 11:7; 12:25-27). Yet the Israelites repeatedly fail to trust in God's provision in the wilderness, even to the point that on several occasions they wish to return to Egypt! (Exod 16:1-3; 17:1-3; Num 11:4-5; 20:1-6; 21:4-5).

- The Israelites get anxious waiting for Moses to come down from the mountain, and so they trade gods, replacing their devotion to Yahweh with devotion to a god made by their own hands (Exodus 32).

- The Israelites fail to trust that Yahweh will be able to establish them in the promised land, and so they wander for forty more years in the wilderness (Num 14:1-35). That their lack of trust is at the forefront of their betrayal of Yahweh is made clear by Yahweh's response (Num 14:11): "How long will this people despise me? And how long will they refuse to believe in me, in spite of all the signs I have done among them?"

- In rebuking David for committing adultery with Bathsheba and murdering Uriah, God begins by reminding David of the tremendous blessing that has been bestowed upon him and then says, "and if that had been too little, I would have added as much more!" (2 Sam 12:8). In effect, God is saying, "Why was my blessing too little for you that you needed to take matters into your own hands and steal that which belonged to another?" David has done no less than "despise" Yahweh and Yahweh's instruction (2 Sam 12:9, 10).

- Similarly, in his explanation of why he will tear ten tribes of Israel away from Solomon, and at the forefront of describing the various ways Solomon has gone astray, Yahweh begins by stating, "This is because he has forsaken me" (1 Kgs 11:33).

- Throughout the prophetic books, the prophets portray Israel's idolatry not simply as a transgression against God's law but more basically as a rejection of God's blessing and love, at times using the analogy of Israel as an unfaithful spouse or lover (see, for example, Hos 2:1-15; Isa 5:1-7; Ezek 16:1-58) or an ungrateful child (Hos 11:1-9). Idolatry is among the worst of sins, not simply because it breaks the commandments but because it is the rejection of God as the source of blessing and the turning to another source for blessing—an infidelity that fosters increasing degrees of corruption and alienation and eventually leads to destruction (in short, the story of the monarchy). Many prophetic oracles of judgment also focus on the greedy hoarding of resources by the rich, an ill-guided attempt to provide for their own blessing apart from God and at the expense of others, and foretell their ruin (see Isa 1:1-31; Hos 6:4-6; Amos 5:1-24)

- As a wonderful counterexample, the psalms revolve around trust in God. Praise and thanksgiving manifest the jubilant expression of trust, and lament presents complaint rooted in trust. Even in those cases in which the psalmist's trust in God's provision appears to be waning, the psalmist—unlike many other biblical figures—remains steadfast in the belief that blessing is found in no one else. The psalmist's gaze, in other words, never wavers from God, and eventually God's blessing is found and lament turns to praise.

- Like the message of the prophets, many of Jesus' teachings also focus on the hoarding of resources, casting greed as essentially a lack of trust in God and God's provision: "No one can serve two masters; for a slave will either hate the one and love the other, or be devoted to one and despise the other. You cannot serve God and wealth" (Matt 6:24; see also Matt 6:19-34; Mark 10:17-22; Luke 12:13-34). Blessing, Jesus teaches his followers, is to be found first and foremost not in material possessions but in one's devotion to God.

- Jesus also chastises the religious authorities for trusting in status, honor, and self-righteousness as keys to blessing, while neglecting God's calling to provide for the least among them. Jesus characterizes their actions as incompatible with true devotion to God (see Matt 5:20, 21:33-46, 23:1-39; Luke 20:45-47). Hence, the trusting child, open to the blessings of God's kingdom, rather than the religious elite, serves as the true model of faithfulness (Mark 9:33-37, 10:13-16; Matt 11:25-27).

- Paul's exhortations to his fellow Christians follow suit. Human depravity has its origins in the lack of honor and thanks to God: that is, the refusal to recognize and trust the Creator as the source of blessing (Rom 1:20-21; see also 3:10-18).

- Conversely, both the Gospels and Paul present *trust* (a better word to translate the Greek *pistis* than "faith") as that which enables believers to take hold of God's gift of grace in Jesus. Repeatedly in the Gospel accounts it is those who trust in Jesus as the one who inaugurates and embodies God's saving rule that are healed of their diseases or ailments (see Mark 5:21–6:6; 9:23; 11:23-24; Matt 9:28; 14:31; 15:28).

Such trust is what enables one to take hold of the good news of God's salvation in Jesus (see Mark 1:15; Luke 8:12-13; John 3:16-18; 5:38). The attainment of blessing—God's salvation—is beyond our ability. It is, as Paul emphasizes, a free gift of God's grace. It all begins with trust (Rom 3:21-26).

- Revelation's naming of Satan as "that ancient serpent . . . the deceiver of the whole world" (Rev 12:9) echoes the story of the Fall as it reminds us of the "lie" that evil has long sought to sow among humankind: that blessing is found in self, wealth, greed, and beast rather than God. Fittingly, the biblical canon ends with a work whose fundamental challenge to the faithful is the same as the challenge dominating the beginning and middle of the biblical collection: in whom or what will you trust as the source of blessing? In Christ, we are brought back to the garden (Rev 22:2) and given the chance to choose God and life all over again.

## 4. God Is Merciful and Gracious, Slow to Anger, and Abounding in Steadfast Love and Faithfulness

If humanity's lack of trust in God as the source of blessing leads to the unraveling of the created order, then it is God's mercy, forbearance, and forgiveness that keep stitching creation back together and giving humanity chance after chance to begin anew. In chapter 3, we discussed the golden calf affair (Exodus 32–34) as one of several instances in which God was so moved by human intercession that God had a change of mind. The story also announces what Israel will come to regard as a fundamental dimension of God's character. J. Clinton McCann Jr. captures well the importance of this story in Scripture's portrayal of God's dealings with humanity:

> Exodus 32:1-14, along with the larger narrative which it introduces (Exod 32–34), is fundamental to understanding the Book of Exodus, the Pentateuch, the entire Old Testament, and indeed, the New Testament and the whole history of God's dealings with humanity.[6]

The story dramatically indicates, as McCann goes on to say, that "'calf-making' is a perennial temptation for the people of God."[7] But as we move toward the conclusion of this story, it is God's mercy that becomes the focus of the narrative, culminating in God's self-disclosure in Exod 34:6-7a. God reveals the divine glory to Moses and, passing by him, proclaims,

> The Lord, the Lord,
> a God merciful and gracious,
> slow to anger
> and abounding in steadfast love and faithfulness,
> keeping steadfast love and faithfulness for the thousandth generation,
> forgiving iniquity and transgression and sin . . . (Exod 34:6-7a)

As discussed in chapter 1, what makes this self-disclosure so remarkable is that it comes on the heels of one of the worst acts of betrayal the Israelites could have committed. They have just recently been liberated by Yahweh from Egypt and have pledged to be in covenant relationship with God (Exod 24:3, 7). Moses is now up on the mountain receiving instructions concerning the tabernacle, that portable shrine in which God's presence will dwell among the people as they journey through the wilderness. But the Israelites tire of waiting and lose faith. So they form a golden calf, bow down to it, and proclaim "These are your gods, O Israel, who delivered you from Egypt!" (Exod 32:4). Yahweh's immediate response is that of furious rebuke and threatened destruction. But as soon as these words leave Yahweh's lips, the narrative moves in another direction. In response to Moses' appeal for forbearance, Yahweh has a change of mind (32:14) and does not destroy the people. We find this same pattern of judgment moving toward mercy and restoration beginning again at the end of Exodus 32. God sends a plague upon the people and then tells Moses that even though God's angel will go before them to establish them in the land as promised, God will not go with them, "or I would consume you on the way, for you are a stiff-necked people" (33:3). The people repent and mourn. Moses pleads for the people, and once again God relents.

> Moses said to the Lord, "See, you have said to me, 'Bring up this people'; but you have not let me know whom you will send with me. Yet you have said, 'I know you by name, and you have also found favor in my sight.' Now if I have found favor in your sight, show me your ways, so that I may know you and find favor in your sight. Consider too that this nation is your people." He said, "My presence will go with you, and I will give you rest." And he said to him, "If your presence will not go, do not carry us up from here. For how shall it be known that I have found favor in your sight, I and your people, unless you go with us? In this way, we shall be distinct, I and your people, from every people on the face of the earth." The Lord said to Moses, "I will do the very thing that you have asked; for you have found favor in my sight, and I know you by name." (Exod 33:12-17)

But Moses isn't finished with his requests. He also asks to behold God's glory. God grants his wish, passes before him, and proclaims the self-disclosure of Exod 34:6-7a.

Now the proclamation of God as "merciful and gracious, slow to anger and abounding in steadfast love and faithfulness" is in tension with other elements of this story, not to mention portrayals of God's judgment found elsewhere in the Old Testament. Even though Moses is likely acting on his own when he calls the sons of Levi to slaughter the revelers (32:25-29), God says, "when the day comes for punishment, I will punish them for their sin," and then God sends a plague on the people (Exod 32:34-35). In addition, God's self-disclosure to Moses in Exodus 34 concludes with the rather ominous countertestimony in v. 7b:

> *yet by no means clearing the guilty,*
> *but visiting the iniquity of the parents*
> *upon the children*
> *and the children's children*
> *to the third and fourth generation.*

The golden calf affair and this confession mirror the very same tension in Yahweh's response to humanity's infidelity throughout the biblical story. The lesson we learn in Genesis 3–6 continues to be played out in the rest of the history of God's people: to trust in something other than Yahweh as a source of blessing is to embark on a path that leads to betrayal, alienation, and increasing degrees of corruption resulting finally in destruction. The biblical story consistently presents serious, even disastrous consequences for God's people when they choose to remove themselves from the domain of God's care. Trusting God really is, as Moses will later emphasize to the Israelites when they are on the verge of entering the promised land, a matter of life and death.

See, I have set before you today life and prosperity, death and adversity. If you obey the commandments of the Lord your God that I am commanding you today, by loving the Lord your God, walking in his ways, and observing his commandments, decrees, and ordinances, then you shall live and become numerous, and the Lord your God will bless you in the land that you are entering to possess. But if your heart turns away and you do not hear, but are led astray to bow down to other gods and serve them, I declare to you today that you shall perish; you shall not live long in the land that you are crossing the Jordan to enter and possess. I call heaven and earth to witness against you today that I have set before you life and death, blessings and curses. Choose life so that you and your descendants may live, loving the Lord your God, obeying him, and holding fast to him; for that means life to you and length of days, so that you may live in the land that the LORD swore to give to your ancestors, to Abraham, to Isaac, and to Jacob. (Deut 30:15-20)

At the same time, and without glossing over the serious consequences of human distrust as presented in these and other passages, it is important to note that the golden calf affair is both *framed* and *remembered* as a story of God's steadfast love and mercy. To see what I mean, get out your Bible and read all of Exodus 31. Then jump to chapter 35 and continue reading. Notice how the narrative flow doesn't skip a beat? In Exodus 31, God concludes the lengthy instructions on the building of the tabernacle, reminds Moses about the importance of the Sabbath, and finally gives Moses two stone tablets containing the instructions he is to share with the people. When we turn to Exodus 35, Moses begins to share God's instructions with the people, beginning with the reminder to honor the Sabbath and followed by the plans for building the tabernacle. We pick up in Exodus 35 right where we left off in Exodus 31. If you were a source or redaction critic, you would likely conclude that at some point in the traditioning process a biblical editor inserted the story of the golden calf (Exodus 32–34) into a cohesive account of the planning and building of the tabernacle (Exodus 25–31; 35–40). Why make this insertion here? In doing so, the editor was able to highlight the egregious nature of the Israelites' sin (as discussed above), coming on the heels of God's deliverance of the people, the people's embrace of the covenant, and preparations for God's presence to dwell among them. But this placement of the story also enabled the editor to emphasize the restorative power of God's mercy. It enabled him to show that despite this awful act of betrayal and because of God's forgiveness, the rest of story still ends up going on just as planned. In Exodus 34, the damage to the relationship is undone: the covenant between God and the people is renewed and a new set of tablets is composed (34:10-27). Then we pick the tabernacle story back up again in chapter 35 with the planning and building of the sacred shrine. It is as though the golden calf affair never happened. But it did, and that's just the point. Despite such extraordinary betrayal, God puts the people's sin aside and the story continues just as God willed from the start. Fittingly, the book of Exodus ends with God entering the tabernacle and dwelling with the people (40:34-38).

The way in which this story is remembered throughout the rest of the Old Testament also affirms our reading of it as a story that focuses on the revelation of God's grace. From this point on in the biblical story, God is known as "merciful and gracious, slow to anger and abounding in steadfast love and faithfulness." This disclosure becomes an oft-recited confession of faith identifying these traits as fundamental dimensions of God's character (see Num 14:18-19; Neh 9:17, 31; Pss 77:7-8; 86:15; 103:8; 116:5; 145:8, 13; Isa 30:18; 63:7; Lam 3:20-32; Jonah 4:2; Joel 2:3). Particularly instructive on this point is Numbers 14. As the Israelites approach the borders of the promised land, Yahweh orders Moses to send out spies into Canaan (Num 13:1-24). When the Israelite spies return, they report to the people the extraordinary abundance of the land and the imposing stature of its inhabitants and the fortification of its towns (Num 13:25-33). In response, the people fail to trust in God's ability to protect them and establish them in the land. More incredibly still, they subsequently hark back to the "good ol' days" in Egypt and begin making preparations to return to Pharaoh.

> Then all the congregation raised a loud cry, and the people wept that night. And all the Israelites complained against Moses and Aaron; the whole congregation said to them, "Would that we had died in the land of Egypt! Or would that we had died in this wilderness! Why is the LORD bringing us into this land to fall by the sword? Our wives and our little ones will become booty; would it not be better for us to go back to Egypt?" So they said to one another, "Let us choose a captain, and go back to Egypt" (Num 14:1-4).

As in Exodus 32, Yahweh again responds to the betrayal of the people with the intention of consuming them, and again Moses intercedes on their behalf. He appeals to Yahweh's covenant relationship with the people, and cautions Yahweh that his destruction of the people will be to the detriment of others as well, for it will lead the other nations to dismiss Yahweh's power and sovereignty. Then, as a final appeal, he cites Yahweh's self-profession from Exod 34:6-7:

> And now, therefore, let the power of the LORD be great in the way that
> you promised when you spoke, saying,
> *"The LORD is slow to anger,*
> *and abounding in steadfast love,*
> *forgiving iniquity and transgression,*
> *but by no means clearing the guilty,*
> *visiting the iniquity of the parents*
> *upon the children*
> *to the third and the fourth generation." (Num 14:17-18)*

Moses cites the confession in full, including the phrases referring to Yahweh's judgment. Yet remarkably, *Moses goes on to focus only on its witness to Yahweh's mercy.* For after reciting the entire confession, he next urges Yahweh to "forgive the iniquity of this people according to the greatness of your steadfast love, just as you have pardoned this people, from Egypt even until now" (Num 14:19). It is clear that Moses understands the confession of Exod 34:6-7 as speaking more prominently to Yahweh's mercy than wrath. As in Exodus 32–34, judgment is also part of this story: none of those doubting Yahweh will live to see the promised land, and Israel's sojourn in the wilderness is extended (Num 14:20-38). But Moses' plea for mercy is successful. Yahweh again changes Yahweh's mind and the relationship between God and the people is preserved.

It is also important for us to note that the way in which Moses remembers and utilizes the golden calf story here in Numbers 14 foreshadows the use of this tradition elsewhere in the Old Testament. Whenever the account of the golden calf affair is remembered in subsequent Old Testament traditions, it is not remembered as a story of judgment, but is celebrated as a story of God's forgiveness and mercy, or of God's relenting from judgment (Neh 9:18-19; Pss 78:36-38; 103:7-8; 106:19-23).

These accounts join with scores of others throughout the biblical story in which God's grace has the final word, and the relationship between God and God's people is preserved. In fact, it serves as one clear instance of a recurring pattern that characterizes much of the interaction between God and Israel throughout the Old Testament:

1. God saves or restores the people.

2. The people respond with thanksgiving and devotion.

3. The people betray God.

4. God rebukes and judges.

5. The people repent.

6. God forgives and restores the people.

Beginning with the golden calf affair, nearly every major development in Israel's history (and many minor ones as well) correspond to this pattern. As we saw in chapter 6, several biblical summaries also reflect at least the general contours of the pattern, such as those found in Judges 2, Psalm 78, and especially the expansive summary of Nehemiah 9, which covers all of Israelite history leading up to the post-exilic period.

What is most important to notice about this pattern is that even though rebuke and judgment are part of the way in which God responds to the people's sin, it is God's grace that in the end makes it possible for the story to go on. In this we encounter Yahweh's covenant faithfulness in the extreme. Yahweh's steadfast love is such that Yahweh remains faithful to the covenant relationship even when Israel is not. Actually, to put it more accurately, so entrenched is Yahweh's fixation on this people that Yahweh repeatedly sets aside the stipulations of the covenant in order that the relationship may be preserved. By the accounting of the covenant mandate (Exod 19:1-6; 24:1-8), Yahweh has been released from obligation to this people by their chronic failure to abide by the covenant promises. The covenant relationship could have, and should have, been nullified a long time ago, save for Yahweh's character as one who is merciful and gracious, slow to anger and abounding in steadfast love and faithfulness (the very point emphasized by Ezra in Nehemiah 9). What this reveals is that the covenant between God and the people is not in the end the most fundamental or crucial component holding their relationship together. The covenant repeatedly fails, but God's steadfast love endures.

In light of the fact that the God of the Old Testament is sometimes pegged by Christians as a judgmental and vengeful God, this is a crucial point to appreciate. From the time of Noah on, through the dysfunctional challenges posed by the patriarchal families to the complaints of the people in the wilderness, the golden calf affair, the dark ages of the judges, and the debacle of the monarchy—throughout the whole history of the relationship between God and the people—it is God's steadfast love and gracious willingness to suffer the consequences of living in relationship with a stiff-necked people that time and time again leads God to forgive and grant the people the chance to begin anew.

Several features of prophetic speech also invite us to cast God's judgment not as the final word God offers in response to human sin. Rather than presenting us a wrathful God coldly matching Israel's waywardness with overflowing vengeance, numerous texts instead speak of God agonizing over the broken relationship with Israel (for example, Ps 78:40-41; Isa 1:2-3; 5:3-4; 63:10; Jer 2:1-3, 29-32; 3:11-14; Hos 6:4-6). Consider Hos 11:1-7:

> When Israel was a child, I loved him,
>     and out of Egypt I called my son.
> The more I called them,
>     the more they went from me;
> they kept sacrificing to the Baals,
>     and offering incense to idols.
>
> Yet it was I who taught Ephraim to walk,
>     I took them up in my arms;
>     but they did not know that I healed them.

*I led them with cords of human kindness,*
    *with bands of love.*
*I was to them like those*
    *who lift infants to their cheeks.*
    *I bent down to them and fed them.*

*They shall return to the land of Egypt,*
    *and Assyria shall be their king,*
    *because they have refused to return to me.*
*The sword rages in their cities,*
    *it consumes their oracle-priests,*
    *and devours because of their schemes.*
*My people are bent on turning away from me.*
    *To the Most High they call,*
    *but he does not raise them up at all.*

Recall also Isa 65:1-7:

*I was ready to be sought out by those who did not ask,*
    *to be found by those who did not seek me.*
*I said, "Here I am, here I am,"*
    *to a nation that did not call on my name.*
*I held out my hands all day long*
    *to a rebellious people,*
*who walk in a way that is not good,*
    *following their own devices;*
*a people who provoke me*
    *to my face continually,*
*sacrificing in gardens*
    *and offering incense on bricks;*
*who sit inside tombs,*
    *and spend the night in secret places;*
*who eat swine's flesh,*
    *with broth of abominable things in their vessels;*
*who say, "Keep to yourself,*
    *do not come near me, for I am too holy for you."*
*These are a smoke in my nostrils,*
    *a fire that burns all day long.*
*See, it is written before me:*
    *I will not keep silent, but I will repay;*
*I will indeed repay into their laps*
    *their iniquities and their ancestors' iniquities together,*
    *says the* LORD;

*because they offered incense on the mountains*
   *and reviled me on the hills,*
*I will measure into their laps*
   *full payment for their actions.*

These and other passages suggest that judgment comes only as a last resort, a last-ditch, desperate effort on God's part to make some sort of future between God and the people possible (see also Nehemiah 9). For this reason, the necessity of judgment is accompanied by God's anguish.

*My anguish, my anguish! I writhe in pain!*
   *Oh, the walls of my heart!*
*My heart is beating wildly;*
   *I cannot keep silent;*
*for I hear the sound of the trumpet,*
   *the alarm of war.*
*Disaster overtakes disaster,*
   *the whole land is laid waste.*
*Suddenly my tents are destroyed,*
   *my curtains in a moment.*
*How long must I see the standard,*
   *and hear the sound of the trumpet?*
*"For my people are foolish,*
   *they do not know me;*
*they are stupid children,*
   *they have no understanding.*
*They are skilled in doing evil,*
   *but do not know how to do good."*
(Jer 4:19-22; see also 8:18–9:3)

God's eventual acquiescence to judgment and continuing concern for and presence with the people in the midst of destruction is well described by Terence Fretheim:

It is striking how commonly the language of God's judgment consists of images involving withdrawal, forsaking, hiddenness, or giving the people up. As the people remove themselves from God, God engages in major efforts at healing the breach, but finally may be forced into a tearful withdrawal, reluctantly allowing all the forces that make for death and destruction to have their way with the people. But while God may give them up, God does not finally give up on them. Into the midst of these suffering judgments, God returns.[8]

The impression given by the consistent pattern throughout the biblical story of judgment leading to repentance and forgiveness is that God's judgment is not only a last resort, but is itself ultimately redemptive for those who would repent of their evil ways and return to God. This also coheres well with how God's judgment is presented by the prophetic books. Numerous passages speak of a remnant of Israel that will be preserved and will flourish after the time of judgment is over (see, e.g., Mic 4:6-13; 5:1-9; Joel 2:30–3:1; Amos 9:9-15; Isa 10:20-27, 65:1-25; Jer 31:1-39; 30:12-17; 33:4-9). Other traditions specifically refer to the "redemptive" intent of God's judgment: to wake Israel up from its sinful stupor and return to Yahweh (see, for example, 2 Sam 7:14; Isa 26:9-11; 29:13-24; Ezek 20:33-44; 33:29; 35:9; Hos 11:1-11).

> As I entered into judgment with your ancestors in the wilderness of the land of Egypt, so I will enter into judgment with you, says the Lord God. I will make you pass under the staff, and will bring you within the bond of the covenant. I will purge out the rebels among you, and those who transgress against me; I will bring them out of the land where they reside as aliens, but they shall not enter the land of Israel. Then you shall know that I am the Lord. (Ezek 20:36-38)

Still other sections of the prophetic corpus repeatedly juxtapose announcements of judgment with calls for repentance and even the proclamation of future restoration (for example, Hos 14:1-3; Joel 1:13-14; 2:12-13; Mic 6:6-8; Isa 1:18-20; 29:1–30:26).

For the survivors of Israel's fall who continued to claim their identity as Yahweh's chosen people, the prophetic explanations of judgment and calls for repentance, along with the painful, real-life consequences of destruction and exile, provided the perspective and motivation they needed to reorder their lives into those that welcomed God's blessing. This is why the words of the prophets were preserved and continued to speak beyond their time: they provided Jews in exile and thereafter with an explanation of why these tragic events took place (judgment), but also gave them instruction on how to respond (repentance), in order that they might move beyond the time of judgment and embrace a new future with God and one another (restoration). Imagine, for instance, the penetrating poignancy of Yahweh's challenge to the beleaguered survivors of the Babylonian invasion, those who in the end chose to listen to the prophets and re-member their lives as God's people.

> Therefore I will judge you, O house of Israel, all of you according to your ways, says the Lord God. Repent and turn from all your transgressions; otherwise iniquity will be your ruin. Cast away from you all the

transgressions that you have committed against me, and get yourselves a new heart and a new spirit! Why will you die, O house of Israel? For I have no pleasure in the death of anyone, says the Lord GOD. Turn, then, and live. (Ezek 18:30-32)

Many generations later, a remnant of Jews would once again respond to the prophetic calls for repentance echoed in the preaching of a retro, Elijah-like prophet along the shores of the Jordan River. He too spoke of woes, winnowing forks, and the burning of chaff in unquenchable fire. Yet to those who dared to listen and hope for Israel's renewal, John the Baptist also spoke of someone far greater to come after him—one who in turn would offer these words about a merciful and gracious God who desired not the death of any, but their return to abundant life.

For God so loved the world that he gave his only Son, so that everyone who believes in him may not perish but may have eternal life. Indeed, God did not send the Son into the world to condemn the world, but in order that the world might be saved through him. (John 3:16-17)

## 5. God's Attempt to Reclaim Humanity Comes to Its Culmination in Jesus, God with Us

In the preceding pages of this and the foregoing chapters, we have already devoted much space to articulating the New Testament's jubilant claim that Jesus brings God's plan of restoring creation and humanity to its fulfillment. More specifically, we have engaged the New Testament's celebration of Jesus as:

- one whose life among us serves as the fullest manifestation of God's desire to live in intimate relationship with humanity (chapters 3 and 4)

- the authoritative teacher of God's torah, whose actions and teachings redefined our understandings of righteousness and who continues to instruct believers on what it means to live in right relationship with God and one another (chapters 3 and 4)

- one whose death and resurrection signal the forgiveness of sins and the defeat of death's power over us (chapter 6)

- one whose life, death, resurrection, and ongoing ministry mark the fulfillment of God's promises to redeem Israel and all of humanity (chapters 6 and 7)

- one who will return to vanquish all evil, gather God's faithful, and lead them into God's eternal kingdom of blessed abundance (chapter 6)

With this final act of the biblical story, we see its main plotline come to resolution: in Jesus, God's attempt to lead humanity back to blessing is being accomplished.

## Implications: Interpretive Integrity in the Midst of Diversity and Ambiguity

Numerous features of the biblical traditions we have explored lead us to two contrasting "interpretive stances" toward Scripture. On the one hand, the plurality of its traditions and the various ways in which the biblical text embodies and invites faithful conversation commend a way of engaging Scripture that is committed to diversity, our dialogue with one another, and Christ's ongoing and reforming instruction. On the other hand, the central plotline and broad contours of the biblical story suggest that these core story lines are fundamental to a "biblical" view of God, God's will for humanity, our calling as God's people, *and* our recital of that story.

The approach to Scripture presented here values both of these interpretive stances endorsed by Scripture's own shaping of sacred tradition. They are both, in my view, integral to a fully biblical mode of reading Scripture. If either one is neglected, it will lead to uses of the biblical text that circumvent its full witness. If, for example, we neglect Scripture's polyphonic testimony to Yahweh's character, our own conceptions of God will remain unenhanced by Scripture's manifold witness and will be anemic in comparison. If we fail to note that in their remembrance of sacred tradition the biblical authors are inspired to varying recitals of their story in different times and places, and that biblical speech is creatively and boldly shaped to address the needs of the moment, then we will likely overlook our calling to proclaim the word boldly and creatively afresh in our time and place. If we refuse to recognize the diversity of Scripture and to admit that at times the biblical authors disagree with one another, then we may try to force upon our own dialogue an artificial unanimity that we pretend characterizes Scripture but is actually detrimental to the kind of conversation Scripture itself models. Or, if we ignore the ongoing and reforming character of God's instruction as evidenced throughout the Scriptures, we will fail to consider the possibility that God's Spirit may be moving us in new directions on certain matters of faith and practice beyond particular statements and portrayals of the biblical writers.

However, if the central story lines of Scripture are not embraced as an integral part of what it means to read Scripture faithfully, dangers also abound. One is that of amnesia. For if the story that Scripture tells is not the story shaping believers and communities of faith, then what ultimately shapes the identity, the worldview of these believers and communities, and how is their mission defined? What serves as the basis for their proclamation and practice, and even their reason for existing? Or, if in our dialogue we neglect the central contours of our sacred story, what can serve as a foundation upon which our discussions with one another can build? Especially in times of contention, to what can we then appeal both to seek agreement and to understand, even honor, our differences? Or, as communities of faith, how can we build up and edify, help one another grow in wisdom, if there is no story that we share, and none that our hearts can more deeply enjoin? Still another danger is that of facile, superficial engagements of the text, those which simply strip-mine the treasure of Scripture for narrow ends, unmindful of the larger movements of the story which define the heart of biblical faith. In such treatments, the biblical story suffers the humiliation of proof-texting as its traditions are milled into fodder for "interpretive" endeavors more concerned with legitimating a predetermined agenda than with humble discernment.

Although integral to a biblically formed mode of engaging Scripture, these two interpretive stances also present us with a pernicious challenge: how to hold them faithfully in tension. Where does the diversity of our sacred tradition end and the unity begin? What elements of the story can we recast in light of what we regard as its main course, and to what extent? Is development of thought to be permitted on matters that are part of Scripture's essential witness, or do they form a normative core that is irreducible? Even if we were to agree on the basic story Scripture tells, what does it mean for us to live into that story in a way that is faithful to both the testimony of Scripture and the ongoing witness of the Spirit? There clearly is a lot of ambiguity in all this! Is this the best an approach to Scripture as sacred dialogue can do?

I am afraid so. The only faithful way I can see through the dilemma necessitated by the character of Scripture is continual remembrance and recital of the story shaped by earnest dialogue and discernment. It is the calling of each community of faith to discuss and discern the story Scripture tells and how that story is to be revered and lived in the freedom of the Spirit. There is no one method than can definitively answer these nagging questions for all Christians. There is no approach that will completely resolve the tension Scripture requires. There is no easy way to navigate the polyvalence that inevitably results when Christian communities gather around the word. All believers can do is diligently remember the story as the one story that really matters, pray a lot, and do their best to figure out with one another how faithfully to live into its witness.

In my own conversation with Scripture, I privilege and treat as normative what I consider the essential plot and the basic story lines, the story as I've summarized it in these last two chapters. In my view, these central story lines form the core, or heart, of the witness that Scripture proclaims, and they are basic to my understanding of God and God's will for humanity. While I hope that my understanding of these core features of the biblical story will continue to grow and develop, I find it difficult to imagine them as anything less than essential to a biblically formed view of the world and my vocation as a follower of Jesus.

Yet the world Scripture unveils—and my world as scripted by God's word—though having these basic contours, leaves much unknown and undetermined. These contours give me a place to stand, an orientation to what is most real and essential, but then the call comes to go forth a find a way in the world that is faithful. This is where I often become far less certain, and far more reliant on God's grace and God's people to show me the way. Scripture is my starting point, my compass, my lamp for this journey, but when I come to those inevitable forks in the path, *answers on which way to proceed do not come without the conversation.* I might wish that they would. Life and faith would be a lot more straightforward and would take a lot less effort, and I am tempted to lament, "Couldn't we just have it all in writing please, the kind of direction that is comprehensive and clear, beautiful in its simplicity, and unambiguous?"

Then again, perhaps the conversation is just as important, just as essential to the journey, as the answers.

# Reading the Bible Biblically

## conclusion

**In the Introduction, I emphasized that the** interpretive approach to Scripture presented in these pages would revolve around three key principles. It would be above all else be canon-centered, story-centered, and Christ-centered. By "canon-centered," I mean that the approach takes seriously both the content of the biblical witness and the tendencies exhibited in Scripture's shaping of its sacred tradition. In short, this approach recognizes that not only does Scripture proclaim the story of Christian faith; it also displays characteristic patterns in telling and reflecting on that story, providing an "instruction manual" of sorts for how we are to read and reflect on it ourselves. The instruction Scripture provides, in turn, is what leads us to appreciate the Bible's conversational character and also guides us into a manner of engaging and conversing about Scripture that is story-centered and Christ-centered. This chapter begins by reviewing the insights presented in the previous chapters concerning the Bible's own instruction on "how to read the Bible biblically." It then offers some practical suggestions on how individuals and communities of faith may make use of these insights in their reflection on Scripture.

### What the Instruction Manual Teaches Us

At the end of the preceding chapter, I summarized the discussion of the book up to this point by describing two contrasting modes of engaging Scripture endorsed by the numerous features of the biblical text we have examined. Let me restate these two "interpretive stances" and gather the insights presented in the preceding chapters. On the one hand, God's "conversational character," the diversity of the biblical traditions, the development of perspectives they display, and the various ways in which the biblical texts invite imaginative, conversation-laden discernment call for our dynamic engagement with our sacred traditions that is open to the ongoing witness of the Spirit and discerning dialogue with God and one another. To unpack this in more detail, the preceding chapters have illustrated the following tendencies of Scripture. First, the bold and honest dialogue between believers and God as displayed throughout the biblical stories and the psalms helps us to see the importance of "bringing it all" to God, and God's readiness to invite and be moved by conversation (chapter 1). Second, divergent perspectives on God's will for humanity and what it means to live as God's people are found among the biblical authors themselves (chapter 2), beckoning us to recognize the dialogue between diverse perspectives that exists within and is valued by the biblical traditions. Third, Scripture's own recasting of torah leads us to grasp the ongoing and reforming character of God's instruction: God is not through teaching us what it means to be God's people (chapter 3). Fourth, the tendencies in Paul's radically imaginative, context- and Spirit-driven conversations about living the gospel commission us to speak with one another in ways that creatively and courageously interlace the proclamation of God's love and faithfulness with the lived reality of our daily, sometimes disturbed, lives (chapter 4). Fifth, the myriad ways in which Scripture invites polyvalence born out of believers' intimate entanglement with the biblical story in their own times and places affirms God's desire to engage each of us in dialogue, and also cautions against our easy dismissal of others who tell the story differently. Instead, we are called to share our recitations of the biblical story with one another that we may more deeply engage its transformative power (chapter 5). Sixth, guided by Jesus' own teaching and the witness of the New Testament authors, we are called to reflect on all of biblical tradition in light of God's will as made known most fully in the cross, resurrection, and ongoing ministry of Jesus (chapters 2 and 4). Finally, as those who share with the New Testament authors the confession that Jesus abides with us still, to read the Bible christocentrically also means that we remain open to the instruction Jesus, the Living Word, continues to offer on how to live as his disciples in our time and place (chapters 2, 3, and 4), even when such instruction recasts and reforms sacred tradition.

On the other hand, numerous features of the biblical text emphasize the centrality of the story Scripture proclaims for discerning God's character and will, claiming our identity as God's people, and proclaiming our faith to one another. Specifically, Scripture's unrelenting commitment to recite, revisit, and otherwise put before its readers the central plotline and broad contours of the biblical story teaches us that any attempt to claim as "biblical" our view of God, God's will for humanity, and our conversation as God's people must be rooted in the prevailing strokes of that story (chapters 6 and 7). Acts of remembrance and recitation that neglect these core story lines will fail to articulate fully and faithfully the good news Scripture proclaims. Moreover, Scripture's repeated portrayal of God's people intentionally inscribing themselves into that story at key moments in their history calls believers to make this story constitutive of their identity and mission as the people of God. In short, this story is to define our understanding of who and whose we are.

Finally, the story of Scripture comes to its culmination in the ministry, death, resurrection, and ongoing ministry of Jesus. It is through his teaching, sacrifice, resurrection, and continuing instruction that we are reconciled to God and one another and also granted the resources we need to live in right relationship with God and one another, thereby partaking in the blessing God intended for humanity from the very beginning. Thus, to embrace this story is to embrace the One in whom it finds its fulfillment as Lord and Savior.

These two interpretive stances, one embracing the call to ongoing discernment of God's will through Spirit-driven dialogue and the other embracing the story of our faith as constitutive of our identity, mission, and conversation, are both embedded in the witness of Scripture itself. Therefore both, I argue, are integral to a biblically formed mode of reading Scripture. Both also emphasize the Christ-centered character of biblical interpretation for the Christian community. In each, it is God's revelation and salvation culminating and continuing in Jesus that serve as the "interpretive lens" for discerning how we are to remember, recite, and live out the story of our faith in dialogue with one another.

However, the discipline of faithfully attending to these two tendencies of Scripture when reading the Bible is far from a straightforward affair. As I stated at the end of chapter 7, holding these two tendencies in faithful tension is one of most troublesome challenges facing the interpreter of Scripture and communities gathered around the word: how in our reflection and dialogue do we remain committed to the biblical story on the one hand, yet open to the ongoing and reforming witness of the Spirit on the other? Where are the lines drawn between these two commitments? What are the parameters for our polyvalent readings? Different readers, of course, will address this challenge and draw these lines in different ways, and hopefully by comparing notes we can learn from one another. Broadly speaking (as I also discussed at the end of chapter 7), I attempt to navigate this tension by privileging and treating as normative what I consider the essential plot and the basic story lines of Scripture, the story as I summarized it in chapters 6 and 7. In my view, it is these central story lines that form the core, or heart, of Scripture's testimony to God's will and ways. I treat these as the center around which our persistent remembrance of the story, imaginative proclamation of the gospel, and ongoing conversation about what it means to be God's people in our time and place are to revolve.

In what follows I lay out some more specific steps and suggestions for reading biblical texts, drawing from the approach to Scripture as sacred dialogue presented in this book. Again, however, I must emphasize that there is no one standard rubric, or formula, or delineated progression of exercises one can employ to steer neatly through and resolve all the challenges posed by the dynamic and tension-filled character of Scripture. *Scripture's persistent call for Spirit-induced conversation cycling around the poles of sacred story and reforming discernment cannot be reduced to technique.* It is more a matter of the heart than a matter of method. Nevertheless, because fellow clergy, students, and layfolk have frequently asked me for guidance on how to read the text in this fashion, I offer the following suggestions on how one might proceed. The initial steps represent methodology commonly employed in the interpretation of biblical passages, the kind of instruction you would find in most good handbooks on biblical exegesis. The aim of these initial steps, here focusing on biblical narrative and the New Testament epistles, is to discern the meaning and function of a text within the larger work in which it resides. The latter guidelines are meant to help the reader bring a passage into conversation with the biblical story as a whole, with our lives as God's people, and with the ongoing ministry of Jesus in the Spirit. Here we discuss the essential practice of embracing the story of our faith as constitutive of our identity and mission, and of remaining open to the ongoing instruction of Jesus in our time and place—the task of engaging the tenacious tension that Scripture presents us. I offer suggestions for how this reflection might take shape within a group of believers gathered around Scripture in a way that values the diverse perspectives of the members of the group yet also seeks to identify which readings best "fit" with the passage in view. Finally, I offer a brief discussion of the story of Jephthah's vow in Judges 11 as a means of further illustrating the steps presented here.

## Getting Started: Discerning the Meaning and Function of a Biblical Text

The first task of interpretation, as many define it, is that of "exegesis." "Exegesis" is from the Greek verb *exēgeisthai* meaning "to lead out," and when applied to literary works it refers to the practice of discerning the meaning "leading out from" a text. In other words, we must first try to discern what it is that the author or final editor of a biblical text intended his readers to get out of it. Now, as I mentioned in chapter 5, some scholars influenced by postmodern thought have abandoned the attempt to discern the "authorial intent" of a passage. In their view, there are simply too many features of the communicative process circumventing the transfer of meaning from an author to a reader that any attempt to figure out what an author intended to say—an attempt to get meaning *out of* a text—is sheer folly. As I said back in chapter 5, I do not share their pessimism. In my view, we do share enough conventions of meaning and features of worldview with the biblical authors that in many cases, though perhaps not all, we do have a good shot at connecting with the gist of what they intended to express. And as those committed to the theological claims of the canon, it seems to me that we are at least to make the effort to discern authorial intent, since it is presumably because of what the authors (or editors) intended to express in these texts that their words were viewed as faithful by the people of God and thus canonized.[1] Still, there are several challenges to reading texts—especially ones as ancient as these—that are important to keep in mind.

### Four Challenges We Face When Interpreting the Biblical Texts

Chief among these challenges is our distance, historically and culturally, from the time in which the biblical texts were written. These texts come from a time and place very different from our own, and for this reason it is important for us to become familiar with the historical and cultural contexts out of which the biblical texts were written. If we neglect these contexts, we can miss important elements that the texts are intending to convey, or, even worse, we can completely misunderstand them. For example, if we are unaware of the Jewish antipathy toward Samaritans in the time of Jesus and the history behind it, the full significance of Jesus' placing a Samaritan in the role of one who truly knows and lives out God's torah in the parable of the Good Samaritan (Luke 10:25-37) will likely escape us. Or, if we do not know that the ancient Egyptians viewed their pharaohs as gods, and also had deities they believed governed nearly every aspect of the natural world, we may fail to note that one of the main functions of the plagues in the exodus story, in addition to proclaiming Yahweh's faithfulness to the covenant, is to make clear that Yahweh and no other—not Pharaoh or any of the Egyptian deities—is Lord of creation. Unfortunately, space does not allow us to provide even a summary of Israelite history and the various cultural tendencies common to each era (that would be another, much longer book!). Fortunately, however, most good biblical commentaries will provide you with historical and cultural information relevant to a particular passage, and I will be cuing you in as we go along on when to make use of those resources in your study of a biblical text.

A second challenge is that the way Scripture is often engaged in many churches encourages us to read passages without attending to their literary context. Most Christian communities will only read small portions of a biblical text each Sunday. Unless the priest, pastor, or lay-person reading the text regularly explains how the passage fits into its larger work of which it is a part, many members of that congregation will likely have the impression that the Bible consists of short, discrete texts with self-contained lessons of faith that are profitably engaged in isolation from one another. But with the vast majority of Scripture, nothing could be further from the truth. To read from biblical narrative, for instance, a passage in isolation from the rest of the story in which it resides is tantamount to having a book discussion group read and discuss only one paragraph out of an entire novel! In both cases, you may get something of value out of the discussion, but not nearly as much as you would if you engaged that passage with the whole narrative in view. You may also find that the passage actually functions quite differently when you view it against the backdrop of its larger, literary context. Many of us are probably familiar with the maxim concerning real estate: "location is everything." With biblical interpretation, *context*—historical, cultural, literary, and canonical—is (nearly) everything.

A third challenge facing interpreters of Scripture is the meaning of "meaning." We addressed this in chapter 5. A common tendency among readers and hearers of Scripture is to jump immediately to the question, "What does the text mean *for me* or *for us*?" without first attending to the question, "What did the author of this text intend it to mean?" The problem of jumping immediately to the question of what a text means "for me/us" is that it leads us to overlook its historical, cultural, literary, and canonical contexts. It is to treat the text as if the author were writing that one passage exclusively for me in my time and place. It is important for us to resist the urge to translate these texts immediately into a contemporary lesson of faith. Instead, we must first allow them to speak on their own terms and out of their own context. Then and only then are we in good position to discern how they might speak anew to us in our time and place.

Finally, and here I offer a thankful nod of acknowledgment to the postmodernists among us, another challenge we commonly face is reading our own preconceived notions about God, faith, and righteousness into the biblical texts. As we observed in chapter 5, this is to some degree inevitable, and we can only do so much to guard against it. Yet this is also to some extent desirable since different readers with different preconceptions and experiences may enrich the community's appreciation of the different dimensions of the passage. Still, we must do all that we can to grant biblical passages enough freedom to speak on their own terms so that when we engage Scripture there is the potential to hear more than simply the echo of our own voices. Humility and a willingness to have our preconceptions challenged and transformed by *God's* voice are prerequisites for faithful interpretation.

In what follows I offer some basic suggestions and guidelines for interpreting biblical narrative (including Old Testament narrative and the Gospels and Acts) and the New Testament epistles.[2] The goal of these reading strategies is to discern the meaning and function of a biblical passage within the larger work in which it resides. They also call readers to be mindful of how historical and cultural realities contemporary to the text may inform their interpretation. While interpreting biblical passages can seem a difficult and even daunting task, keep in mind that carefully engaging these texts involves many of the same skills that you have likely already spent a considerable amount of time cultivating in reading of other forms of literature.

## *Reading Biblical Narrative*
### Some General Suggestions

1. Christians have a tendency to read the Old Testament through a "christological" lens. What this means for some is that they frequently find references to Jesus in the Old Testament, as if particular Old Testament passages predict specific features of Jesus' ministry. But is important to read Old Testament passages first on their own terms—to try to understand them as the original Israelite/Jewish audiences would have understood them. Otherwise we disconnect these passages from their historical and literary contexts and likely construe their meaning in ways that their authors did not intend. Then, as a following step, one can reflect on how Jesus fulfills and at times recasts the general hopes and expectations announced in these Old Testament passages and in the Old Testament as a whole.

2. One of the most important elements of biblical interpretation is to ask questions of the text that it was composed to answer. If we ask questions of the text that are unrelated to its intention, we may come up with some interesting stuff, but it won't really be a reflection of what the text itself intends to say. If you bring the following set of questions to any biblical text, you'll be putting yourself in a good position to get from the text what it was meant by its authors, final editors, and compilers to convey.

   What does this text have to say about
   • God's will and God's character?
   • God's undying effort to restore humanity throughout human history, culminating in Jesus? (That is, what is the role of the story in this larger history?)

- what it means to walk in God's ways, to partake in God's intentions for humanity?

3. If possible, photocopy the text from your Bible or download the text from online, so that you can feel free to underline key phrases, circle key words, note repetition, draw lines connecting parts of the passage, jot down notes or questions in the margins. But keep your Bible open, so that you can review the broader context as well.

## Engaging the Text

1. Read the text several times through to get a general sense of the action depicted in the story. Jot down questions and elements of the text that strike you as significant. Make asking questions and noting observations your regular mode of engagement with the text.

2. Take careful note of repeated words, concepts, or phrases. What seems to be of particular interest to the narrator?

3. Try to get a sense of what the passage intends to express about the activity and persons it portrays.
   - Discern the role of its characters, the relationships between them, and the significance of their movements and interaction. Respond thoughtfully and carefully to the question: What is going on in the passage?
   - Focus in on how characters are being portrayed in this passage, including God and/or Jesus. What elements of their character is the author "sketching"? How do their actions and/or words relate to or respond to the action, problems, and concerns at work in the story? How do you think the narrator is intending the readers to regard the characters and their actions? Positively or negatively? How are others responding to him/her? How do the actions of the characters fit with how they act elsewhere in the narrative?
   - In the case of a saying/teaching/parable of an esteemed character, such as God, Moses, a prophet, or Jesus, what main points are emphasized, and what appears to be its purpose (to rebuke, inform, encourage)? What is being communicated about the reign of God or what it means to take part in it?

4. How would you characterize the tone of the passage? (It may be helpful to read the passage out loud, trying out different intonations). Is the language correcting, combative, lamenting, comforting, joyous?

5. It is not inappropriate to consider how the passage makes you feel. How might the author be employing "pathos" (emotion) to guide readers' reactions to the story?

6. Are any earlier biblical traditions in view? If so, how are they being used to characterize the persons or events taking place in the narrative? Has the tradition in view been "tweaked" or reworked in a particular way? For examples of this, recall those provided in the introduction.

7. Determine how the story contributes to the surrounding narrative.
   - First, investigate the "immediate context." How might the material immediately preceding and following the passage under study add to your understanding of it? Is it a new development or a fulfillment of what was expected? Is it a digression from the main flow of the narrative, or is it a continuation of what the narrative has been focusing on up to this point? With the Gospels especially, how does the sequencing of the episodes in the surrounding narrative affect your perception of this passage?
   - Next, investigate the "larger context" of the entire section or Gospel. How does what takes place in this passage relate to the major themes or story lines of the work as a whole?

8. Try to discern what customs, cultural values, or historical settings might be helpful to keep in mind as you study the passage. How might this information help you better understand certain details in the text as well as the narrator's intentions in shaping the text? A good biblical commentary can provide you with this information.

9. Gather up all of the details you have discerned in the passage about the action presented and the portrayal of characters in relation to the surrounding narrative and summarize your findings. In your view, what does this passage intend to express about the character and will of God, God's relationship with the people, and God's hopes and expectations for humanity?
   - Avoid interpretations that rely heavily on one insight at the expense of others. Your goal is a balanced interpretation that incorporates all of the relevant information.
   - Consulting one or more biblical commentaries may be helpful at this point as well. Compare your interpretation with that of others to see what elements of the passage you may have overlooked. If the sources you consult offer an interpretation different from yours, don't immediately accede to the "experts." Assess the

strength of their arguments (take them seriously), and then decide if you should revise your interpretation.

### Reading the New Testament Epistles
### A General Suggestion

As we saw in chapter 4, most of the New Testament letters are highly *occasional* documents; that is, they are written to *particular* individuals or groups in order to address *particular* situations and concerns. Moreover, when reading these letters we need to be mindful of the fact that we are listening in on one part of a conversation. Consequently, the interpreter must explore several layers of contexts when seeking to understand what a given passage is intending to communicate and how it is functioning within the letter as a whole.

### Engaging the Text
1. Explore the Passage
   - Read the passage over several times, attempting to discern its primary thrust. If the passage is lengthy, break it up into paragraphs, sentences, or smaller "thought units." Try to determine if the boundaries that have been selected for the passage actually constitute a distinct unit of thought.
   - More carefully investigate the passage. Seek to determine its logical progression, that is, how the argument is being developed in order to prove a point (how the "thought units" flow from and to and relate to one another). Try to perceive the tone of the passage (conciliatory, lamenting, sarcastic, rebuking, exhortative). Note what ideas seem most prominent, looking for repeated words, phrases, or concepts. Write down or spell out in your own mind what the point of the passage seems to be.
   - One technique that I have found useful with many epistle texts is to list all of the words/phrases that are repeated throughout the passage along with what the author says about each of those concepts. This is especially helpful with passages that have three or more repeated expressions. Focusing, then, on those words or phrases, one should piece together how the author relates them to one another. For example, with Gal 3:6-18, I would list "belief/faith, law, Abraham, promise, Christ, God, justified/ righteous," and a brief description of what Paul has to say about each of these concepts. Then I would try to discern the connections he draws between them. This provides a good starting point for determining the overall intent of the passage.
   - Determine if earlier traditions are cited or referenced. If so, how are they being used to support or advance the author's perspective or

to illustrate a point? Has the tradition in view been "tweaked" or reworked in a particular way? For examples of this, see the discussion of Paul's shaping of Old Testament texts in chapter 4.

2.  Explore the Immediate Context (the surrounding argument)
    Investigate the immediate context of the passage, seeking to determine how the passage under study functions within the surrounding argument. Does the passage mark a new development, a digression, or serve as an illustration or a proof? Be sure to note transitional words or phrases. Reflect on how the immediate context can shape your understanding of the passage.

3.  Explore the Larger Context (the entire letter)
    Incorporate what you have discerned about the passage into your understanding of the letter as a whole. How, in other words, does the passage in its immediate context relate to the prevailing topics, concerns, and character of the letter? If you need help with this, consult a commentary on the epistle and read through the relevant parts that discuss the letter as a whole. Or, if you have a study Bible, review its introduction to the letter.

4.  Explore the Situational Context (the occasion) and Historical Context
    Try to determine what aspects of the community situation the passage addresses and how this might help you better understand the meaning and function of the passage. In addition, are there any features of the wider cultural or historical context that could shed light on certain elements the passage? A good biblical commentary can provide you with this information.

5.  Putting It Together
    • Once you have examined all of these contexts, then you are ready to utilize these observations to describe how this passage functions as one piece of one part of a larger conversation. This becomes, then, the point of departure for discerning how the message of the passage is to be brought into conversation with the canon as a whole.
    • As with other biblical genres, consulting one or more biblical commentaries may be helpful at this point as well. Again, compare your interpretation with that of others. Have you overlooked something in the passage? Remember, take the arguments of others seriously, but do your own thinking.

## Bringing the Passage into Conversation with . . .

I have emphasized that the overarching purpose of Scripture is to proclaim the character and will of God; God's undying effort to redeem a wayward humanity throughout human history, culminating in Jesus' ministry; and what it means to be God's people. And so, if we continually ask of the biblical passages we encounter what they are revealing about God and God's will, God's undying attempt to redeem humanity, and what it means to be God's people, then we are reading Scripture in a manner that is consonant with its purpose. Moreover, reading a biblical passage with these questions in mind also helps us to bring into conversation with the passage the canon as a whole and our time and place.

### . . . the Rest of the Canon

This step involves taking what we have discerned a passage under study proclaims about God, God's efforts to redeem humanity, and what it means to be God's people (while realizing that different passages will speak to some of these matters more so than others), and bringing it into dialogue with the dominant story lines of Scripture. Again, there is no one, clearly defined way to engage in this reflection. With this step and those to follow (and all the previous), interpretation is much more of a Spirit-formed art than a science. Perhaps the best way to become acquainted with and more adept at this approach is simply to practice it and converse with others who are doing the same thing. Even so, here are some lines of inquiry that might be helpful to pursue.

1. Does the passage under study speak to dimensions of God's character and will, God's attempt to redeem humanity, and our calling to be God's people that are common throughout the biblical story?

2. If so, are there ways in which the passage nuances your understanding of these basic matters of biblical faith? Is there some element that the passage casts in sharper relief? How does its instruction relate to the New Testament's proclamation concerning Jesus? What lines of continuity would you draw between them? How does the passage's instruction on these matters contribute to our understanding of the biblical story as it culminates in Jesus ministry, crucifixion, resurrection, and ongoing ministry?

3. If the passage presents a view of these basic matters of faith that appears to be in contrast with the dominant threads of the biblical story:
   - Try to define specifically what the differences are.
   - How might the circumstances depicted in the passage help us to understand its portrayal of God and/or what it means to be God's people? At this point in time, what is taking place in the history of God's people? Is God responding to the actions of certain characters? Is there a particular crisis in view?
   - Is the passage's depiction of God, God's attempt to redeem humanity, or our calling similar to that found in other stories in Scripture? How might these stories together help to fill out our understanding of these basic matters of faith? More to the point, how might the stories help us to see another side of God or what it means for us to be God's people that we might have neglected? Discovering additional perspectives can enrich our grasp of the biblical story. With such reflection, it is important for us to be open to the ways in which the story may be widening our view of God, God's attempt to redeem us, and what it means to be God's people. In other words, we need to be especially mindful that the preconceptions we bring with us to Scripture don't get in the way of learning something new.
   - If we are dealing with an Old Testament passage, how might the culmination of the biblical story in Jesus' ministry, teaching, and resurrection provide us with some perspective for gauging the relevance of the passage within the flow of the biblical story? For example, is the passage speaking to realities that Jesus addresses and recasts in his own teaching, such as what it means to be counted among God's people? Do we find in the New Testament traditions development of thought beyond what is presented in this passage (such as the role of the law in Jesus' teachings and Paul's letters)? If so, how does this qualify the role we grant to the passage in helping to define our view of God and/or what it means to be God's people? Still, even if we view some particular features of the text as belonging to an earlier era in the history of God's people (such as the requirement of circumcision, or dietary restrictions), how might the passage—given its place in the biblical story—still contribute to our understanding of God's character and faith? (That is, we are to be a people called to live in right relationship with God and one another, and set apart for a particular vocation.)

4. If you are still sensing that the story is presenting a view of God or what it means to be God's people that is incompatible with the dominant story lines of Scripture, and not simply a matter transcended in the ministry and teaching of Jesus:

   • Once again define that difference as specifically as you can. Review carefully how your understanding of the core story lines of Scripture would be affected if you embraced the contrasting view of God and faith portrayed in the passage. What specific teachings of Jesus or the writers of the New Testament seem counter to this perspective?

   • If you come to the conclusion that the intent of the passage cannot be reasonably reconciled with the essential story lines of Scripture, reflect on what this teaches us about the character of Scripture, and why the editors of the canon decided to include this tradition. How might this passage, and your reflection on it, be a testimony to the dynamic character of Scripture as sacred dialogue?

   • It may also be profitable to reflect on why the biblical author thought it important to portray God and faith in this fashion. What sense do you get of his motivations? How might we find similar motivations at work in believing communities today?

In my experience, the type of reflection described in (2) above is by far the most common in our reading of Scripture. Bringing a passage into conversation with the rest of Scripture is usually characterized by that constructive task of discerning how a passage contributes to or fills out our understanding of God, God's act of salvation in Jesus, and what it means to be God's people. Less common is our encounter with passages that seem to be in contrast with the dominant trends of Scripture. Yet with many of these cases we can either appreciate the text as speaking to elements of God's character and will that we may have neglected, or make sense of the passage as presenting a conception of God and God's will that was common to a particular time and place for God's people but was transcended in later instruction (such as we saw with some of the Old Testament law codes in chapter 3). Less common still are those passages that seem to be so at odds with the character of God as depicted throughout the biblical story and in the ministry of Jesus that it appears impossible to draw any significant lines of continuity between them. Still, they have crucial value in that they are one of several features that help us to understand the nature of Scripture as dynamically formed dialogue.

### . . . Our Time and Place

Asking what a passage of Scripture reveals about God and God's will, God's undying attempt to redeem humanity, culminating in Jesus, and what it means to be God's people, also lays a foundation for discerning and announcing the witness of that text for believers in our time and place. Much has been made of the fact that there often exists a troubling disconnect between the work of critical exegesis and the engagement of Scripture for believing communities. The picture offered is that of a pastor or priest dutifully engaging in complex exegetical work only to set much of that aside as he or she then painstakingly tries to wring from the examined passage some message of relevance for believers in the pew. But this need not be the case. It all comes down to which set of questions an interpreter brings to the text and for what ends the tools of exegesis are employed. Accordingly, the approach presented on the preceding pages marshals exegetical technique for explicitly confessional ends. It leads the interpreter—as part of the interpretive process—to grapple with how a passage is part of and relates to the larger story that Scripture tells about God and God's relationship with humanity. What results is not a dumbing down of the text so that church folk can understand it, but a way of engaging Scripture that leads the interpreter more deeply into the heart of the story Scripture was composed to proclaim. And having been led there, the interpreter stands in a much better place from which to help others engage and converse about the story.

Still, the practice of inscribing ourselves into the story of our faith does have its share of challenges, as I noted above. It too is a learned art, driven by a Spirit-led imagination, and much is to be gained from pursuing it in community with other believers. Here again are suggestions for some lines of inquiry one might want to pursue, perhaps while preparing for preaching or in the context of a small group Bible study.

1. Gather together what you have discerned the passage proclaims about God and God's will, God's undying attempt to redeem humanity, culminating in Jesus, and/or what it means to be God's people. Allow the particular focus and nuances of the passage to come to the fore. Ask yourself, "What does this passage contribute to my understanding of the biblical story? How does it help me better appreciate God's will or character, God's effort to restore humanity, and/or what it means to walk in God's ways?"

2. Have as your goal discerning ways of engaging and talking about the passage that will best enable us to mirror its witness in our own conversation about God and our lives of faith. Shape connections between our lives and the circumstances and characters of the text that will

help give expression to the particular witness of the passage. How is it that we may—in our own lives—more fully recognize, experience, and testify to the truths about God and faith the passage proclaims?

3. Creatively reflect on how we might deeply inscribe ourselves—in our time and place—into the view of God and faith this passage offers.
   - Imagine the passage "replayed" in our contemporary setting. Look for patterns in our own lived experience that in some way parallel the activity, experience, and circumstances in view in the passage. Hold those experiences and circumstances—that of the passage and our lives—together in dynamic relationship. How is our contemporary experience or circumstance in view illuminated by the witness of the biblical text? What would it mean to frame and respond to our experience or circumstance in a manner inspired by the testimony to God and God's will offered by the passage? How might the testimony of this passage transform our understanding of this experience or circumstance?
   - Imagine how characters presented in the passage would respond to the contemporary circumstances or experiences you have in view. For example, if the passage is from a New Testament epistle, how would the epistle writer respond to this situation in a way that parallels his instruction in the passage? How about the community to which he is writing? If a narrative text, how might we imagine faithful characters reacting in a manner that mirrors their actions and attitudes in the passage? What might this imagining help us to discern about how we ourselves could similarly bear witness to God's character and will?
   - A similar line of inquiry one might pursue, especially with a narrative text, is to consider which characters in the story are those with whom we most readily identify. At times we may associate with characters who act in accord with God's will and we may feel inspired to unite with them in faithful witness. In such instances, it may be fruitful for us to ask, "What would it mean for us to join them in living out the story of our faith our time and place? In what situations and circumstances are we called to do as they do and speak as they speak?" At other times—perhaps during our more honest moments—we may find ourselves identifying with characters with whom we would rather not be associated but who are, at least in some ways, much like us. At such moments, it might be helpful for us to reflect on how their actions are mirrored in our own and what it would mean to shape our lives toward greater faithfulness.

4.  A word of caution. Although we can find, in most cases, some significant points of connection with the testimony and experiences depicted or presented in a biblical passage, there are passages that will speak more readily to some communities than others. And some passages may reflect situations so far removed from our particular context that we may not do them justice if we try to put ourselves in their setting (for example, for us in America, stories of persecution leading to martyrdom, and for many of us, stories that console the poor). But this can become an opportunity for telling the stories of our brothers and sisters whose lives do reflect these realities, and considering how we might more faithfully assist them in responding to these challenges and be edified by their witness.

5.  Discerning how a passage speaks to us in our time and place can also be pursued with passages that present a view of God and faith in sharp contrast with the larger contours of the biblical story and the ongoing instruction of Jesus in our midst. With such passages, it may be fruitful to inscribe ourselves into the circumstances expressed or assumed by the passage in order to appreciate and understand the motivations behind the perspective it offers, and perhaps even realize ways in which we ourselves might share them. Then the crucial task is to discern how the teachings and example of Jesus counter and transform this perspective and lead us more deeply into God's kingdom.

### . . . Jesus, through the Spirit

Prayer is the gift from God that more than any faculty or craft we possess enables our faithful interpretation and proclamation of the gospel. It is also the means by which we are most attentive and receptive to the ongoing ministry of Christ in our midst. Every facet of our interpretation—whether as individuals or as a community—should be centered around prayer, so that we may faithfully inscribe ourselves into the story it proclaims and open our hearts to the words Christ has yet to reveal to us, and the words we need Christ to repeat to us. As emphasized in chapter 3, granting Christ the sovereignty due to him as Lord entails being open to the new things Christ may be working in our midst. Christ alone is the Word that is to be the recipient of our worship and devotion.

In my view, the "fruits of the Spirit" are evident in those whose reflection on Scripture revolves around prayerful attentiveness to Christ's ongoing instruction in their midst. Their deliberation and discussion of Scripture are characterized by a steadfast confidence in the truth of God's love made known in Jesus, a generous spirit toward others, and openness to the new and even surprising ways the Spirit may be at work among them. Their use of Scripture is not for the purpose of proving the rightness of their claims over those of others. Instead, it is to discern the ways in which Jesus is calling them and their communities to entrust themselves more completely to God and one another. Indeed, discerning God's will for us and affirming what we believe are important. And, as we see embodied in Scripture itself, our discussion about God and God's ways will at times be contentious. But in every act of reading and conversing about Scripture, especially during our times of disputation, our confidence and conviction must be matched by a humility that knows that Christ may yet have more to teach us.

### . . . the Community of Faith

All of the above strategies are those that would be fruitful for individuals in their reading of Scripture, whether doing so devotionally or for the purpose of becoming better acquainted with our sacred traditions (or both). With some guidance, reading Scripture can be for individuals a blessed experience of more deeply embracing the story of our faith and hearing more clearly Jesus' call to discipleship. And yet, as valuable as individual reflection on Scripture can be, I believe that Scripture is most fully and faithfully engaged when read prayerfully within a community of believers. One of the most consistent and tangible benefits of a community gathered around the story I have experienced is that people from different walks of life are able to illuminate different dimensions of the passage in view. What results is an engagement with Scripture that is much richer and often more readily brought to bear on the context of our own lives. Another benefit is that the experience of being shaped by Scripture and the Spirit in and through their dialogue with one another strengthens the fellowship of those believers and their commitment to one another. Finally, and most important still, is the promise of Jesus that "where two or three are gathered in my name, I am there among them" (Matt 18:20). It is in community that we are most fully enabled to receive Christ's presence and embrace Christ's ongoing word.

Now I realize that some, perhaps many, of us have been part of small-group Bible studies that in various ways have failed to measure up to the idealized portrait I just offered. I have too. Even the best of groups will have its share of trying moments or periods when inspiration seems rather lean. The following suggestions are geared toward helping group leaders and participants facilitate discernment that invites members to share their unique gifts and insights as they gather around Scripture and seek to live into its story more faithfully.

1.  Pray at the beginning and close of each session, asking for insight, faithful discernment, generosity toward others, and humility.

2. Avoid patterns of interaction in which the group looks to one individual to provide "the answers." This, unfortunately, is the role many groups impose upon their pastor. Several of my clergy colleagues complain that their Bible studies with church members are often reduced to a running monologue or sermon because the participants don't want or feel equipped to share their own ideas about the text. Other pastors may relish this role as one that exalts their knowledge of Scripture and pastoral authority. In my view, however, this way of doing Bible study circumvents many of the blessings this time of exploration and reflection has to offer. It also has the potential to be quite lifeless and boring.

3. The following techniques have helped me as a group facilitator to encourage participation within a Bible study group.
   - The first and best thing to do, especially if you sense that group participation could be a problem, is to emphasize the conversational character of the group when you first start meeting. This may not be necessary if the group has been meeting for some time. Nevertheless, it may be helpful to set aside one meeting or part of a meeting for the purpose of talking about the value of having as many group members as possible make contributions to the discussion and discernment. In any case, addressing in an open and straightforward manner the importance of valuing the input of all members, respecting the perspectives shared by one another, and maintaining a disposition of humility and generosity toward one another may go a long ways toward resolving many of the group dynamics that inhibit rich dialogue and reflection.
   - One common method of helping participants find their voice and encouraging participation is to divide the participants up into smaller groups, have them discuss certain features of the passage, and then reconvene as a larger group, asking for input from each of the smaller groups. If possible, pair quieter members not with talkers, but with those who you think will be able to draw out the ideas and reflection of the quieter members. I have found that providing the small groups with specific questions on which to ruminate—at least as a starting point for their reflection—often facilitates more productive discussion.
   - Sometimes group members will have something to say, but just need to be asked to do so. Don't be afraid to ask direct questions of participants. Or, if one member hasn't participated in the discussion, simply ask that person if there is anything he or she would like to share with the group.

- If, despite your best efforts to encourage participation from all members, one or two people continue to dominate the discussion, either because they simply like to talk or because no one else will, it may be useful to speak with them individually. Rather than asking them to refrain from talking, however, ask them to help you encourage the other members to participate.
- I have found four things especially important for maintaining good group morale and creating an environment conducive to discussion and discernment: (i) affirmation of all group members' contributions to discussion; (ii) straightforward emphasis on the importance of group participation; (iii) a profound respect for the blessing this time of reflection provides; and (iv) a good sense of humor.

4. While encouraging participants to share their perspectives, the group should also have as one of its main goals the discernment of read ings that thoughtfully engage the text in view. For this reason, the strategies of interpretation introduced in the preceding sections are offered to help groups discern the intent of the biblical author or editor and also to encounter biblical texts as an invitation to sacred dialogue. The group may also want to make use of resources that will help them navigate through the passages they study, such as a discussion guide (available for Lectionary texts, individual biblical books, and topical studies) or commentaries written for a lay readership. At the same time, the group should be encouraged not to defer automatically to the perspective of these resources or to turn to them without having first spent a considerable amount of time engaging the passage on their own. The primary goal is not to explore what others outside the group think about the biblical texts in view, but to have the group members explore the texts themselves, sometimes with the assistance of others.

5. As we discussed in chapter 5, people will come away from biblical texts with different perspectives and reactions. This is a blessing that should be valued, for varied responses to the text, held together in creative tension, can lead us to see different dimensions of the passage and better discern how they speak to the central story lines of Scripture as well as to our lives. Still, there will likely be times when the interpretations group members present are so at odds with one another that it is difficult to see them as simply emphasizing different dimensions of the passage in view. It is also important for the group to identify readings emerging from their discussion that seem too disconnected from the passage under study. This is not an easy task. It is difficult to know where exactly to draw the line

in terms of which readings helpfully illuminate different aspects of the passage, and which ones obscure or even oppose the witness of the passage. Once again, Mark Allan Powell's rubric of "polyvalence within parameters" is helpful to consider (see chapter 5). Our openness to various perspectives is crucial to ensuring lively, rich, and illuminating discussion, the kind of polyvalence that leads to faithful discernment in Christian community. There may be a range of "acceptable" readings that could emerge from a passage. At the same time, there is a wider range of readings that may have little to do with the passage in view or may construe it in ways that severely circumvent its potential to bear witness to God, God's undying attempt to redeem humanity culminating in Jesus, and what it means to be God's people. It is important for us to point out (thoughtfully and humbly) when interpretations offered by members seem too disconnected from the witness of the passage or strike a chord at odds with its testimony to God's character and our call to faithful service.

6.  In situations of disagreement, it is essential for the group to talk through their differences of opinion with both honesty and humility. Both are needed to ensure that members freely offer their perspectives and that others receive them *open to the potential that their own perspectives may be altered in the exchange*. What matters most is not that any one member's viewpoint (including our own!) is adopted as the more faithful interpretation. Rather, what matters most, and what in the end will lead to the blessing of greater understanding for all members as they gather themselves around God's word, is prayerful, discerning, and gracious dialogue. It is this medium of engagement with God and one another—as the preceding pages have labored to show—that more than anything else connects us deeply with God and God's will and leads us to shape our lives into fertile ground for God's work among us. If you get the "right answer," but sacrifice the conversation in the process, much has been lost.

### By Way of Example: The Story of Jephthah's Vow (Judges 11)

The purpose of this brief discussion of Jephthah's vow is to illustrate some of the suggestions and guidelines presented in the preceding discussion, specifically those having to do with the interpretation of biblical narrative and bringing the passage into conversation with the biblical story as a whole and with our time and place. A truly in-depth examination of the passage would fill many pages, but I hope that my summary is enough to provide a helpful illustration of the guidelines presented above. I have selected this story in order once again to address a passage that seems to be at odds with the dominant features of God and God's will as depicted throughout Scripture. However, even if you do not find yourself agreeing with my interpretation of the passage, I hope that the exercise of walking through it for illustrative purposes will still be useful.

### Engaging the Text

I have selected a portion of the text (Judg 11:29-40) that includes the story of Jephhtah's vow and is similar to the length of passages commonly read in worship and examined by Bible study groups.

> Then the spirit of the Lord came upon Jepthah, and he passed through Gilead and Manasseh. He passed on to Mizpah of Gilead, and from Mizpah of Gilead he passed on to the Ammonites. And Jephthah made a vow to the Lord, and said, "If you will give the Ammonites into my hand, then whoever comes out of the doors of my house to meet me, when I return victorious from the Ammonites, shall be the Lord's, to be offered up by me as a burnt offering." So Jephthah crossed over to the Ammonites to fight against them; and the Lord gave them into his hand. He inflicted a massive defeat on them from Aroer to the neighborhood of Minnith, twenty towns, and as far as Abel-keramim. So the Ammonites were subdued before the people of Israel.
>
> Then Jephthah came to his home at Mizpah; and there was his daughter coming out to meet him with timbrels and with dancing. She was his only child, he had no son or daughter except her. When he saw her, he tore his clothes, and said, "Alas, my daughter! You have brought me very low; you have become the cause of great trouble to me. For I have opened my mouth to the Lord, and I cannot take back my vow." She said to him, "My father, if you have opened your mouth to the Lord, do to me according to what has gone out of your mouth, now that the Lord has given you vengeance against your enemies, the Ammonites." And she said to her father, "Let this thing be done for me: Grant me two months, so that I may go and wander on the mountains, and bewail my virginity, my companions and I." "Go," he said and sent her away for two months. So she departed, she and her companions, and bewailed her virginity on the mountains. At the end of two months, she returned to her father, who did with her according to the vow he had made. She had never slept with a man. So there arose an Israelite custom that for four days every year the daughters of Israel would go out to lament the daughter of Jephthah the Gileadite.

As we read through the text, there are a number of observations and questions we are likely to raise. The following is just a sample.

- "Then"—what just took place in the preceding narrative, and how is this story related to it (v. 29)?

- What is the relationship between the coming of the "spirit of the LORD" upon Jephthah and his immediately following actions, including the vow (vv. 29-31)?

- Was the spirit of the Lord commonly given to the other judges? How did the spirit impact or empower their actions?

- Is the vow seen as a faithful or unfaithful act by the narrator?

- Is Jephthah vowing human sacrifice, or does he have an animal in mind?

- Why does Jephthah make the vow to begin with? Is this an attempt to bargain with God, or to express his devotion to God?

- Jephthah defeats the Ammonites and returns home. He fulfills his role of delivering God's people (vv. 33-34).

- The narrator emphasizes (note the redundancy) that Jephthah's daughter is his only child (v. 34b).

- Jephthah is grief-stricken that he must sacrifice his daughter, yet he will honor his vow (v. 35).

- The narrator seems to be using pathos (emotionally charged narration) here to help us recognize the tragedy of the scene (vv. 34-40).

- The daughter displays amazing devotion to God and her father, courage and piety (vv. 36-37, 39).

- How did she know the content of her father's vow (v. 37)?

- Jepthah appears to respond to his daughter with compassion, allowing her to delay for two months (v. 38).

- Why does the narrator emphasize the daughter's virginity (vv. 37-40)? To heighten the sense of tragedy, or to point out that Jephthah will have no heir?

- This is such an important story that it led to a ritualized remembrance to honor the daughter (v. 40).

- Jephthah is named "the Gileadite" (v. 40).

As we continue to work our way through the passage, many of these points will resurface, especially the ones that seem most relevant for helping us understand the focus of the passage: Jephthah's making and keeping of his vow. Perhaps chief among the questions, and the one preoccupying nearly all published discussions of this text, is how are we meant to regard Jephthah's vow? Are we meant to see it as admirable or as incredibly and cruelly wrongheaded? The fact that the biblical author does not come out and tell us his perspective on the matter is not surprising. As we noted in chapter 5, the authors of Old Testament narratives are characteristically reticent, especially when it comes to direct assessments of characters' actions. More often than not they compose their narratives in such a way that they subtly guide us toward an appraisal of a character's actions without expressly stating it. What is troubling about the Jephthah story, in my view, is that even though it is a story about human sacrifice, the author does not provide us with any clear indication, directly or subtly, that we are to regard Jephthah's and his daughter's actions as unfaithful.

In fact, there are numerous details of the passage that present Jephthah and his vow in a positive light. The author informs us that Jephthah is filled with the spirit of the Lord, and it seems that all of his actions recorded in the immediately following verses up through his defeat of the Ammonites and including his vow stem from this inspiration (vv. 29-33). There are no breaks in the narration or sequencing of the events to suggest otherwise. His remorse for his daughter appears genuine, and he also shows compassion in allowing her to delay her death so that she may spend her final days with friends. His daughter's own piety only serves to reinforce this positive appraisal of the vow. Without questioning her father, she commits herself to whatever the vow requires and emphasizes the importance of her father's fulfilling the vow he made to the Lord (vv. 36-37). Moreover, the repeated reference to the "Lord" in their dialogue suggests that they have God as their focus. While the daughter's death is clearly portrayed as tragic, both for her and the soon-to-be-childless Jephthah, there is no hint from the narrator that this tragedy is not at the same time to be regarded as honorable. On first sight, it seems that the author wished to express through this poignant and disturbing tale that faithfulness to the commitments we have made to God is of first and greatest importance, beyond our commitment to anything or anyone else.

### Engaging the Text in Its Literary Context

When we broaden our purview, we find that the surrounding literary context also suggests the author's positive assessment of Jephthah. A son of Gilead, yet born to a prostitute, Jephthah is eventually spurned by his father's other sons and is driven out of the town of Gilead lest he inherit the household. He, not unlike David, becomes a mercenary and mighty warrior (Judg 11:1-3). When the Ammonites threaten to attack and take over the region, the leaders of Gilead, including those who had banished him, seek Jephthah's aid. In exchange for his military prowess they promise to make him head over them and all the inhabitants of Gilead. Jephthah accepts the terms (vv. 4-11). Before the onset of battle, however, a lengthy diplomatic exchange takes place between Jephthah and the king of the Ammonites (vv. 12-28). Here the narrator devotes a major section of the story to sketching out a marvelous view of Jephthah's character. We might have thought, given his background as an exiled prostitute's son and his renown as a mighty warrior, that Jephthah would be ill-equipped to bandy words with a head of state. But this is far from the case, as the eloquence and clever rhetoric of Jephthah's diplomacy surprisingly show. More remarkable, however, is that Jephthah is fully versed in the history of Israel's conquest of the land and joins with other leading characters throughout the historical books in testifying to Yahweh's faithfulness and sovereignty: Jephthah repeatedly upholds Yahweh's covenant with Israel and Yahweh's victory on Israel's behalf as that which establishes their basic claim to the territory the Ammonites want for themselves (vv. 12-28). Likewise, in the narrative that follows the vow story, Jephthah credits the LORD for his defeat of the Ammonites (Judg 12:3). If this were Joshua speaking, we would hardly be surprised. But during a period of Israel's history when God's people seemed unable or unwilling to remember much at all about their covenant relationship with and dependence on Yahweh (see the summary of Judg 2:6-23), Jephthah stands out as an exceptional champion of faith. This positive portrayal of Jephthah, including his acknowledgment of Yahweh's faithfulness and Israel's dependence on God for victory, provides the proper context for discerning the nature of his vow. He offers it not because he has ignored God's spirit or to manipulate Yahweh to action. Rather, as one who knows of Yahweh's help in the past and is filled with God's spirit, he offers his vow as a confident pledge to acknowledge the victory that Yahweh will impart to Israel through him. It is more a vow to praise (such as we find in the psalms) than a conditional statement.

Of course, it is difficult for us to stomach the notion that God's spirit would impel someone to make a pledge that could be interpreted as, or at least possibly result in, human sacrifice: "whoever comes out of the house to greet me when I return. . ." We cannot be sure of the specific intentions of Jephthah's vow. Archaeological evidence from this time and region shows that it was common for animals to reside in rooms connected to houses, and so whether Jephthah had an animal or a family member in mind for the sacrifice is uncertain. But should not Jephthah have thought it very possible that a human, like his devoted daughter, might be the first to run out and greet him? Or, if not Jephthah, shouldn't the spirit of God have known better? The author's portrayal of Jephthah as astute and gifted in speech *and* guided by God's spirit tells against a careless vow on his part and instead suggests that he presumed the sacrifice would be one of his own family.

If we turn to other treatments of the passage, we find that most interpreters do not believe that the author of Judges meant to uphold Jephthah's sacrifice as an example of honorable devotion to God. The tragedy of the sacrifice, as well as the consistent prohibitions against human sacrifice throughout the Old Testament (see Lev 18:21; 20:2; Deut 12:31; 18:9-10; Jer 3:24; 7:31; 9:4-6; 32:35), and an assessment of the vow as an unfaithful act "desiring to bind God rather than embrace the gift of the spirit" are common reasons given in support of this view.[3] As we have seen, however, the surrounding context emphasizes Jephthah's faithful regard of Yahweh and Yahweh's deliverance of Israel in the past. That Jephthah would suddenly offer a vow as if to bargain with God does not cohere with his characterization by the narrator, and there is nothing to signal us that his disposition has changed or that he has become suddenly fearful. In addition, the sequencing of the text in Judg 11:29-33—which begins with Jephthah's reception of the spirit, then moves on to his approach to battle, his vow, and his defeat of the Ammonites—makes it difficult to justify pulling out the vow as the one element of that sequence that the spirit did not inspire. Elsewhere in Judges the spirit of God impels and empowers characters to do things that we might otherwise think counter to God's will. Gideon receives the spirit (Judg 6:34) but then repeatedly demands, in the famous story of the dew on the fleece, further proof of God's willingness to lead him to victory, proof that God then graciously provides (Judg 6:36-40). The spirit leads Samson to dismember a young lion (Judg 14:6) and later empowers him to kill (murder) thirty men simply for their garments to settle a lost bet (Judg 14:19)! Our assumptions of what the spirit of God would or would not empower and inspire may not be the same as those of the writer of Judges. While we and many writers of the Bible may find human sacrifice reprehensible, it appears that the writer of Judges was willing to grant this exception for the very reason that—in his view—it was not offered by Jephthah in the attempt to manipulate God, but in faithfulness to a pledge made by an honorable man, with an equally honorable daughter.

### Engaging the Text in Its Historical Context

If we consider the historical context in which this story was likely put into its final form, the exilic or early post-exilic periods, we can see how it might be meant to speak to Israel in that time and place. On one level, the story joins with others throughout Judges serving as reassurance that if they, like Israel, repent (see 10:10-16), no matter how far they have strayed from God's ways, God will empower leaders among them who will restore their fortunes. On another level, in Jephthah the author presents one who fully acknowledges God's power and strength and is willing, in response, to devote himself to God no matter what the cost. For a people cast into exile because of their unrelenting faithlessness to God, Jephthah and his daughter serve as models of the type of single-minded devotion that the exiles themselves are now to emulate. Jephthah's sacrifice of his daughter poignantly speaks to the depth of commitment that Israel itself is to have for the covenant promises renewed by Yahweh. What matters most, above every other commitment, even above one's devotion to one's children, is faithfulness to God.

### Bringing the Passage into Conversation with the Canon

There are numerous points of contrast between the Jephthah story and the rest of the canon. As noted above, the Old Testament consistently denounces human sacrifice, not to mention the unprovoked killing of other persons, and it is a common criticism that the prophets level against the Canaanites and some of Israel's own kings. While God's command for Abraham to sacrifice Isaac may seem to provide a parallel to this passage, God's intervention shows that the sacrifice itself was not what God sought, but Abraham's demonstration of his trust in God and loyalty. In the case of Jephthah, God does not call for the sacrifice or, sadly, intervene to stop it. More important still, it is difficult to reconcile the tale with one of the major story lines emerging from the creation story and coursing throughout the Scripture: God's desire for creatures to have life and have it abundantly. Against this backdrop, the death of Jephthah's daughter appears as such a waste and notably one that prevents God's will for her to "be fruitful and multiply."

Jesus' actions and teachings present a perspective on the value of human life that contrasts sharply with Jephthah's fulfillment of his vow. There are numerous passages we could bring into conversation with the Jephthah story, but two that seem especially appropriate, given their focus on two daughters, are the interlaced accounts of Jesus healing Jairus's daughter and a women suffering a hemorrhage in Mark 5:21-43. Jairus, the synagogue leader, begs Jesus to heal his beloved daughter, who is at the point of death. Jesus immediately goes with him (vv. 22-24). While on the way, a woman who has suffered from a flow of blood for over twelve years and has spent all that she had searching for a cure pushes her way through the crowd toward Jesus, thinking "If I but touch his clothes, I will be made well" (vv. 25-29). When she catches an edge of Jesus' cloak, she is immediately healed. Jesus stops in his tracks, and spins around to find the one who touched him. After some delay, the woman comes forward with fear and trembling (suffering from a flow of blood, she had just made Jesus and many others in the crowd unclean [see Lev 15:25-30]), and tells Jesus the whole truth. In a moving scene, Jesus embraces the impoverished, socially outcast woman as "daughter," commends her faith, and sends her forth healed of her disease (vv. 30-34). Meanwhile, messengers from the leader's house come to Jairus with painful news. His beloved daughter has died. He need not trouble Jesus any longer. But Jesus continues the journey, telling Jairus not to fear but to trust in him. Upon arriving, he enters the house, and raises the little girl to life (vv. 35-43).

In each story, the emphasis on faith in Jesus as the embodiment of God's saving power is apparent. Both the woman suffering a hemorrhage and Jairus trust Jesus to the point that they open themselves to receiving God's blessing. In this sense, their faith parallels that of Jephthah, who also knew to trust in God's deliverance. However, in stark contrast to the Jephthah story, these stories (and many others throughout the Gospels) celebrate human trust as that which opens the way for *God's gift of healing and new life.* Here faith led to the deliverance of two beloved daughters from death by the grace of God, not to their sacrifice in order to display the faithfulness of their fathers. In short, trust in God leads us to embrace God's gift of life for ourselves and others—this is the essence of the Gospel. And as seen most clearly in Jesus, *God makes the sacrifice that saves us and leads us to faith so that we may share together in God's blessing.* The revelation of God's will and ways in Jesus helps us to see that Jephthah's sacrifice of his daughter is not what the LORD required of him, and it circumvented the blessing God would have been pleased to provide for both of them.

Of course, there are numerous New Testament passages in which Jesus and others call believers to remain steadfast in their faith, even if it leads to persecution and death. Choosing to die for the sake of Jesus and the gospel is upheld as an admirable sacrifice. However, this is a choice that arises as a result of the rejection of Jesus and his followers by those who oppose God's reign. In other words, God's adversaries create the circumstance in which believers are either forced to renounce their faith or suffer persecution and perhaps even death. Such was not the case with Jephthah. He knew his enemies would be vanquished and Israel spared. Yet the one who knew so much about God failed to understand this dimension of God's will: sacrifice of human life simply as an unprovoked display of devotion is not what God desires. It becomes a sacred act only when circumstances demand it, when the only alternative would be to deny the truth of God's love. Moreover, this is always a choice that believers are to make for themselves, not on behalf of others. In a contrast painful to behold, Jephthah does not offer up his own life as a sacrifice, but that of another.

Therefore, when brought into dialogue with the rest of the biblical canon, including the ministry and teaching of Jesus, Jephthah's vow and sacrifice are revealed as the result of a tragic misunderstanding on the part of Jephthah, his daughter, and the writer of Judges of what God seeks from us and wills for us. To be sure, there are several admirable elements of Jephthah's and his daughter's character and actions that cohere well with our calling as God's people. But from a vantage point different from theirs and looking back over the whole period of the judges, we see that Jephthah's vow and his daughter's embrace of her role in it ably capture the struggle of God's people during this dark era of their history to sustain faithful devotion to God and true wisdom.

### Bringing the Passage into Conversation with Our Time and Place

Even if the writer of Judges meant to present Jephthah's vow and sacrifice of his daughter as an example of admirable devotion to God, this does not entail that we should dismiss this text as an unworthy resource for preaching or reflection. Rather, the contrast we have discerned between the text and the rest of the canon and what that conversation highlights about the tragic deficiencies in Jephthah's and his daughter's understanding of God's will can serve as the focus for discerning how this passage may speak faithfully to us in our own time and place. For instance, questions I might be led to raise in my faith community are the following: What in our lives and the lives of our church community reflects our own misplaced piety? What actions and attitudes have we championed in the name of faith that are actually opposed to God's ways? Like Jephthah, how have we treated others as objects, whose lives can be offered up for the sake of displaying our honor or to serve our vocation? How through self-absorption have we circumvented God's blessing for others? Or, like Jephthah's daughter, how have we allowed others to chart our course in ways that render us unable to use the gifts and vocation God has granted us?

Moreover, if the interpretation I offer above holds true, then this passage is among others we have examined in this book that stand in opposition to the dominant features of God and God's will presented throughout the canon. The valuable lesson we learn from these passages is that God's word is comprised of many voices, some of which strike a note in sharp discord with the harmony composed by the whole.

The reasons these stories found their way into Scripture is not because God was sloppy when guiding our creation of the canon or suffered a lapse of attention (though with us among God's creatures, we could certainly understand why God might get distracted from time to time). They were included because Scripture stands as a witness to God's call for our ancestors in the faith to join God and one another in a sacred dialogue, a conversation that gathers many voices around the one story of God's saving grace. These passages also serve as God's invitation to us. For they, along with the rest of Scripture, call us to join our harmonious and discordant voices to that ancient and ongoing conversation among God and God's people, and to discern the wondrous melody rising above the discordance. They call us to speak with God and one another and to listen, that we might hear the footfalls of Jesus and clumsily trudge our way more deeply into God's blessing.

# Notes

-------

## Introduction: Scripture: An Invitation to Sacred Dialogue

1. For a helpful and often-cited discussion of the canonical processes leading to the formation of Scripture, see James A. Sanders, *From Sacred Story to Sacred Text: Canon as Paradigm* (Philadelphia: Fortress Press, 1987).

2. Paul J. Achtemeier, *Inspiration and Authority: Nature and Function of Christian Scripture* (Peabody, Mass.: Hendrickson, 1999), 76–77.

3. For example, see ibid., 91–121.

4. Terence E. Fretheim, *The Pentateuch*, Interpreting Biblical Texts (Nashville: Abingdon, 1996), 169.

5. Richard Bauckham, "Reading Scripture as a Coherent Story," in *The Art of Reading Scripture*, ed. Ellen F. Davis and Richard B. Hays (Grand Rapids: Eerdmans, 2003), 43–44.

## Chapter 1: Having Words with God

1. In my discussion of this and other biblical stories to follow, I am concerned with exploring the account as it is presented by the biblical author, not with trying to reconstruct the history behind it. My intent throughout this and other chapters is to discern and illustrate what the biblical authors and compilers claimed about God, God's will for humanity, and what it means to be God's faithful people through the stories and instruction they record.

2. Scholars differ over whether or not the Israelites were intending to replace Yahweh with a different god or simply attempting to force Yahweh or Yahweh's messenger to be present among them through the creation of an idol in Exodus 32. Yet so consistently is the creation of idols linked with the worship of other deities throughout the Old Testament that I think the most natural way to understand the action is as an attempt to replace devotion to Yahweh with the worship of other gods (see Exod 20:2-5). This is also suggested by the author's use of *elohim* in this context (lit. "gods") to refer to the object of the people's worship in contrast to the nearly singular use of *YHWH* (translated "Lord") for Yahweh in 32:1-14. Although *elohim* is often used for Yahweh, it is also frequently employed to designate gods other than Yahweh. Finally, Ps 106:19-20 clearly refers back to this event and understands what took place as an idolatrous act of *replacing* Yahweh with the worship of another god: "They made a calf at Horeb and worship a cast image. They exchanged the glory of

God for the image of an ox that eats grass. They forgot God, their Savior, who had done great things in Egypt, wondrous works in the land of Ham, and awesome deeds by the Red Sea." Nevertheless, in either case, the end result is nearly the same: the people are setting the terms for their relationship with G(g)od, and their ritual indicates that what they now worship is a far cry from the God revealed to Abraham's descendents and through the Exodus.

3. The phrase "Most Moved Mover" is borrowed from the title of Clark H. Pinnock's fine work *Most Moved Mover: A Theology of God's Openness*, Didsbury Lectures 2000 (Grand Rapids: Baker, 2001).

4. Ibid., 7.

5. Ibid., 27.

6. For an excellent discussion of the psalms as instruction for human dialogue with God, see J. Clinton McCann Jr., *A Theological Introduction to the Book of Psalms: The Psalms as Torah* (Nashville: Abingdon, 1993).

7. It is likely because they were meant to serve this function that most psalms offer only general descriptions of the situation at hand, enabling them to be utilized in response to a variety of experiences and situations.

8. Walter Brueggemann, "The Costly Loss of Lament" *Journal for the Study of the Old Testament* 36 (1986): 57-71, here 62.

9. Walter Brueggemann, *The Message of the Psalms: A Theological Commentary* (Minneapolis: Augsburg, 1984), 86.

10. Anna Carter Florence, *Preaching as Testimony* (Louisville: Westminster John Knox, 2007), 74-75.

11. Scholars frequently note that even the Evangelists did not always cast the meaning of a parable in the same way, as is evidenced by differences in their editing of a parable and their placement of it in the narrative (see the parable of the great banquet in Luke 14:15-24 and Matt 22:1-10).

12. Pinnock, *Most Moved Mover*, 7.

### Chapter 2: Sacred Traditions in Tension

1. Most biblical scholars believe that the prophetic oracles contained in Isaiah 40–66 come from the exilic and post-exilic period (after 587 B.C.E.), given their frequent references to the destruction of Jerusalem, the Babylonian exile, and return from exile. These latter chapters are commonly referred to as "Second Isaiah," or divided into "Second Isaiah" (Isaiah 40–55) and "Third Isaiah (Isaiah 56–66). Some scholars have postulated that these later oracles were produced by an Isaianic school or looser group of devotees which preserved the oracles of the eighth century prophet and added others to his collection that they deemed consistent with his message. Others argue that the later oracles are the work of an individual prophet who believed that the prophecies of the eighth-century Isaiah were being fulfilled in his day and desired to expand upon that ancient witness to God's work in the present.

2. Ben Witherington III, *Conflict and Community in Corinth: A Socio-Rhetorical Commentary on 1 and 2 Corinthians* (Grand Rapids: Eerdmans, 1995), 199.

3. This is known as the "two-source" or "four-source" theory and is one proposal of how to resolve what is known as the "Synoptic problem." Matthew, Mark, and Luke are known as the "Synoptic Gospels" because they present such a similar portrayal of Jesus: they see (*optic*) together (*syn*). So similar are their portrayals, often even down to the level of syntax and word choice, that scholars presume that there must be some literary relationship among them: that is, someone must have copied

from someone else. The question of what exactly is the nature of the literary relationship among the three Gospels is the "Synoptic problem": "problem" in the sense of an "issue" needing to be resolved. In the minds of most scholars, the explanation best supported by the evidence is that Mark was written first. Some of the reasons commonly cited in support of this view are the following: (1) Mark's Gospel is written in a less polished style of Greek, and when writers in antiquity copied from one another, they did not usually rewrite their sources in a poorer style. (2) There are many passages where it seems that Matthew and Luke have tightened up and polished Mark's account. (3) Matthew and Luke contain far more stories and teachings about Jesus, including infancy accounts, parables, and miracle stories, and it is hard to see why Mark would have excluded such material if he was copying from Matthew or Luke. (4) There are also a few places where Matthew seems to have reshaped portions of Mark's account in order to give some explanation for an event or to make it seem less scandalous (Jesus' baptism by John [Matthew has John protest], the request of James and John [Matthew reports that it was their mother that made the request], Jesus' teaching on divorce [Matthew includes the qualification of unchastity]).

4. Allen Verhey, *Remembering Jesus: Christian Community, Scripture and the Moral Life* (Grand Rapids: Eerdmans, 2002), 62.

## Chapter 3: The Dynamic Character of God's Instruction

1. To these could be added the several differences in the articulation of the Decalogue, or Ten Commandments, as they are found in Exod 20:2-17 and Deut 5:6-21. Regarding these, Peter Enns (*Inspiration and Incarnation: Evangelicals and the Problem of the Old Testament* [Grand Rapids: BakerAcademic, 2005], 87) states, "God seems perfectly willing to allow his law to be adjusted over time. Perhaps Israel, standing virtually on the brink of the promised land in Deuteronomy, needed to hear the fourth commandment a bit differently." Enns's discussion of diversity in the Old Testament (71–112), in which he cites several examples beyond the ones offered here, is insightful and well worth reading, though he and I understand its implications for discerning the nature of Scripture somewhat differently.

2. Terence E. Fretheim, *The Pentateuch*, Interpreting Biblical Texts (Nashville: Abingdon, 1996), 169.

3. James D. G. Dunn, *The Theology of Paul the Apostle* (Grand Rapids, Mich.: Eerdmans, 1998), 657.

4. See Karl Allen Kuhn, "Natural and Unnatural Relations between Text and Context: A Canonical Reading of Romans 1:26-27," *Currents in Theology and Mission* 33 (2006): 313–29, here 313–19. Much of the following discussion draws heavily from this article.

5. Paul J. Achtemeier, *Inspiration and Authority: Nature and Function of Christian Scripture* (Peabody, Mass.: Hendrickson, 1999), 155.

6. Robert A. J. Gagnon (*The Bible and Homosexual Practice: Texts and Hermeneutics* [Nashville: Abingdon, 2001], 443) argues that the New Testament "nowhere affirms slavery as an institution; the best that can be said is that it tolerates slavery and regulates it even in Christian households." So also Kathryn Greene-McCreight, "The Logic of the Interpretation of Scripture," in *Homosexuality, Science, and the "Plain Sense" of Scripture,* ed. David L. Balch (Grand Rapids, Mich.: Eerdmans, 2000), 242–60, here 258.

7. Some readers will note that the texts addressing slavery I discuss below all come from Paul's "disputed" letters; namely, those which many scholars (if not most) believe

Paul did not actually write (the disputed Paulines include: 2 Thessalonians, Colossians, Ephesians, 1 and 2 Timothy, Titus). Instead, many claim that they were likely written by followers or admirers of Paul after the apostle died, as if to say, "If Paul were still among us, this is what he would teach us about these matters." Does this give us reason to take the disputed letters as less inspired and authoritative than those letters considered by most to be Paul's authentic letters (1 Thessalonians, Galatians, Philippians, Philemon, 1 and 2 Corinthians, Romans), thus providing us an excuse to set aside the parts of these letters we don't like? Not in my view. To do so would be to elevate (in this case) Pauline authorship—the discernment of which is dependent upon the speculative practice of scholarly conjecture—as the chief criterion for the canonicity of these letters. The early Christians who valued, preserved, and gathered the texts that make up the New Testament and the church that throughout the centuries has equally valued these writings did not make authorship their sole or even primary criterion for inclusion in the canon (as is evidenced by the existence of numerous writings bearing the names of faithful Christians that were not included in the canon and the inclusion of others that are anonymous). Rather, what seemed most important to them was whether or not a writing conformed to the *regula fidei*, rule of faith: in other words, whether or not it faithfully proclaimed Jesus, his significance, and what it meant to be his disciple. Throughout the centuries, the church has embraced the disputed Paulines as conforming to that *regula fidei* and faithfully contributing to the witness of the whole canon. I believe that dialogical approach presented here is a much more biblically grounded way of addressing these "problem texts" in the disputed Paulines rather than simply marginalizing them because they were not written by Paul. As we shall see, Paul's undisputed letters have their problem texts as well.

8. See Gagnon, *Bible and Homosexual Practice*, 441-52.

9. I. Howard Marshall, *Beyond the Bible: Moving from Scripture to Theology*, Acadia Studies in Bible and Theology (Grand Rapids, Mich.: Baker, 2004), 78.

## Chapter 4: Theologizing in the Thick of Things

1. Others have strenuously criticized attempts to systematize Paul's thought into a coherent whole or to identify an abiding center, claiming that what we find in Paul is not theology per se but deeply contextualized, pastoral reflection characterized by a spontaneity, incompleteness, and even contradiction that resists coherence. See, for example, E. P. Sanders, *Paul, the Law, and the Jewish People* (Philadelphia: Fortress Press, 1983); and Heikki Räisänen, *Paul and the Law* (Philadelphia: Fortress Press, 1986).

2. David J. Lull, "Salvation History: Theology in 1 Thessalonians, Philemon, Philippians, and Galatians: A Response to N. T. Wright, R. B. Hays, and R. Scroggs," in *Pauline Theology*, Volume 1, *Thessalonians, Philippians, Galatians, Philemon*, ed. Jouette M. Bassler (Minneapolis: Fortress Press, 1991), 247.

3. J. Christiaan Beker, *Paul the Apostle: The Triumph of God in Life and Thought* (Philadelphia: Fortress Press, 1980), 11.

4. This near-exclusive concern with the content of Paul's theology dominates Pauline studies, including the debate on whether or not reconstructing Paul's theology is even possible. There are, however, some notable exceptions to this tendency. Both Richard B. Hays *(Echoes of Scripture in the Letters of Paul* [New Haven, Conn.: Yale University Press, 1989]) and Morna D. Hooker ("The Authority of the Bible: A New Testament Perspective," *Ex auditu* 19 [2003]: 45-64) argue that Paul's manner of engaging in contextual theology—his method of "doing theology" (or hermeneutics)—should also be regarded as instructive for Christians.

5. James D. G. Dunn, *The Theology of Paul the Apostle* (Grand Rapids, Mich.: Eerdmans, 1998), 170.

6. Hays, *Echoes of Scripture*, 2.

7. See Hays, *Echoes of Scripture*, 36-83, for discussion of how several passages from Romans contain allusions that recall Jesus' death and resurrection and relate them to the grand narrative emerging from the Jewish Scriptures. See also the chapters offered by N. T. Wright ("Putting Paul Together Again: Toward a Synthesis of Pauline Theology [1 and 2 Thessalonians, Philippians, and Philemon]"), Robin Scroggs ("Salvation History: The Theological Structure of Paul's Thought [1 Thessalonians, Philippians, and Galatians]"), Richard B. Hays ("Crucified with Christ: A Synthesis of the Theology of 1 and 2 Thessalonians, Philemon, Philippians and Galatians"), and Lull ("Salvation History") in *Pauline Theology,* vol. 1, ed. Bassler (Minneapolis: Fortress Press, 1991), for their emphasis on Paul's conception of Jesus and the gospel in relation to God's past and present dealings with Israel.

8. For other examples of Paul creatively recasting Old Testament passages, see Gal 3:15-18; Rom 5:12-21 and 9:19-33.

9. See, for example, the helpful article of Dan Cohn-Sherbok, "Paul and Rabbinic Exegesis," *Scottish Journal of Theology* 35 (1982): 117-32.

10. Leander E. Keck, *Paul and His Letters,* 2nd ed., Proclamation Commentary Series (Philadelphia: Fortress Press, 1988), 37.

11. Hays, *Echoes of Scripture*, 161.

12. Ibid., 168-69. Hays's concluding chapter, entitled "The Word Is Near You," offers a helpful assessment of Paul's interpretive strategies (hermeneutics) and their potential implications for the way Christians are called to read Scripture today.

13. Ibid., 189.

14. Beker, *Paul the Apostle*, 34.

15. Hays, *Echoes of Scripture*, 189.

## Chapter 5: God's Word in Many Voices

1. Mark Allan Powell, "The Forgotten Famine: Personal Responsibility in Luke's Parable of 'Prodigal Son,'" in *Literary Encounters with the Reign of God,* ed. Sharon H. Ringe and H. C. Paul Kim (New York: T&T Clark, 2004), 265-87.

2. Ibid., 266-67.

3. When Powell challenged the Russian students' focus on the famine as the primary cause of the son's plight, they replied that during a severe famine even the rich will die from hunger.

4. Powell, "Forgotten Famine," 279-85.

5. Mark Allan Powell, "The Timeless Tale of a Prodigal Son: What It Means both Near and Far," Founders' Day Lecture, Lakeland College, Sheboygan, Wisconsin, February 6, 2007. Powell also reports on the Tanzanian response to the parable in his *What Do They Hear? Bridging the Gap Between Pulpit and Pew* (Nashville: Abingdon, 2007) 26-27.

6. See Mark Allan Powell, *Chasing the Eastern Star: Adventures in Biblical Reader-Response Criticism* (Louisville: Westminster John Knox, 2001), for additional studies illustrating the reality of polyvalence in our reading of Scripture.

7. Robert Alter, *The World of Biblical Literature* (New York: Basic, 1992), 65.

8. Walter Brueggemann, *Theology of the Old Testament: Testimony, Dispute, Advocacy* (Minneapolis: Fortress Press, 1997).

9. Ibid., 145-266.

10. Ibid., 293.

11. Ibid., 242.

12. Ibid., 271.

13. Origen, *Homilies on Genesis and Exodus*, trans. Ronald E. Heine, *Fathers of the Church* 71 (Washington D.C.: Catholic University of America Press, 1982), 239–40.

14. John J. Collins, *Introduction to the Hebrew Bible* (Minneapolis: Fortress Press, 2004), 20.

15. For a helpful defense of pursuing the "authorial intent" of biblical passages as a chief aim of biblical interpretation, see Stephen E. Fowl, "The Role of Authorial Interpretation in the Theological Interpretation of Scripture," in *Between Two Horizons: Spanning New Testament Studies and Systematic Theology*, ed. Joel B. Green and Max Turner (Grand Rapids, Mich.: Eerdmans, 2000), 71–87.

16. Cited by Bruce M. Metzger, *The Canon of the New Testament: Its Origin, Development and Significance* (Oxford: Clarendon, 1997), 154–55.

17. Joel B. Green, "The (Re-)Turn to Narrative," in *Narrative Reading, Narrative Preaching: Reuniting New Testament Interpretation and Proclamation*, ed. Joel B. Green and Michael Pasquarello III (Grand Rapids, Mich.: Baker, 2003), 17.

18. Shared with the author in personal conversation with Mark Allan Powell.

19. Allen Verhey, *Remembering Jesus: Christian Community, Scripture and the Moral Life* (Grand Rapids, Mich.: Eerdmans, 2002), 70.

## Chapter 6: Coherence in the Conversation

1. For a helpful review of the role historical criticism in biblical studies and its marginalization of literary and theological dimensions of the text, see Hans Frei, *The Eclipse of Biblical Narrative: A Study of Eighteenth and Nineteenth Century Hermeneutics* (New Haven, Conn.: Yale University Press, 1974); and Walter Brueggemann, *Theology of the Old Testament: Testimony, Dispute, Advocacy* (Minneapolis: Fortress Press, 1997), 1–60. For noteworthy discussion and illustration of the important role historical criticism has and can continue to play in theological assessments of the biblical materials, see John J. Collins, *Encounters with Biblical Theology* (Minneapolis: Fortress Press, 2005); and James A. Sanders, *From Sacred Story to Sacred Text: Canon as Paradigm* (Philadelphia: Fortress Press, 1987).

2. See, for example, *The Postmodern Bible: The Bible and Culture Collective*, ed. Regina M. Schwartz et al. (New Haven, Conn.: Yale University Press, 1995), especially the introduction. For a helpful critique of both perspectives, see Richard Bauckham, "Reading Scripture as a Coherent Story," in *The Art of Reading Scripture*, ed. Ellen F. David and Richard B. Hays (Grand Rapids, Mich.: Eerdmans, 2003), 38–53.

3. Another literary form serving a similar function is the genealogy, which is also found throughout both the Old and New Testaments. Because it possesses a distinct form, I do not include it in the listing below. But it too serves the purpose of knitting together major segments of the biblical story by showing the relations between key figures in those stories. In the Pentateuch, genealogies also testify to the fulfillment of God's promise to bring forth numerous descendants from Abraham and to remain in relationship with God's people, Israel.

4. Here are a few of the many references to the exodus: Exod 20:1-2, 32:11, 34:18; Lev 11:45, 23:43; Num 14:22, 20:16; Deut 1:30, 20:1; Josh 2:10, 24:5; Judg 2:1, 6:8; 1 Sam 8:8, 10:8; 2 Sam 7:6; 1 Kgs 6:1, 9:9; 2 Kgs 17:7, 21:15; 1 Chr 17:21; 2 Chr 5:10, 6:6; Neh 9:9; Pss 78:12, 105:38; Isa 10:26, 11:16; Jer 2:6, 23:7; Ezek 20:5; Dan 9:15; Hos 2:15, 13:4; Amos 2:10, 9:7; Mic 6:4, 7:15; Hag 2:5; Zech 10:11; Acts 7:34, 13:17; Heb 3:16, 8:9; Jude 1:5.

5. Luke Timothy Johnson, "Imagining the World that Scripture Imagines," in Luke Timothy Johnson and William S. Kurz, S. J., *The Future of Catholic Biblical Scholarship: A Constructive Conversation* (Grand Rapids, Mich.: Eerdmans, 2002), 139.

## Chapter 7: Deep Harmony

1. Terence E. Fretheim, *Exodus,* Interpretation Commentary Series (Louisville: John Knox, 1991), 25.

2. Ibid., 27.

3. Walter Brueggemann, *Theology of the Old Testament: Testimony, Dispute, Advocacy* (Minneapolis: Fortress Press, 1997), 192.

4. Ibid., 195.

5. For a helpful presentation of this perspective, see Douglas John Hall, *Imaging God: Dominion as Stewardship* (Grand Rapids, Mich.: Eerdmans, 1986).

6. J. Clinton McCann Jr., "Exodus 32:1-14," *Interpretation* 44 (1990): 277.

7. Ibid.

8. Terence E. Fretheim, *The Suffering of God: An Old Testament Perspective,* Overtures to Biblical Theology (Philadelphia: Fortress Press, 1984), 126.

## Conclusion: Reading the Bible Biblically

1. In saying this I do not intend to imply that biblical passages cannot be rightly viewed as conveying a "fuller sense" (*sensus plenior*) than what they express in their original literary and historical context. On the contrary, the interpretive task of bringing the passage into conversation with the wider canon, our contemporary context, and the Holy Spirit within the community of faith is an attempt to explore its fuller sense. I would argue, however, that determining the meaning and function of a passage in its original context is the best starting point for discerning how the passage may speak to us anew as part of the larger witness of the canon.

2. For an accessible and more developed treatment of exegetical technique written for students, pastors, and lay readers, see Michael J. Gorman, *Elements of Biblical Exegesis: A Basic Guide for Students and Ministers* (Peabody, Mass.: Hendrickson, 2001). Another helpful guide, written from an evangelical perspective, is Gordon D. Fee and Douglas Stuart, *How to Read the Bible for All Its Worth: A Guide to Understanding the Bible,* 2nd ed. (Grand Rapids, Mich.: Zondervan, 1993).

3. See Phyllis Trible, "The Daughter of Jephthah: An Inhuman Sacrifice," in *Texts of Terror: Literary-Feminist Readings of Biblical Narrative* (Philadelphia: Fortress Press, 1984), 93-116, here 97. Although engaging in a feminist-critical mode of investigation, Trible asserts that the narrator shapes the narrative to present the vow as an act of unfaithfulness. See also, for example, E. John Hamlin, *At Risk in the Promised Land: A Commentary on the Book of Judges,* International Theological Commentary (Grand Rapids, Mich.: Eerdmans, 1990), 118; Dennis T. Olson, "The Book of Judges," *New Interpreter's Bible,* ed. Leander Keck et al. (Nashville: Abingdon, 1998), 2:830-36. Esther Fuchs ("Marginalization, Ambiguity, Silencing: The Story of Jephthah's Daughter," *Journal of Feminist Studies in Religion* 5 [1989]: 35-45) sees Jephthah's actions along the lines of a tragic mistake and helpfully points out that "the daughter actively participates in the processes leading to her own demise" (39).

# Auther and Subject Index

# Scriptural Index